D1175936

The Abandoned Ones

Advisor in Criminal Justice to Northeastern University Press

Gilbert Geis

The Abandoned Ones

The Imprisonment and Uprising
of the Mariel Boat People

Mark S. Hamm

Northeastern University Press • Boston

Northeastern University Press

Copyright 1995 by Mark S. Hamm

Library of Congress Cataloging-in-Publication Data

Hamm, Mark S.
    The abandoned ones : a history of the Cuban prison riots at
Oakdale and Atlanta / Mark S. Hamm.
        p. cm.
    Includes bibliographical references and index.
    ISBN 1–55553–230–6 (alk. paper)
    1. Prison riots—Louisiana—Oakdale. 2. Prison riots—
Georgia—Atlanta. 3. Prisoners—Cuba. 4. Cubans—United
States. 5. Oakdale Federal Alien Detention Center (Oakdale,
La.)—History. 6. United States Penitentiary, Atlanta
Georgia—History. I. Title.
HV9471.H29 1995
365′.641—dc20   94-25285

Designed by Lisa Diercks

Composed in Meridien by Coghill Composition Company. Printed and bound by The Maple Press Company in York, Pennsylvania. The paper is Sebago, an acid-free stock.

MANUFACTURED IN THE UNITED STATES OF AMERICA
99 98 97 96 95   5 4 3 2 1

Dedicated to the Cuban Detainees:

Past, Present, and Future

Contents

Preface   xi

Part I • Foreground

1. The Riots   3

2. The Siege   15

3. The Lessons   30

Part II • Background

4. The Freedom Flotilla   45

5. The Resettlement   53

6. The Moral Crusade   70

7. The Pains of Imprisonment: Atlanta, 1984–1987   84

8. The Adaptation and Equilibrium   102

9. The Human Rights Offensive   120

Part III · Action Theory
for Administrative Reform

10. The Oakdale and Atlanta Riots Revisited   153

Notes   183

References   207

Chronology of Events   219

Index   229

What happens to a dream deferred?

Does it dry up like a raisin in the sun?

Or fester like a sore—And then run? Does it stink like

rotten meat? Or crust and sugar over—Like syrupy sweet?

Maybe it just sags like a heavy load.

Or does it explode?

—Langston Hughes, "A Raisin in the Sun"

• • •

Slogans mean nothing to a young man facing 352 years hard

labor in Angola. For a crime he did not commit.

It's freedom of speech.

As long as you don't say too much.

—Neville Brothers, "Sons and Daughters"

Preface

This study has been years in the making. Following the 1987 riots of Cuban prisoners at the U.S. Federal Detention Center at Oakdale, Louisiana, and the Federal Penitentiary at Atlanta, several hundred prisoners were transferred to the maximum security penitentiary at Terre Haute, Indiana. As part of the negotiated settlement to the riots, the Cubans were guaranteed what the federal government called a "full, fair, and equitable review" of each prisoner's case to determine whether they were appropriate candidates for release into the community.

Early in 1988, representatives of the Atlanta-based Coalition to Support Cuban Detainees came to my office in the Criminology Department at Indiana State University to ask if I would be willing to train and lead a group of students to serve as legal representatives for the Cubans during their release hearings. I agreed. Over the next two years, my students and I represented some two hundred Cuban prisoners in their parole reviews before the U.S. Immigration and Naturalization Service (INS).

During the course of these hearings, I became witness to an extraordinary saga of human struggle which went far beyond that which is common to all immigrants arriving on America's shores—the struggle to assimilate into mainstream society. Unlike the great majority of Latin American, Caribbean, Asian, and Third World immigrants who *have* successfully gained access to the economic, political, and educational institutions of American society in recent decades, the Cubans at Oakdale and Atlanta had been locked out of the mainstream. Instead, they had been locked up in maximum-security prisons by a cruel and complex body of legislation that left them with little practical hope of ever being released. For them, the migration to America had become a colossal misadventure, causing nothing but pain and suffering. Depression, lethargy, and resort to self-mutilation and suicide had become a way of life for them. As I probed deeper into the causes of their anguish and the ways in which they related to the riots, I also became witness to a chronicle of massive political corruption and administrative bungling.

This book tells that story.

My attempt to puzzle out the Oakdale and Atlanta riots has not been an easy task. To borrow a simile from the 1960s, it has been at times like "trying to catch the wind." Finding reliable information on *any* prison riot defies most standard methods of gathering data on human behavior. I shall rely, then, on an array of reconstructions of events and circumstances surrounding the prisoner rebellions. In addition to interviews with Cuban prisoners involved in the riots, the words of guards, prison administrators, lawyers, judges, priests, FBI agents, and non-Cuban convicts also stand witness to these events. I shall also draw on scholarly research, government documents, legal evidence, and journalists' accounts in a balanced fashion (of the 208 sources cited, 41 percent are legal or scholarly publications, 39 percent are media reports, and 20 percent are official documents).

By these methods, I will endeavor to provide a critical analysis of the riots against the backdrop of social, political, administrative, and legal change. Along the way, I will explain why the Cubans became such a serious problem for the U.S. Bureau of Prisons and suggest how a similar crisis may be avoided in the future.

Because of obvious disjunctions in this research between goals and means, a short examination of the reliability of information is necessary. For instance, the reader may find the interviews with Cuban prisoners to be especially brief and to the point, and there is a good reason for this: At the time I conducted these interviews, any information about a Cuban prisoner who had been involved in the riots could be used against him in his INS parole hearing. ("Him" because all prisoners involved were men.) It was therefore to the prisoner's advantage to say nothing about the riots, even to his legal representative. Their reflections on the uprisings often came in one-word answers, rendered like frightened children. The more courageous offered a sentence or two. But most of the time, they said nothing about the riots at all.

The same may be said about the interviews with guards and prison administrators. Often they would react to questions about the rebellions with obvious embarrassment, or would say they "weren't allowed to talk about it" because of ongoing Justice Department investigations. Compounding these problems, there were important structural constraints placed on the data. Most official records on the Oakdale prisoners were destroyed in the fire that consumed that institution on the night of November 21, 1987. The integrity of other prison records was plagued by misfiled documents, or by documents that had been copied and recopied so many times as to be unreadable.

While the official government reports used in the study were always well-typed and legible, they also had shortcomings. Information published by the Departments of Justice and State and by the Senate and the House of Representatives all was collected for specific bureaucratic purposes and may not contain the degree of accuracy and objectivity required for academic research (a problem similar to using the *Uniform Crime Reports* to predict street crime). Such data also may have been deliberately tampered with to legitimize the goals of the data-collecting agencies. Finally, data collected over time, such as those published by the Justice and State Departments, are subject not only to changes in record-keeping procedures but also the vagaries of federal law and the contentions of political Washington.

Nor is the legal evidence used in this study without fault. Mechanistic and micro in nature, it usually misses the larger structural beat of things. And even the novice student of the social sciences is aware of the hazards associated with using newspaper, magazine, and television reports to explain such a complex problem as prison violence.

To repeat: Explaining a prison riot is not an easy task. Explaining two that occurred at the same time, six hundred miles apart, is twice as difficult. It's like "trying to catch the wind" because such a project defies most methods of gathering data on human behavior. Scholars attempting to unpack the experiential setting of the near-legendary riots at Attica and in New Mexico have wrestled with similar problems—which will no doubt continue as we begin to see studies emerge on the more recent prisoner uprisings at Talledega, Alabama (1992), Lucasville, Ohio (1992), and the Colorado State Prison (1994).

Every researcher who undertakes a study of prison rebellion must confront these fundamental problems of reliability. I have employed two methods. First, I have attempted to triangulate the findings. When I have recounted the spoken words of a Cuban prisoner, for example, I have corroborated the statement with legal, scholarly, official, and journalistic evidence. The same corroborative process holds true when I question official reports; I try to back them up with original interviews, scholarly and legal research, journalistic evidence, and so on.

The second strategy came through my good fortune in finding a number of scholars and professionals in the fields of civil rights, criminology, corrections, immigration law, and political science who were kind enough to talk to me at length about maximum security confinement and the Cuban situation, or who read certain selections of the manuscript and offered critically constructive comments.

• • •

To the extent that I have caught the winds of Oakdale and Atlanta, I have many to thank for assistance and inspiration. Long before I undertook this project, I spent more than a dozen years working the cellblocks of prisons and juvenile institutions in Arizona. In 1982, I was appointed Assistant Superintendent of the Arizona State Prison Complex at Tucson. Were it not for my fellow wardens—Tom Korff, Duane Vild, Joe Martinez, Kelly Spencer, and Bob Zorn—I would have never understood the brutal realities of life inside the maximum security prison. And I will never forget the Tucson riot of August 1983. (Who could forget a steel shank ripping a bloody stomach onto the blistering desert sidewalk and the shrill death-cry that followed?)

Though these were important background experiences, nothing really had prepared me for the Cubans of Oakdale and Atlanta. I cannot thank enough the people who made this study possible.

If it were not for the tireless and compassionate efforts of Carla Dudeck, Gary Leshaw, and Sally Sandige of the Coalition to Support Cuban Detainees, I would never have met the "abandoned ones." If not for Shela Van Ness, who played a major role in organizing the defense at the INS hearings, I would never have slowed down enough to get to know them. And were it not for the cooperative guards and administrators at the Terre Haute Penitentiary, who gave me access to the Cuban files and cell houses, I never would have understood the pains of their imprisonment.

Judge John Kite, Michael Gradison, the late Christ Perry, and Richard Waples enabled me to understand the legal road that brought the prisoners to Oakdale and Atlanta, and Cuban scholars Gaston Fernandez, Michael Erisman, and Esteban Morales helped me to comprehend how they coped with it all.

Criminologists Gregg Barak, Thomas Castellano, William Chambliss, Francis Cullen, Jeff Ferrell, Mark Fleisher, John Klofas, Coramae Mann, Tony Platt, Herman Schwendinger, Kenneth Tunnell, Patricia Van Voorhis, Ralph Weisheit, Marjorie Zatz, and especially Professor Jim Thomas made it possible for me to stake out a scholarly theory.

The recent impassioned pleas for justice by former President Jimmy Carter and author Kate Millett helped me to understand how the United States government was able to violate the prisoners' human rights—and how it continues to get away with such violations to this very day.

And without the fundamental lessons in democracy that I learned long ago from my family and friends—especially from Lou, J.D., Marla, and Cassady—I never would have bothered in the first place.

Part I

Foreground

Prisoners of conscience convicted of their political activities have been languishing in Cuban prisons deprived of all freedom for nearly a quarter of a century. Some prisoners convicted in the last year can expect to be in prison well into the 21st century if the present system in Cuba survives that long. . . . Think about that.

—*Ronald Reagan: January 5, 1984*

MIKE INMAN (GENERAL COUNSEL FOR THE U.S. IMMIGRATION AND NATURALIZATION SERVICE): It is our desire to in effect protect the citizens of this country and to return the detainees to Cuba as the law requires and hopefully in the future the relationship with Cuba will permit that.

TED KOPPEL: You raise an interesting point, because just today I read, I guess it was in this morning's *New York Times,* that there are apparently now talks beginning . . . between our government and the Cuban government concerning deportation. . . . You'd like to send those folks back, right?

INMAN: Absolutely.

—*ABC Nightline: July 3, 1987*

Chapter 1

The Riots

The events slowly unfolded, like the snow that was gently falling from the late autumn sky. On November 20, 1987, Tom Brokaw calmly reported on the NBC "Nightly News" that a treaty had been signed in Mexico City between the United States and Cuba concerning the repatriation of Cuban prisoners in the custody of the Federal Bureau of Prisons (BOP). For most viewers, the report meant very little. After all, what did it mean to "repatriate" a convicted criminal from a communist country? Even if we knew, who really cared? It was the Reagan era.

Yet within minutes of Brokaw's announcement, a drunken Cuban detainee at the Federal Detention Center at Oakdale, Louisiana, staggered into the prison dining room and moved to the front of the serving line. He picked up an empty food tray and hurled it at the forehead of a food service supervisor, drawing blood.[1] This act of violence, proclaimed the Cuban, was a protest against the repatriation accord. Excited by the disturbance, most of the other Cubans eating dinner began shouting and throwing their trays, food, and silverware onto the floor and against the walls. The staff signaled for help and within minutes the dining room was secured by guards who returned the prisoners to their housing units without further incident.

The next morning (Saturday, November 21), Oakdale administrators ordered the institution's Special Operations Response

Team (SORT) to report for duty in full riot gear, including helmets, gas masks, tear gas canisters, and riot batons. SORT officers positioned themselves on the yard near the front gate of the prison and were instructed to be prepared to respond to any emergency that might occur. At 7:30 A.M., the Cubans were turned out of their housing units and reported to their scheduled work details. For the next hour and a half, things went smoothly, like any other morning. Then, around 9:00, a detainee went to the yard captain's office and reported that a number of Cubans had makeshift weapons and were planning to break through the front gate at sundown.

Throughout the afternoon, word continued to filter into the yard captain's office that something was going to happen that evening and even that female staff members might be taken hostage and raped. In an attempt to relieve their fears, the warden issued a written statement to the detainees assuring them that while he knew very little about the treaty, he would provide more information as it became available. By late afternoon, many detainees had quit cooperating with their work detail supervisors. They began to huddle in small groups to discuss the treaty. Meanwhile, the yard captain received information that detainees were hording food, packing personal belongings, and dressing in multiple layers of clothing. After work, waiting lines at the prison telephones became unusually long, and an ominous silence fell on the yard as the Cubans began to confer in hushed tones.

As a precautionary measure, administrators ordered day-shift staff members to remain at the institution throughout the evening. Security officers and counselors were designated "team leaders" and assigned three guards apiece. Each team was issued handcuffs and tear gas canisters, and told to report to areas outside the perimeter, in the vicinity of the housing units. They were instructed to prevent any attempt by the Cubans to scale the fence. At about 4:30, all female staff members were quietly removed and administrators requested standby alert assistance from the Federal Border Patrol Tactical Team (BORTAC) in El Paso, Texas. At 5:00, the evening meal was served without incident and all prisoners were returned to the housing units by 6:30.

Fifteen minutes later, approximately 250 Cubans exited the

housing units and gathered together in the middle of the yard. From beneath their coats and jackets, they quickly pulled home-made clubs, knives, and machetes. In unison, they began chanting *"Somos los Abandonados!"* ("We are the Abandoned Ones!")

Then all hell broke loose.

The Cubans charged toward the front gate, and the SORT squad responded by firing a dozen volleys of tear gas at the feet of the oncoming mob. The Cubans retreated to the center of the yard, where they split into two groups. One group went off toward the support services buildings where it began breaking windows and starting fires with gasoline-soaked rags. The second group readied itself for another assault on the front gate, which occurred at 6:55, and was again successfully repelled with tear gas canisters laid down by the SORT squad.

Two minutes later—the brief time that it took to catch their breaths—the Cubans mounted a third attack; it also was turned back by tear gas. A fourth attack took place five minutes later and again it was repelled with tear gas. But the Cubans were unrelenting. Five minutes later they mounted a fifth assault but were again forced back.

Meanwhile, another group of detainees broke into the Mechanical Services Building and armed itself with fireaxes, picks, shovels, crowbars, sawblades, and gasoline. Back near the front gate, dozens of Cubans, their faces wrapped in wet bandanas, picked up the searing tear gas canisters and threw them back at the SORT squad. Others returned to the housing units, only to reappear on the yard with a larger cache of homemade machetes, knives, and clubs.

By 7:15, the squad had exhausted its tear gas supply and had retreated to a position outside the front gate. Hundreds of detainees then went on a rampage, breaking windows and setting fire to nine of the fourteen prison buildings. By this time, staff members who had remained inside the institution had been chased down and captured by yet another group of detainees.

At 7:30, the Cubans again approached the front gate, but this time they moved more forcefully. Uninhibited by tear gas, they screamed their slogan, throwing rocks and smashing windows in the Administration Building as they went. Reaching the front gate, they were forced to retreat when the SORT squad aimed automatic assault rifles at them and threatened to fire if they came any closer. The detainees again retreated to the middle of the yard, where they stood in a circle and with great exhilaration chanted over and over *"Somos los Abandonados!"* Inspired by their revolt, they turned and charged the front gate once more—because they could. By this time, the Cubans held control of Oakdale.

Once again, however, they were forced to retreat from the front gate under the threat of SORT firepower. By 8:30, detainees had taken twenty-eight hostages and had set fire to two more buildings—the hospital and the Administration Building. Another small band of detainees, using two hostages as cover, attempted to cut the perimeter fence behind one of the housing units with bolt cutters, but were forced back by a guard armed with a shotgun.

At about 8:45, a group of twelve white American prisoners ran to the front gate and reported that nine correctional officers were trapped in the Food Service Building (which was not burning) and would not come out unless they received assistance from administrators. The captain agreed to go onto the yard and rescue the officers. The American prisoners gave him a detainee jacket and ski cap to conceal his identity. Surrounded by the Americans, the captain went in and removed the officers through a rear exit of the Food Service Building. Simultaneously, several staff members trapped in the burning hospital were freed by a group of friendly detainees.

At 9:00, staff members assigned to the prison's control center were forced to evacuate their post as detainees smashed the Plexiglas windows surrounding them. Running from the control booth beneath the advancing smoke and flames from the Administration Building, one guard was caught by several detainees. Flushed with excitement, the Cubans threw him into a laundry cart and paraded him around the burning yard, laughing and banging on the cart with their clubs. Not only did the Cubans now control Oakdale, some of them were beginning to truly enjoy it.

Shortly after 9:00, two hours after the initial assault on the front gate, the director of the Bureau of Prisons and the U.S. attorney general were notified of the riot. All staff members were directed to secure the perimeter and prevent further escape attempts. The release of hostages and recontrol of the prison would be settled through negotiations.

An hour later, at about 10:00 P.M., two detainees came to the front gate under a white flag and reported that two detainee patients were locked in rooms in the burning hospital. An Oakdale psychiatrist agreed to assist in their release and accompanied the detainees back to the hospital, but was unable to unlock the thick metal door of the building. Several detainees then used sledgehammers in an unsuccessful attempt to smash through the outer walls. Frustrated, the Cubans took the psychiatrist hostage, but within minutes other prisoners descended on the scene and set him free. They escorted him back to the front gate, where the captain, in return for freeing the civilian psychiatrist, gave them a key to the hospital door. The detainees returned to the burning building and were able to release the patients without injury.

At 10:30, FBI agents from the regional office in Lake Charles, Louisiana, arrived by helicopter to evaluate the situation. They immediately called in support units from various branches of the federal government. By midnight, the captain, in consultation with the warden and the FBI agents, had communicated with the leaders of the revolt over captured security radios and arranged a meeting with them at the front gate.

This first attempt at negotiation focused exclusively on freeing the hostages and did not deal with the larger issue of repatriation to Cuba. The Cubans therefore rejected the proposal and declared they would continue to hold hostages until the issue of repatriation was settled. Furthermore, they warned, any effort to use force against them would result in the immediate death of the hostages. In order to maintain the bargaining value of the hostages, the detainees quickly established a security force within their own ranks to periodically move hostages from place to place within the occupied prison.

Attorney General Edwin Meese III and Bureau of Prisons Director Michael Quinlan assumed the role as the government's chief negotiators in the developing crisis, and at 2:30 A.M. on Sunday, November 22, a fifty-man FBI Hostage Rescue Team (HRT) and thirty BORTAC officers arrived at Oakdale on their orders.

At sunrise a lone Cuban came to the front gate waving a white flag. He read a prepared statement announcing that five hostages would be killed if all vehicles were not immediately removed from the perimeter fence. The warden assured the messenger that as long as the hostages were safe, force would not be used to enter the compound. The vehicles were nevertheless moved away from the perimeter fence and no hostages were injured.

At 7:05, an announcement was made over the institution's public address system: "Any Cuban detainee who wants to leave the prison can do so by reporting to the front gate immediately!" There were few takers; only a meager group of Cubans surrendered. Most of the Cubans were, in the argot of black prisoner subcultures, "down for" the revolt. To demonstrate their commitment, between 10:00 and 10:30 the Cubans burned the prison library to the ground. But their passion was just beginning to build.

At noon, a group of detainees took two laundry carts filled with wood, paper, and gasoline to the front gate. By this time, an FBI team had arrived at Oakdale and snipers were aiming automatic assault rifles at the detainees. The Cubans were ordered to withdraw their carts, or they would be shot. After a brief conference, the detainees complied.

About 2:00, administrators cut off electricity and water to the prison. A half-hour later, another lone Cuban took instant camera pictures of the hostages to the front gate to show that they were all alive and well. In exchange for this vital information, the Cuban asked that the electricity and water be restored. Administrators refused, and so began a period of siege mentality in which nearly a thousand detainees and their twenty-eight hostages were forced to live without electricity and water in an institution already suffering from catastrophic physical damage.

By sundown, more than five hundred armed BOP and FBI agents were guarding the Oakdale perimeter, waiting for the next move. It occurred at 9:00 P.M. when Director Quinlan was contacted by an assistant to Bishop Agustin Roman of the Catholic Diocese of Miami, Florida. Roman indicated his willingness to go to Oakdale and help resolve the crisis. For years, the bishop had been a strong supporter of Cubans incarcerated in federal prisons, arguing consistently that most were not criminal offenders and that there was no legal basis for their incarceration. A majority of the Cubans confined in Oakdale were from or had ties to Miami, and were familiar with the bishop's message. Moreover, Bishop Roman was a widely acknowledged religious leader in the Cuban-American community and a well-known and highly respected figure to many of the prisoners who now held control of the Oakdale facility.

Meese and Quinlan rejected Bishop Roman's offer because the bishop asked to be directly involved with the Cubans in their negotiations with government officials. It was in Meese's and Quinlan's interest that the bishop act only to clarify the issues that would be resolved exclusively by the two warring parties—the detainees on one hand, and BOP officials on the other. Furthermore, because the bishop's concerns were adversarial and he was primarily concerned with the status of detainees as refugee-prisoners, his involvement was not seen as productive by the attorney general and the director. Bishop Roman was eliminated from the negotiations.

At about 9:30, the yard captain contacted detainee representatives by radio and asked them to come to the front gate, where they were handed a Xerox copy of a three-sentence letter from Attorney General Meese offering the detainees, in exchange for the hostages, an indefinite moratorium on repatriation to Cuba and a "full, fair, and equitable review" of each detainee's case. The Cuban representatives returned to the housing units to discuss the offer with their constituents. A short time later, they returned to the front gate and refused the proposal. As one detainee later explained, "We didn't trust Meese. He's a liar. We wanted Bishop Roman all the way!"

The Winds of Rebellion

The Oakdale rebellion became a major national news story on Sunday, November 22. Among those who learned of the riot were 1,394 Cuban detainees at the Federal Penitentiary in Atlanta, Georgia. At 7:30 A.M. on Monday, November 23, the prison work call was sounded and cell houses were opened for detainees to report for work. Unlike most mornings, many of the Cubans left their cells wearing tennis shoes instead of standard prison-issue safety shoes. Many were also wearing extra layers of clothing and some were carrying Sunday newspapers featuring stories about the Oakdale riot.

Between 8:30 and 9:00, work detail supervisors in the institution's giant Federal Prison Industries shop (UNICOR) began noticing that detainees were more quiet than usual and slower in their work. Small groups began walking away from their work stations, huddling around newspapers, and discussing the events at Oakdale. At 9:10, the UNICOR supervisor received a report that detainees were warning some staff members of trouble, and that it would be a "good idea" if female staff members were immediately escorted from the prison.

The UNICOR supervisor began to walk around the shop, speaking to small groups of detainees about the implications of the repatriation treaty and Oakdale. Like the Oakdale warden two days before, the supervisor advised the detainees that the Bureau of Prisons did not yet have much information about the treaty but expected to find out more about it later in the day.

At 9:15, the Atlanta warden ordered all female personnel to discreetly leave the prison and began calling in about forty off-duty staff members in case of an emergency. The warden then directed all day-shift staff members to "saturate the institution with talk" about the treaty in an attempt to calm the detainees.

At about 10:30, a small group of detainees started a fire in the UNICOR shop as a larger group raced out of the prison dining room and began to overpower staff members all over the yard. Other groups began capturing personnel inside the UNICOR shop and in the dining room. Then, more than eight hundred Cubans appeared on the yard brandishing homemade clubs, knives, and machetes, as well as boards, chains, blowtorches, bolt cutters, and gasoline. They joined the detainees who had captured staff members on the yard and seized radios, keys, and handcuffs.

Another riot had begun.

The next ten minutes were pandemonium. As the detainees began chasing staff members, tower guards opened fire at Cubans holding weapons. One detainee, thirty-two-year-old José Peña

Perez, was shot in the head and killed as he chased an employee with a machete. Five other Cubans were struck by gunfire, leaving them seriously wounded on the ground, but the guards suspended their fire when a small band of detainees approached the wall, holding a knife at the throat of a hostage and threatening to kill him if the shooting did not stop.

At 10:40, administrators implemented emergency procedures and called for the assistance of the Atlanta-based FBI SWAT team as well as local law enforcement. Five minutes later, a group of detainees attempted to open the huge steel-grilled gate leading to the main corridor of the Administration Building. Guards on the other side of the gate laid down a volley of tear gas, forcing the Cubans back. Fifteen minutes after that, the regional director, acting on information from the warden, phoned Director Quinlan and told him that Atlanta was "coming apart!"

Over the next hour, the UNICOR building became engulfed by raging flames and the detainees successfully captured a total of seventy-nine staff members, who were taken to the chapel and to the dormitory usually occupied by American prisoners. Another twenty-six staff members were taken hostage in the hospital and sixteen employees were trapped inside the Cuban Segregation Unit (Cell House E, where inmates had remained locked down all morning and which rioters had not yet penetrated). Essentially, the Cubans had taken control of the maximum-security prison in less than two hours.

At 1:00, a BOP lieutenant made contact with detainee representatives by radio and began negotiating for the release of hostages. A single Cuban was then permitted to leave the dining room and enter the main corridor of the Administration Building for a discussion with the lieutenant and other administrators. He was given a Xerox copy of Attorney General Meese's letter promising an indefinite moratorium on repatriation to Cuba and a review of each detainee's case, in exchange for the hostages. Once again, the Cuban representative said the Cubans did not believe Meese's assurances and were unwilling to release their hostages. And, as before, hostages would be killed if any attempt was made to rescue them.

Throughout the afternoon, several small groups of detainees

turned themselves in at the main gate. But again, the majority of Cubans stayed inside and out of view. Meanwhile, BOP administrators directed the FBI SWAT team to plan and carry out the rescue of staff members trapped in Cell House E. By 5:00, sparks from the raging UNICOR building had ignited the food service warehouse, and it also began to burn out of control. Then the Cubans set fire to the Recreation Building. Over the next hour, the fires intensified to massive proportions, engulfing the institution in huge billows of black smoke.

At 5:30, the SWAT team successfully rescued the employees trapped in Cell House E by scaling an adjoining wall under cover of heavy firepower. At precisely the same moment, Atlanta television newscaster Marc Pickard of WSB-TV went on the air with a special report on the developing crisis. As part of the report, the station broadcast CNN's live coverage of Attorney General Meese's earlier statement.

Television sets inside the occupied Atlanta compound received the transmission and limited negotiations were briefly established, leading to the release of three injured staff members and ten injured Cubans who were taken to a nearby hospital. Meanwhile, National Guard helicopters began flying criss-cross patterns over the compound and dropping water on the raging fires.

Shortly after 6:00 P.M., two important events took place. First, Meese and Quinlan appointed Diader H. Rosario, an agent in the FBI's Atlanta office, as chief on-site negotiator for the government in its attempt to retake the prison. Rosario, a Puerto Rican-born, eighteen-year veteran of the FBI, was selected because he spoke fluent Spanish and was familiar with the Cuban situation at Atlanta. Second, the detainees sent out a message asking for Gary Leshaw, longtime legal representative for the Atlanta detainees, to represent them in their negotiations. Rosario called Leshaw's involvement "an excellent idea." The detainees also asked to be represented by newsman Marc Pickard, who was to be allowed into the prison to film the negotiations. Rosario also approved of this, signaling the beginning of the Cubans' reliance on television to disseminate information on the riots to the outside world—information that would become increasingly important in the days ahead.

Negotiations began at 7:30 in an office off the main hallway of the Administration Building (an area that had not yet fallen to the Cubans). The corridor leading to the office was lined with armed FBI SWAT team officers. Four Cuban representatives were allowed into the corridor. They walked past the SWAT officers and into the office, where they took a seat at the negotiating table alongside Rosario, Leshaw, Pickard, and several FBI and BOP officials. Unbeknownst to the Cubans, or to Leshaw or Pickard, a video camera hidden in the ceiling lights was transmitting the scene to the Washington office of Director Quinlan.

For the first ten minutes, Leshaw dominated the conversation, attempting to establish trust between the two sides. But then the detainees became agitated and emotional, bringing up the shotgun killing of José Peña by the tower guards nine hours earlier, and all four detainees, who were in their twenties, began weeping. "My God," cried one, "they even killed one of our own!" As Leshaw calmed them down, Rosario convinced the young Cubans that the SWAT team members should be allowed to take Peña's body to the local morgue.

Ten minutes after the four detainees left the negotiation table and returned to the yard, another group of Cubans carried Peña's body to the Administration Building, where two BOP guard strapped the corpse to a gurney, photographed it for Pickard's use in his TV news report, and removed it from the prison.

After this, the Cuban representatives re-entered the Administration Building and resumed negotiations. Leshaw and Pickard tried to convince them to sign Attorney General Meese's agreement quickly and to release all hostages so they would be able to get their message protesting forced repatriations on the eleven o'clock news, thereby reaching a worldwide audience. Leshaw and Pickard explained to the Cubans that interest in the Oakdale and Atlanta riots had already reached international proportions.

But this was not to be. The four detainees left the negotiation table, returned to the yard, and discussed the government's offer with the other prisoners. Essentially, their distrust of Meese's promised moratorium and full review of each detainee's case ran too deep. As a result, the Cuban representatives returned to the

Administration Building and rejected the proposal. Negotiations broke off at about 10:00.

Meanwhile, six hundred miles away in Oakdale, detainees and administrators had established a simple arrangement: Officials agreed to suspend any maneuver to enter the compound and detainees promised not to injure any of the hostages. And as the final minutes of November 23 ticked away, it became obvious to both detainees and officials at Oakdale and Atlanta that negotiations were deadlocked—a situation that would last for a week and a half. During this period, a series of events would occur that were unprecedented in the annals of American penology.

Chapter 2
The Siege

The revolt went on for eleven days. It did so, in large part, because of three interrelated strategies employed by the detainees between November 24 and December 4. The first related to a formidable series of theatrical events used by the Cubans to subject hostages to intense psychological torture. These theatrics were meant to send a clear message to the government's ultimate negotiators, Attorney General Meese and Director Quinlan: hostages would lose their lives if detainee demands were not taken seriously. The second strategy involved the sophisticated organizational structure developed by the detainees. And the third strategy involved a profound sense of spirituality that guided the rebellion from start to finish.

Theatrical Events:
"They Would Behead Us if You Come in with Force"

This phenomenal chapter in the history of American prisons began shortly after 3:00 A.M., Tuesday, November 24, when a dozen detainees at Oakdale openly constructed a small platform near the smoldering ruins of the Administration Building. A chair was placed in the center of the platform and the makeshift construction was surrounded with rags and mattresses soaked in gasoline. A message was delivered to the front gate to the effect that

FBI and National Guard helicopter flights over the compound were creating havoc among the detainees and that this could result in harm to the hostages. If the flights were not immediately suspended, the Cubans threatened to strap a hostage to the execution chair and burn him to death. After this, fly-overs became less frequent (though they did continue) and no hostages were burned alive.

The execution chair was only the first in a series of successful theatrical events used by the Cubans to demonstrate the fact that their wager between life and death was real. With the success of each event, the detainees gained confidence in their ability to hold out against remarkable odds.

Twelve hours after the execution chair incident, Oakdale detainees rolled a laundry cart containing six acetylene tanks to an area beside the Administration Building. SORT and HRT snipers "locked and loaded" their assault rifles and took aim at the detainees from behind the fence. The Cubans were ordered to withdraw the tanks, or they would be shot. They complied by rolling the loaded cart back as far as the execution chair, where they were joined by another group carrying a load of cinder blocks. Beside the execution chair, they defiantly constructed a six-foot-high cinder block wall to protect their acetylene tanks.

The SORT squad turned high-pressure firehoses on the execution chair and the wall in an attempt to knock them down, while HRT sharpshooters moved within firing range of the central compound. In response, detainees took two hostages to the front gate. They put machetes to their throats and threatened to kill them unless the firehoses and the snipers were withdrawn. To sustain the psychological blackmail, the captain also received a radio transmission from a hostage: "They have us handcuffed and have machetes at our throats and would behead us if you come in with force!" Again, officials complied with the detainees' demands and no hostages were injured.

More such theatrical events, though not as dramatic, continued throughout the Oakdale siege. For example, at 4:36 A.M., November 28, a guard working near the perimeter fence saw a detainee stab another detainee and drag him into a nearby housing unit. But the stabbing was staged in a deliberate attempt to deceive officials into thinking that the Cubans were capable of extreme acts of violence.

Similar events were employed by the Atlanta detainees. At 2:45 P.M., November 24, a detainee spokesman radioed officials from the second floor of the chapel that hostages would be killed if the BOP and FBI made any attempt to recapture the prison. In the background, another detainee was overheard giving orders to "throw hostages out the window" should FBI and National Guard helicopters resume their flights over the compound. Several hours later, a group of detainees entered the chapel with acetylene tanks and threatened to "blow up the whole place," killing both hostages and detainees in the process. Over the next four days, detainees released more than a dozen hostages who witnessed this event so that they could report it to officials on the outside.

The next morning at 11:55, Quinlan ordered the Atlanta warden to cut off the water. At 9:20 P.M., a detainee began banging a metal club on the door to the main corridor of Cell House B. From a distance, it sounded like gunfire. SWAT sharpshooters "stood up" in preparation for action. Later, however, it was found that this loud banging was intended only to continue the psychological blackmail. The next day, November 26, at 6:55 A.M., detainees began moving groups of hostages from one area of the prison to another. Then they moved them all back to their original locations in the chapel and the dormitory that usually housed American prisoners. Two days later, after detainees and hostages had gone without water for three days, a Cuban spokesman radioed a message that three hostages would be immediately killed if the water was not turned back on. The following day, water pressure was restored and no one was murdered.

Finally, during the early morning hours of December 2, a detainee spokesman near the prison textile factory reported to Rosario that they had discovered a dead body. They demanded that a physician and a stretcher be sent onto the yard. Rosario complied, but after an hour the detainees still had failed to produce the dead body. Nevertheless, four detainees were then spotted carrying the stretcher back and forth across the yard for no apparent reason at all.

The Damage Done

Despite the psychological torture the hostages endured as a result of the theatrical events, the detainees provided adequate care and protected them throughout the siege. After the takeover, only one known injury was found to have been inflicted on a hostage at Oakdale. At Atlanta, a total of 102 staff members was held hostage during the siege and none of them were injured. After the ordeal had ended, a number of hostages stated that they were warned in advance of the planned insurrection and were told by detainees that they should immediately leave the prison. As the events at Oakdale and Atlanta unfolded, other detainees expressed confusion and frustration over the fact that certain staff members had remained in the prisons to be captured.

After the siege, nearly all the hostages indicated that they were well cared for during the disturbance. They were given regular showers, access to medicine, and the opportunity to exercise. Some hostages even put on weight during the revolt because detainees fed them more than enough food. Several hostages also were treated with great compassion. On the afternoon of November 24, a teacher being held hostage in Atlanta was released after complaining of chest pains. Later in the day, the safety manager and his assistant were released from their office in the burned-out ruins of the UNICOR building by several detainees who worked for them and were allowed to escape to the outside. Five additional hostages were released around midnight because of medical complications. And on November 25, a staff psychologist was released because of yet another medical problem.

Prisoner Organization: Handcuffs and "Happy Birthday"

The successful staging of events and the responsible treatment of hostages were made possible by the sophisticated level of organization that developed among the detainees. Although no strong individual leader emerged, the Cubans who maintained control of Oakdale and Atlanta adopted orderly procedures and duty assignments reminiscent of BOP operations. During the siege, detainees at both prisons were designated as cooks, guards, unit managers, lieutenants, and drill sergeants. Meal schedules were followed and a rationing system was established. Medical services were provided and a remarkably advanced communications network was set up.

Beyond these important measures, detainees at both prisons established a simple system of law and order. Detainees who guarded the hostages were separated from the general population. Boundary lines were drawn on the floors of the various hostage holding areas, from which hostages could not leave and other detainees could not enter. Detainee police forces were organized to enforce this law.

At both Oakdale and Atlanta, the detainee police force used regular eight-hour shifts and patrols, not only to enforce the hostage law but also to observe various areas of the prisons and to prevent other detainees from surrendering. Within these police forces there also emerged a distinct countersociety system of social stratification. That is, those "policemen" who carried more than one or two sets of handcuffs (some carried as many as a dozen) were considered more important than those who did not. If a detainee was caught violating the hostage law or trying to escape, he was handcuffed by the policemen and taken to a recreation area where he was ordered to engage in strenuous physical exercise such as countless push-ups and running in place.

The Cubans needed no other law. Stealing and fighting were rare, and the vast majority of detainees came to accept the fact that everyone, especially the hostages, should be treated with dignity and respect. "The Oakdale and Atlanta riots," recalls Leshaw, "were not an act of anarchy." Indeed, they were not. In Atlanta, shortly after noon on November 24, an American prisoner named Thomas Silversteen was released by the detainee police force from a "side pocket" security cell (reserved for the mentally handicapped) in Cell House A. Atlanta officials considered Silversteen to be an "extremely dangerous high security inmate." Others close to the scene have described him as "one of the most dangerous prisoners in America," or as simply "out of his fucking mind." Once released from his side pocket, Silversteen began organizing a group of some twenty detainees in an effort to take over the rebellion and direct it onto a more violent course. Members of the detainee police force reacted by calling Silversteen "too crazy" for their purposes. The policemen huddled together for a moment, then attacked Silversteen. They wrestled him to the ground, handcuffed and shackled him, and forced drugs down his throat. Once the cuffed and shackled "crazy man" had passed out from the drugs, detainee policemen turned Silversteen's limp body over to guards at the Administration Building.

One reason for this remarkable organizational stability was that the detainees and their hostages had enough to eat during the siege. After the fires at Oakdale and Atlanta were extinguished, both prison dining rooms and commissaries remained standing. In the days before the riot, the freezers at Oakdale had been filled with their quarterly supply of meat, and when detainees took control of the institution, approximately forty thousand pounds of meat were in storage. During the Atlanta siege, meals often were festive and orderly events. Detainees working in the dining rooms of both prisons wore plastic gloves and caps and offered enough food to provide three meals a day for detainees and hostages throughout the crisis.

This intricate level of prisoner organization created conditions conducive to healthful living, safety, stability, and intense playfulness. Simply put, many detainees thoroughly enjoyed the independence they gained from taking care of themselves and their hostages during the state of siege. This led to their favorable publicity in the media, which, in turn, not only reinforced the safety and stability of the detainee organizational structure, but also shaped the nature of the siege itself. For example:

• Throughout their years of incarceration in federal prisons, personal photographs had always meant a great deal to the detainees. At noon, Friday, November 27, final arrangements were concluded by the BOP for live television coverage of the situation at Oakdale. The fact that detainees would actually be able to appear on TV caused animated excitement. The next morning, as TV cameras moved into position near the front gate, several detainees demonstrated their enthusiasm by playfully tossing pool balls at National Guard helicopters hovering above the central compound.

• On Saturday night, November 28, four Atlanta detainees were spotted on the roof of the hospital waving flags, laughing, and shouting toward a group of family members and supporters in the street in front of the prison.

- The same day, Atlanta detainees figured out how to use the institution's public address system. They began to regularly broadcast their own commentaries on the riots over what they called "Radio Mariel."

- The Cuban playfulness reached its peak on the evening of December 1, when more than a hundred detainees gathered on the cold hospital roof to sing "Happy Birthday" to Carla Dudeck, founder of the Coalition to Support Cuban Detainees. As a birthday present to Dudeck, the Cubans released one hostage.

These events created even more media interest in the Cubans. Yet this intense interest ultimately served two counterpurposes. On one hand, the media became a prime source of frustration and anxiety for the detainees, government officials, and hostage families by presenting information that was highly inaccurate. More important, the media portrayed the hostages as being in great danger when in reality they were not, and it portrayed the detainees and the federal authorities as being ruthlessly violent, when actually both sides were remarkably peaceful throughout the siege.

For instance, on the evening of November 24 an Atlanta television station mistakenly reported a routine BOP shift change as an official assault on the occupied Atlanta compound. This report was, of course, broadcast to television sets inside the prison itself. Following the incident, Pickard observed that the detainees "went bonkers. They went bananas. The prison people were petrified [about what might happen], absolutely petrified." Because of the incident, Rosario complained that "We wasted a lot of time saying, 'No, no, no, we're not going to assault.' "

Later in the evening, a CNN reporter called Dudeck about a story CNN was planning to air on the morning of November 25. This story, if broadcast, could have significantly altered the riot's outcome. The reporter said he had heard that the BOP was sending Cuban detainees who had defected from the Atlanta revolt (about fifty-five at this point, though the number would climb to

290 over the next week) to Dobbin Air Force Base in Georgia for immediate deportation to Cuba. This was, of course, not true. Both Dudeck and public information officers from the Departments of Justice and State immediately denied the story, and the CNN broadcast was quashed before it did any damage.

On the other hand, the media played a crucial role in communicating a series of events that would ultimately reveal the secret to unlocking a peaceful solution to the state of siege. At 5:00 P.M., November 24, WSB-TV broadcast CNN's coverage of a press conference held earlier in the day by Michael Quinlan. This broadcast was, again, seen by the detainees who now were in control at Atlanta. Quinlan said that the safety of the Oakdale and Atlanta hostages "is paramount" and that his "patience is endless." He also promised that "no intrusive efforts" would be made on Oakdale or Atlanta as long as the hostages remained safe. After this, the hostages noticed a marked improvement in the treatment they received from the detainees.

But the power of the media cuts both ways. At about the same time that Quinlan was holding his press conference on CNN, one of the hostages at Atlanta sent a radio message indicating that they were "all doing well" and that the detainees were considering the release of all hostages if Leshaw and Pickard (with his TV cameras) were allowed into the prison to speak with them. This request was denied.

Yet, four days later, on Saturday night, November 28, a Spanish broadcast on WRFG-FM (Radio Free Georgia) in Little Five Points a few miles away made an appeal to the Cubans to end the stalemate. The program host, Ernesto Perez, implored the detainees to show "good faith" by releasing some hostages. Within an hour, they released four. The writing was on the wall: The Cubans were showing their willingness to negotiate an end to the siege through a friendly third party.

On November 27, CNN filmed a group of detainees sitting atop the dining hall in occupied Oakdale. They held a banner reading, "Dear Citizens of the United States, Thank You For Your Hopes and Prayers, We Do Not Want To Blow It!" Later in the day, they unfurled a second banner reading, "We Want To Talk To Someone

We Can Trust!" The one person they did *not* trust was Edwin Meese III.

Spirituality: "You Are All My Brothers"

By all accounts, the days following the riots at Oakdale and Atlanta were frustrating ones for Michael Quinlan. The Cubans had violently seized control of two of his federal prisons, taking nearly 150 hostages in an attempt to gain a moratorium on deportations to Cuba. On the authority of Attorney General Meese, Quinlan had promised the Cubans an indefinite moratorium and a "full, fair, and equitable review" of each detainee's case to determine who would be deported. He had also promised them "endless patience" and had successfully implemented a management of restraint that is historically unprecedented in such situations. But the Cubans still would not surrender hostages because they did not trust the attorney general's assurances. The deadlock remained despite Quinlan's best attempts to overcome this deep mistrust.

On November 26, Quinlan took a group of three prominent Cuban Americans from Miami to Atlanta, in the hope they could assist in the negotiations: Jorge Mas Canosa, chairman of the Cuban-American National Foundation; Robert Martin Perez Rodriguez, Cuba's longest-serving political prisoner; and Armando Valladares, a writer who had spent twenty-two years in Cuban prisons and was then the U.S. ambassador to the United Nations Commission on Human Rights. Their attempted intervention proved to be useless.

By this time, Rosario, on the authority of Quinlan and Meese, had banned Leshaw and Pickard from the negotiation table because they were regarded as irrelevant third parties. Hence, the Atlanta Cubans were left alone to negotiate with Rosario and the three Cuban-American dignitaries from Miami. After a full day of negotiations, it appeared that the detainees were ready to release fifty hostages in exchange for a press conference with Pickard and live television coverage, but the proposal fell apart when the detainee negotiators presented it to the Cuban inmate population as a whole. According to Rosario, "the detainees said, 'forget it!' They were insulted." And Leshaw recalls that when the detainees saw Armando Valladares on the Atlanta yard, "they booed him." Moreover, the detainees were confused about the government's decision to bring three conservative emissaries from Miami to the negotiation table in Atlanta. "The detainees," said Leshaw, "[wondered] what the hell . . . these three guys were doing here. They had nothing to do [with the riot or the deportations]. They had never been sympathetic to the [Atlanta] Cubans. Why are they [Meese and Quinlan] trying to use them to negotiate?"

All this changed, however, when on November 28 Quinlan was able to convince Meese that it would be in their best interests to reconsider their position on directly involving Bishop Roman—the original third party figure—in the negotiations.

This came to fruition at 7:00 A.M., Sunday, November 29 (eight days after the Cubans stormed the front gate), when guards set up large video stands at several places around the Oakdale perimeter and detainees were asked to gather in front of the TV monitors for an important message. At 8:00, Bishop Roman's videotaped message was played three times over the monitors and his message was loud and clear: He implored detainees to accept the indefinite moratorium on deportations offered by the attorney general and to immediately release the hostages.

At 8:28, detainees carried a large sign to the front gate that read: "We Want the Bishop, Our Legal Representatives, and National Press Inside Before We Sign Or There Will Be No Agreement." About five minutes later, a large group of detainees gathered in the middle of the yard and began arguing about the government's proposal. The emerging consensus, communicated to the front gate, was that the Cubans would not proceed with the negotiations until they were given a face-to-face meeting with the bishop. Sensing a possible breakthrough, Quinlan ordered a National Guard crew to bring Roman to Oakdale.

At 1:15 P.M., a National Guard helicopter carrying Bishop Roman landed outside the Oakdale perimeter. At the sight of him, the Cubans began clapping, crying, and hugging one another in joy. Roman stood in the back of a BOP pickup truck and was slowly driven around the perimeter in clear view of the detainees.

He continually made the sign of the cross as other detainees came running out of various areas of the compound to see him.

At 1:50, Roman addressed the detainees over the prison loud-speaker system from the back of the truck, which had been parked near the front gate. He said once again that Attorney General Meese's proposal was a good one and that hostages should be immediately released. Though it was precisely the same message that government officials had been delivering to the detainees for more than a week, there was now a different messenger.

Fifteen minutes later, more than nine hundred detainees laid down their weapons and all hostages were set free. Bishop Roman then blessed the detainees and hostages with a mass.

Of War and Peace
News of the Oakdale settlement reached Atlanta four hours later. Face-to-face negotiations among three detainee representatives, Rosario, and the three Miami dignitaries briefly resumed. The detainees asked for the same concession granted to Oakdale prisoners—the assistance of Bishop Roman to help them negotiate an end to the siege. Because of his significant accomplishments at Oakdale earlier in the day, Bishop Roman expressed his interest in coming to Atlanta. Remarkably, however, Quinlan, acting on orders from Meese, denied the bishop's request on the grounds that Roman could contribute most to the negotiations by waiting until an agreement had been finalized between Rosario and the Cubans. In turn, after learning that Roman had been denied access to them, the detainees broke off their discussions.

The Atlanta siege would continue for another week. By this time, the resources amassed by the federal government had reached staggering proportions. A total of 406 special BOP staff members had been temporarily dispatched to the penitentiary to assist some seven hundred regular staff members in safeguarding the perimeter. Another 623 FBI agents had been deployed to Atlanta, where they established a command post, gathered information, and requested a continuous flow of resources from other agencies.

Together, the BOP and the FBI also provided an enormous stockpile of equipment, including automatic assault rifles, various types of tear gas, riot gear, radios, closed-circuit television cameras and monitors, sound-amplification listening devices, additional telephone lines, and picture-file hostage-identification systems. In addition to this show of force, Meese arranged for the Pentagon to dispatch a hundred U.S. Army anti-terrorist specialists to Atlanta—bringing with them airplanes, helicopters, armored personnel carriers, mountain-climbing gear, plastic explosives, dynamite, hand grenades, rocket launchers, automatic assault rifles with infrared sniper scopes, crash saws, sledgehammers, cutting torches, chain saws, and enough ammunition to blow the Atlanta Penitentiary to hell and back several times over.

The U.S. Air Force and the Coast Guard also provided various aircraft, and a large number of the forces surrounding the prison had been dispatched by the U.S. Marshal's Service, the Border Patrol, the Public Health Service, the Immigration and Naturalization Service, the Georgia Bureau of Investigation, the National Guard, the Fulton County Sheriff's Department, the Atlanta Police and Fire Departments, the Salvation Army, and the Red Cross.

This tremendous display of force waited "with endless patience" as the negotiations ground to a halt following Quinlan's denial of Bishop Roman's offer to help resolve the Atlanta conflict. Between Monday, November 30, and Wednesday, December 2, neither side gave an inch as the Cubans held out for Roman's involvement and Quinlan waited for the detainees to release the hostages in accordance with the attorney general's plan. There were two essential reasons for the holdout.

The first reason was that the detainees were absolutely terrified of the mass of military hardware waiting for them outside the walls of the prison. As one detainee said, "We were afraid. We thought we would be killed." Another said, "We didn't want to give in—we thought we would be killed if we did." And still another insisted that "One man can't fight against a whole troop!"

The second reason relates to the profound sense of mistrust among the Cubans for the government's promises in general and for Attorney General Meese's promises in particular. At issue was the subject of deportation. The detainees were adamant about adding an absolute "no deportation" clause to the agreement instead of the Justice Department's "indefinite moratorium" on repatriation. In the former case, detainees would never be deported to Cuba; in the latter, they could be repatriated *legally* at any time after the revolt was over. And the Cubans had little faith in the American legal process.

They were also highly skeptical about the Justice Department's offer of a "full, fair, and equitable review" of each detainee's eligibility to remain in the United States. For years, and especially during the Meese era, the Justice Department had made similar attempts at providing a review of each Cuban's case. But they came to little avail. As one detainee complained, "All I ever got from the government was pocket freedom."* Another said, "I have been in prison for six years. For what? I didn't do nothing but be a Cuban." And an American prisoner said about the Atlanta detainees, "They'd heard it all before. All this shit about parole reviews, halfway houses, and whatever. Most people don't know the worst of what they were put through."

These two powerful forces—fear and mistrust—interacted to produce conditions that would sustain the revolt. As a strong "us versus them" mentality descended on the Cubans, their clandestine prisoner subculture became tighter and more resilient against the forces trying to undo it. Likewise, the government's show of force became stronger, causing inmates to turn further inward in search of organizational sustenance. On the morning of December 2, a week and a half after detainees captured control of Atlanta, these forces reached critical mass. At this point, equally strong forces were needed by the federal government to overcome it. Fortunately, they were available. But these forces did not arise from the lethal power of military hardware, but from democratic and spiritual sources.

Shortly after 9:00 A.M., December 2, Director Quinlan—on his own—gave a briefing on the Cuban riots to a joint committee of the United States Congress. After this briefing, Quinlan immediately contacted Bishop Roman and asked him to send to the

---

*Pocket freedom is a term used by Cubans to signify their possession of a piece of paper (which they can pocket) showing that they are eligible for release, although they cannot be released because they do not have a community sponsor.

Atlanta warden via FBI courier an audiotape pleading with detainees to accept the government's proposal.

At 4:30, a three-minute audiotape of Bishop Roman's message supporting Meese's proposal was broadcast throughout the Atlanta Penitentiary. The bishop also said he stood willing to come to Atlanta to personally witness the signing of the agreement to end the siege and a subsequent surrendering of hostages.

Less than twenty-four hours later, Cuban negotiators reported to officials that a vote had been taken among the Cuban detainee population concerning the "indefinite moratorium on the deportation of Cuban nationals" and the full, fair, and equitable review of each detainee's case. The vote was 1,100 in favor of the agreement and 270 against. However, the actual signing of the agreement, they said, was contingent upon Bishop Roman's presence. They further stipulated that Attorney General Meese be present at the signing.

At 9:45 P.M., a National Guard helicopter carrying Bishop Roman landed outside the Atlanta perimeter. Along with Leshaw and Rosario, Roman was escorted into the negotiating room, where he was introduced to a group of eight Cuban detainees waiting for him. Wearing a black, double-breasted raincoat, the diminutive priest said in Spanish to all present, "You're all my brothers and let's be peaceful and reach an agreement." At 12:25 A.M., media teams, including Marc Pickard's WSB, were escorted in to record the settlement. Two final and dramatic theatrical events then followed.

First, the eight detainee representatives at the table announced that they wanted to go back into the occupied institution to consult one last time with their fellow prisoners. After initial reluctance by Rosario, the Cubans disappeared into the night and re-entered the compound. Bishop Roman bowed his head in prayer. Twenty minutes later, the detainees returned to the negotiation table. But they had not spent the twenty minutes commiserating with their fellow prisoners about the government's proposal. Instead, they had spent the time re-dressing for the occasion. One of them wore a suit and tie and carried a briefcase with a Bible inside. Another returned to the table wearing a Cuban flag draped over his right shoulder and an American flag over the left; in his hands was a crucifix.

Second, in a final theatrical event at 12:50, another group of detainees carrying machetes quickly moved toward the prison chapel. But again, there was really no reason for this because ten minutes later Bishop Roman had convinced the detainee representatives to sign an *immediate* agreement with BOP Regional Director Gary McCune, rather than waiting for Attorney General Meese's signature on the document. In a phone call with an assistant to Meese, one of the detainee negotiators was told that "the attorney general and the government will stand behind this package." The agreement was then signed by McCune and the Cuban representatives and was witnessed by Bishop Roman, Leshaw, Pickard, and Rosario. Within an hour, all eighty-nine remaining hostages were released from captivity and 1,370 Cuban prisoners laid down their weapons and surrendered. At 2:00 A.M., Bishop Roman climbed aboard the National Guard helicopter and returned to Miami. The longest prison riot in the history of American penology was finally over.

Chapter 3
The Lessons

Since 1970, there have been more than three hundred prison riots in the United States. Each has been shaped by a unique set of social and political contentions, prevailing public attitudes toward crime and punishment, and various internal struggles for prison reform. The best way to make sense of one riot, then, is by comparing it to others. By probing into other cases, we are able to understand the unusual character of the first case—if, in fact, it is unusual at all. If it is not, then there is no reason to waste our time trying to understand the first case because its lessons have already been articulated in the vast body of literature on prison riots. However, if it is found to be unusual, then identifying its outstanding features can contribute to our understanding of the phenomenon. This understanding, in turn, can be used to search for effective ways to prevent the recurrence of a similar tragedy.

The rebellions at Oakdale and Atlanta are historically unprecedented if for no other reason than that they lasted for nearly two weeks. But other riots have also earned a place in history. Every prisoner, correctional administrator, and student of the American prison system is familiar with the uprisings at Attica and Santa Fe. The BOP officials surrounding the perimeters of Oakdale and Atlanta certainly were aware of them. As one Atlanta official said: "We didn't want another Attica on our hands. We'd seen the films and read the books. We'd talked about it in training sessions and discussed it with [other administrators]."[1] An Oakdale guard who escaped capture said: "I'd read all about the riot at Santa Fe. I did my master's thesis on it. But the Cubans were nothing like that. They had something very different going on. I think it had more to do with their belief in Santeria" (an Afro-Caribbean religion that blends African ancestor worship with Roman Catholicism).[2]

There are at least four important differences between the revolts at Oakdale and Atlanta and the riots at Attica and Santa Fe.

Nonviolence

The most important lesson, or the major legacy of the Oakdale and Atlanta riots, is that they were relatively peaceful events. Although the Cubans were responsible for millions of dollars in damages to the institutions, their revolt did not lead to the extraordinary levels of gratuitous violence and human carnage witnessed at Attica and Santa Fe.

The riot at the New York State Penitentiary at Attica began shortly after 9:00 A.M., September 9, 1971, when 1,281 of Attica's 2,243 prisoners took thirty-eight hostages in protest against inhumane treatment and deplorable living conditions. During the siege, three prisoners were beaten and stabbed to death after being marked as informants, or "snitches." On September 13, two hundred New York State troopers launched an armed assault on the prison in an attempt to retake the hostages. In less than one minute, more than eighty prisoners were wounded by a barrage of gunfire, leaving twenty-nine dead. Ten guards also were killed—not by prisoners but by the crossfire of the attacking troopers.[3]

The Santa Fe riot has been described as nothing less than a "killing ground."[4] In the early morning hours of February 2, 1980, a group of alcohol-intoxicated prisoners at the New Mexico State Prison near Santa Fe spontaneously retaliated against a smaller group of inmate snitches. They engaged in an orgy of violence that left thirty-three prisoners dead and another two hundred raped, beaten, mutilated, and dismembered. More than a dozen prisoners were knifed or beaten to death with pipes and clubs. One prisoner had his eyes gouged out, a screwdriver driven through his forehead, and his testicles hacked off and stuffed into his mouth. One prisoner was decapitated with a shovel. Several others had their penises and testicles burned from their bodies by acetylene torches, dying horrible and agonizing deaths. Twelve guards were taken hostage; they were stripped, bound, blindfolded, harassed, and brutally beaten.[5]

The same precipitating and predisposing conditions that led to the Attica and Santa Fe rebellions were present at Oakdale and Atlanta during the final days of November 1987. From the time they were first incarcerated in federal prisons, the detainees had been exposed to inhumane treatment and substandard living conditions. There were also many informants within the detainee populations. And the potential for human carnage was certainly present. The lethal forces amassed by the government at Oakdale and Atlanta were far more destructive than the shotguns and deer rifles used by the New York State troopers at Attica, and knives, clubs, screwdrivers, shovels, pipes, and acetylene torches were available to any detainee who wanted to use them as weapons against either staff or fellow inmates.[6]

Yet no one was killed, raped, beaten, harassed, or mutilated during the longest siege in the history of American penology.

Organization and Morality

As in most prison riots, the Santa Fe rebellion was characterized by prisoner disorganization and rapid dispersion by armed forces of the state.[7] By contrast, Oakdale and Atlanta resembled the Attica riot in that prisoners were highly organized, and herein lies its second lesson.

In what is no doubt the most learned and most critically acclaimed study of American prison riots, Bert Useem and Peter Kimball describe the prisoners who took control of Attica in this way:

> Inmates laid the foundation of an inmate countersociety, with a degree of formal organization, articulation of political principles, democratic participation, and law enforcement. . . . Rules were followed. There was no use of drugs, no fighting, and no sexual activ-

ity. The inmates had a defense force, internal police force, and on-call work gangs.[8]

Like Attica, the Oakdale and Atlanta riots were highly structured and deliberate attempts to capture control of prison administration in the pursuit of a specific goal. But more instructively, the Cubans employed an extremely moral approach to rioting in which the outstanding feature was respect for life and human dignity. A demonstrable belief in Roman Catholicism became the emotional taproot of their organizational resilience throughout the crisis. This faith was made explicit in their continued reliance on Bishop Roman and by the fact that the prison chapel at Atlanta was never burned. Instead, the chapel became the detainee operations center, the major hostage holding area, and the most highly protected part of the prison compound. Moreover, the Cubans maintained peace throughout the crisis by employing fundamental principles of psychological blackmail, paramilitarism, spirituality, democracy, and law. These are the essential characteristics of successful guerrilla warfare.[9] A conversation with an Atlanta guard demonstrates the effectiveness of the Cuban countersociety.

> *Guard:* I'd say they were unbelievably organized. They took over [the current yard] with military precision.
> *Question:* Do you think there was anything the Bureau could have done to prevent it?
> *Guard:* At that point, no. Maybe things could have been done earlier, but not then. They had their minds made up that was the way things were gonna go.

The exceptional nature of these events can be best understood by returning to the comparison with Attica and Santa Fe. Because of the spiritual morality that guided the Oakdale and Atlanta revolts, the detainee countersociety held together until an acceptable solution could be achieved. At Attica, the prisoner countersociety fell apart during the crucial hours of the negotiation process. According to Useem and Kimble, "In the later stages [of the Attica siege] there was a return to sexual activity and drug use . . . and an increase in [prisoner-on-prisoner] stabbings and slashings."[10]

At Santa Fe, there was no inmate countersociety; mistrust

between prisoners was rampant and morality was not an issue. Shortly after seizing control of the institution, a group of primarily Hispanic inmates headed straight for the prison pharmacy. Using keys confiscated from the control center, they unlocked the door and raided the supply of pharmaceutical drugs, which were then freely distributed throughout the prisoner population. "Their [primary] concerns," note Useem and Kimball, "were with the expansion of the riot, the consumption of drugs or food, self defense, or the pursuit of personal vendettas."[11] That the Santa Fe riot lasted for only thirty-six hours has been explained by the fact that most of the inmates became so intoxicated that they were physically unable to continue their orgy of carnal violence.[12]

An equivalent cache of pharmaceutical drugs was available to the Cuban prisoners inside Atlanta, yet the detainees set up elaborate procedures to control its dispensation. In fact, one of the first staff members to be taken hostage was the prison pharmacist who, with the assistance of the detainee police force, maintained strict control over the pharmacy throughout the siege.[13] There was nothing carnal about the Cuban violence. Instead, it was in their minds a highly moral act against physical property designed to capture the attention of a larger human audience—the United States government.

Negotiation and Management: "Endless Patience"

The third lesson of Oakdale and Atlanta is that spirituality and patience can interact to play a crucial role in the management and negotiation of a prison riot. At Attica, negotiations for an end to the siege were forged by a public panel, including the journalist Tom Wicker of the *New York Times,* law professor Herman Schwartz, local politician Arthur Eve, and community activist Bobby Seale of the Black Panther Party, together with Russell G. Oswald, the liberal and reform-minded commissioner of the New York Department of Corrections. History teaches us that their negotiations were an utter failure.[14] The Santa Fe riot, on the other hand, was successfully negotiated to an end by New Mexico's veteran Criminal Justice Secretary Felix Rodriguez, though the end had less to do with Rodriguez's negotiating skills than it did with massive prisoner defections from the riot and exhaustion due to severe drug intoxication.[15]

But journalists, civil rights attorneys, community activists, and even public officials were reduced to secondary roles in bringing an end to the sieges at Oakdale and Atlanta. Instead, a religious leader emerged as the key peacemaker. Hence, there are meaningful differences between the negotiation and management techniques used in these four prison riots.

The public managers of the Attica rebellion were Commissioner Oswald and his superior, Governor Nelson Rockefeller.[16] They asked for, received, and analyzed several proposals from the Attica prisoners to end the riot and release hostages. They called in more than thirty experts on penology to help prisoners and administrators reach an end to the crisis by adopting one of the proposed solutions. But a peaceful solution never came about. Instead, Oswald and Rockefeller turned to the New York State Troopers, who used shotguns and deer rifles to kill twenty-nine prisoners and ten hostages within fifty seconds. That is how Attica ended—in a bloodbath.

After prisoners were captured and recontrol of Attica was established, guards and administrators went on a rampage of violence against the prisoners. About these staff members, Useem and Kimball write:

> Many of them engaged in a day-long frenzy of verbal and physical
> brutality toward inmates. Inmates were kicked in the head and the
> privates; wounded inmates were beaten and knocked to the
> ground; inmates were made to run a gauntlet of guards and beaten
> the length of it. Forty-five percent of the inmates . . . suffered
> bruises, lacerations, abrasions, and broken bones.[17]

Useem and Kimble conclude that the major lesson of the Attica riot is that violence could have been avoided if Oswald and Rockefeller had waited longer and given negotiations a chance to work themselves back and forth between prisoners and officials. "Waiting," they argue, "would have been an advantage to the state."[18]

This is precisely the strategy employed by Edwin Meese and Michael Quinlan to end the Oakdale and Atlanta sieges. Where the Attica managers were impatient and used a disorganized and low-tech approach to ending the riot, Meese and Quinlan used high-tech devices controlled by professionalized military personnel to wait "with endless patience" until the detainees laid down their weapons and surrendered. When faced with a negotiation impasse, Oswald and Rockefeller reacted with an unprecedented display of state violence. Although there was great rivalry over the issue, Meese and Quinlan ultimately responded to the same dilemma by seeking the assistance of a nonviolent spiritual leader. Once prisoners at Oakdale and Atlanta were captured, they were not beaten or ridiculed. Instead, they were blessed with Mass and given showers and a good night's sleep in clean beds.[19]

Meese and Quinlan had learned the primary lesson of Attica. Because of their doctrine of endless patience—and their willingness to let Bishop Roman assist with the negotiations—Meese and Quinlan deserve credit for managing what must certainly be one of the most nonviolent prison riots in American history.

Goals and Outcomes

Finally, the Cuban revolt is distinguished by facts related to prisoner goals and the various outcomes that have obtained in the aftermath of the riots. The Attica and Santa Fe uprisings indicated that prisoners were especially discontented with the rhetoric of prison rehabilitation and the reality of prison life. In order of importance, the root causes of the Santa Fe riot have been traced to an acute state of disorganization within the ranks of the prison's security force, the institutionalized use of a snitch system, poor food, crowding, a lack of educational programming, inadequate recreation, and general mismanagement by New Mexico's correctional administrators.[20] But the inmates who reacted to these conditions were neither ideologues nor progressive reformers.[21] Intoxicated on prison "hootch" and drugs, the Santa Fe rioters were nothing more than a gang of cold-blooded killers.[22]

Attica also was a rebellion against the forlorn hope of failed rehabilitation and bad living conditions, but according to Commissioner Oswald it was waged by "a very sophisticated and determined coalition of revolutionaries who were trying to exploit public sympathy to achieve their political objectives."[23] Useem and

Kimball have gone so far as to assert that "Attica could boast the best concentration of prison revolutionaries and experienced jail and prison rioters east of the Sierras."[24]

And it is on this point that the Cubans can be distinguished from their counterparts at Attica. More than anything else, the Attica rebellion was driven by radical black nationalist and leftist ideas. After they seized control of the institution, the Attica revolutionaries demanded "complete amnesty" for the riot and the "transportation of inmates to a non-imperialist country"—such as Castro's Cuba.[25]

By contrast, the Cubans in Oakdale and Atlanta hated Fidel Castro.[26] Indeed, they were staunch supporters of President Ronald Reagan and his interpretations of capitalism and imperialism.[27] They sought legal guarantees to stay in the United States, even if that meant being confined to prison cells where they were afforded deplorable and inhumane conditions with little chance for release. Instead of focusing on their "posture as prisoners" and their own personal suffering at the hands of prison officials, the Cubans waged a united guerrilla war against the political forces that had abandoned them in the suites of Washington. The Cuban riots were not about a lack of rehabilitation opportunities. Nor were they about crowded cells, snitch systems, guard brutality, poor food, bad management, or pocket freedom. The goal of the Oakdale and Atlanta revolts was to focus public attention on the plight of all Cuban nationals incarcerated in federal prisons who were singularly affected by the U.S.–Cuban diplomatic accord of November 1987.

And in this regard, nearly every account published to date shows that the revolts at Oakdale and Atlanta have one important thing in common with the riots at Attica and Santa Fe: They all teach us that *significant changes in carcereal control are possible through collective acts of violence.*

According to Useem and Kimball, even the senseless Santa Fe debacle led to positive changes:

The [Santa Fe] riot was directly responsible for significant improvements in living conditions in the New Mexico prison system, including elimination of overcrowding, suppression of guard brutal-

ity, increased programming, less reliance on "snitches" for information and fewer restrictions on personal property.[28]

Similarly, the Attica riot led to improvements in visiting conditions, fewer restrictions on mail privileges, installation of pay
phones for prisoners, greater access to recreation and religion, the
establishment of an inmate grievance procedure, a statewide effort to hire black and Puerto Rican guards, and a major expansion
of educational programs.[29] About the decision to engage in prison
rioting, Useem and Kimball conclude that "one question . . . is
why inmates since Attica have not made this choice more often."[30]

The Cuban detainees at Oakdale and Atlanta made this choice,
and they also were successful. Before receiving awards from the
American Correctional Association and the Bureau of Prisons for
his exemplary efforts at Atlanta, Attorney General Meese said that
"When details of the agreement that freed eighty-nine hostages
are fully understood, it will become clear that it was fair and
proper."[31]

Not only did the nonviolent detainees win their moratorium on
deportations to Cuba and their individual review of each case, but
the details of the final agreement also granted them immunity
from prosecution for damaging prison property.[32] But the overriding goal of the Oakdale and Atlanta revolts was to capture and
focus public attention on the plight of all Cuban nationals in federal prisons.

And it is here that the Oakdale and Atlanta riots can be most
clearly distinguished from the insurrections at Attica and Santa
Fe. Today we hear little about the conditions of confinement behind the walls of Attica and Santa Fe. But the primary goal of the
Oakdale and Atlanta revolts has sustained itself and has grown
into something wider, something that has enlarged the horizons
of prisoners and public officials alike.

In recent years, the legacy of Oakdale and Atlanta has drawn
attention to inequities in U.S. immigration laws that allow Cubans
to be indefinitely detained in federal prisons without recourse to
an adversarial system of justice. These inequities have been discussed in special sessions held by the United States Congress, the
United Nations Commission on Human Rights, Amnesty Interna-

tional, the American Bar Association, the American Civil Liberties Union, the Catholic Conference of Europe and North America, various state legislatures, and numerous appellate courts within the American judicial system.[33]

The Cubans involved in the Oakdale and Atlanta riots came to the United States aboard the Freedom Flotilla of 1980. The chief governmental architect of the boatlift was President Jimmy Carter. On December 6, 1993, thirteen years after the Freedom Flotilla and six years after the Oakdale and Atlanta revolts, Carter reflected on the plight of Cuban nationals in federal prisons:

> The day before yesterday, I was talking to a reporter who was investigating more than 1,800 Cuban refugees who came to my country [in 1980].
>
> They committed some crimes—small or large. They have long ago finished their sentences and still are being detained in prisons in my country. And the judicial system, combined with the Immigration and Naturalization Service, has not found yet a way to give these immigrants justice.
>
> Every nation that grossly violates human rights justifies it by claiming they are acting within their laws. The way we are doing it now is the same kind of human rights violation that we'd vehemently condemn if it was perpetrated in another country.[34]

Carter's sympathy with the plight of the Cuban detainees has received support at the highest levels of the American legal order. For example, Senator Howard Metzenbaum has recently urged Attorney General Janet Reno to take "immediate action to end the deeply troubling situation."[35] Without the Oakdale and Atlanta riots, it is far from obvious that there would have been such a public impulse for meaningful correctional reform.

Conclusions: "A Propitious Moment"

In addition to the extended length of the siege, then, these four lessons—*nonviolence, organization and morality, negotiation and management,* and *goals and outcomes*—combine to make the Oakdale and Atlanta uprisings historically unusual. While they have certain features in common with other historically unprecedented riots, the differences among them are not negligible. In fact, it is probably safe to conclude that Oakdale and Atlanta were the most successful revolts ever undertaken in the annals of American penology, if not world penology. One of the reasons they were so successful, it seems, is because certain elements of the events collide head-on with preconceived notions we hold about the act of collective aggression.

As such, the Cuban revolt constitutes what the world-renowned French penologist and philosopher Michel Foucault referred to as "a propitious moment." Foucault argued that unparalleled historical events in penology must not be ignored because they reveal a basic truth about the dialectics of imprisonment: The struggle between good and evil, between order and disorder. He stipulated that "truth" appears as the singular product of "propitious moments" and "privileged places" where a ritualized "ordeal" can unfold.[36]

Following Foucault's path, we may view the prisons at Oakdale and Atlanta as "privileged places" where inmates reacted to a crisis, the repatriation treaty of 1987. This created the "propitious moment" from which several extraordinary human "ordeals" manifested themselves. These included elaborate theatrical events, unprecedented acts of playfulness, and profound human compassion delivered from the well-organized grip of guerrilla warfare. On this basis, the Cubans have revealed to us a basic "truth." That is, a new age of prison protest has begun.

The remainder of this work is dedicated to exploring the social and political contours of this possibility. This demands, first of all, a thorough accounting of the complex series of events that brought the Cubans to Oakdale and Atlanta in the first place. Who were these *Abandoned Ones?* Why did they come to the United States? And what did they do to wind up in a federal prison?

Then analysis turns to the intricate course of internal change and conflict that influenced both staff and inmates at Oakdale and Atlanta in the period preceding the climactic riots. Beyond the repatriation treaty of 1987, what were the precipitating and predisposing factors that triggered the riots? Could the riots have been avoided? If so, should they have been? And, perhaps most important, beginning in the early hours of the revolt and extending right up to the signing of the final document, why did the detainees steadfastly maintain their mistrust of Attorney General Meese?

The answer to this final question cannot be underestimated in the geometry of the Oakdale and Atlanta revolts, because Meese's reluctance to involve the trustworthy Bishop Roman was the major reason the revolt lasted as long as it did. If it had not lasted for nearly two weeks—if Roman had become involved earlier—the revolt would not have achieved historical presence. Perhaps more significant, there would have been no lessons about nonviolence, organization and morality, negotiation and management, and goals and outcomes.

Finally, there is the obvious question: What caused the Cuban detainees to so aggressively oppose deportation to their homeland?

Part II

Background

Since 1959 you [the people of Cuba] have been called upon to make one sacrifice after another. And for what? Doing without has not brought you a more abundant life. It has not brought you peace. And most important, it has not won freedom for your people.

—*Ronald Reagan: January 5, 1984*

El exilio: a Spanish term used to refer to a bizarre, phantasmagorical state of mind, what Czeslaw Milosz calls "the memory of wounds" and the Argentine Julio Cortazar [calls] "the feeling of being not all there."

—*Ilan Stavans: "Cuba and the Night"*

MR. REAGAN IF <u>YOU</u> DENY OUR FREEDOM YOU KILL US!

—*Banner displayed at the Oakdale riot*

Chapter 4
The Freedom Flotilla

The 2,400 inmates involved in the rebellions at Oakdale and Atlanta came to this country as part of the "Freedom Flotilla" that brought more than 120,000 refugees to the United States from the tiny port city of Mariel, Cuba, between April and June 1980. These people, soon to be called "Mariel Cubans" or "Marielitos," came to the U.S. as a result of an intricate set of factors related to economic, social, and political developments in Cuba during the late 1970s and early months of 1980.

Economic Forces

As the 1970s drew to a close, the Cuban government found itself in a thicket of economic trouble. To begin with, unemployment rates in the nation had reached a high for the decade. Between 1970 and 1979, the percentage of unemployed workers in the Cuban labor force rose from a postrevolution low of 1.3 to 5.4, leaving nearly 188,000 laborers out of work by 1979.[1] The unemployed represented surplus labor, caused by an unprecedented combination of natural disasters and demographic change. These included the destruction of at least 25 percent of the nation's 1978 and 1979 sugar crops by blight, the loss of almost the entire 1979 tobacco and coffee crops because of "blue mold"; a recurrence of African swine fever which literally wiped out pork production, a

25 percent decrease in fishing revenue caused by an oil tanker spill on Cuban shellfish beds, and an increase in the number of well-trained youth who began making claims on jobs and promotions in the labor market. There was also spectacular growth in the number of women who entered the labor force as a result of expanded educational opportunities and recent increases in material incentives (such as the availability of more durable consumer goods).[2]

Additionally, real economic growth for the average Cuban had not kept pace with population growth. In 1979, the growth of the country's economy declined sharply as the growth rate fell from 9.4 percent the previous year to 4.3 percent. Growth of individual wealth fell from 8.2 percent in 1978 to 3.1 percent in 1979, and was projected to fall to 1.8 percent in 1980.[3] Accordingly, on December 21, 1979, President Fidel Castro told the Cuban people very directly that economic hardship would prevail in their country for years to come.

> We are sailing in a sea of difficulties. We have been in this sea
> for some time and we will continue in this sea, sometimes more
> stormy and other times more calm, but the shore is far away. . . .
> We will march through a sea of difficulties; we will not be
> crossing it.[4]

The Cuban people were thereafter placed on a strict system of rationing that allowed each individual to purchase only two pounds of meat, one and a half pounds of chicken, and five pounds of rice per month, and two ounces of coffee every two weeks. Milk was available only to children under ten years old.[5] In essence, the opportunity for purchasing food in Cuba was 20 percent lower in 1979 than it was in 1965.[6] This rationing system was the result of agricultural disasters and low productivity in 1978–1979, a decline in world sugar prices, inflation in the prices of essential imports such as oil and coal (which are not naturally available in Cuba), continued high interest rates on the world market, and a growing unwillingness on the part of the international banks to extend credit to Fidel Castro.[7] By the end of the 1970s, Cuba's financial situation was, on balance, one of the worst within the Soviet bloc and its per capita debt was estimated to be the largest in Latin America: four times that of Brazil and three times that of Mexico.[8]

In an attempt to restore economic stability, Cuban government officials implemented reforms to deal specifically with the problems of surplus labor and low productivity. Effective July 1, 1979, the government reorganized categories of wage earners, raised the minimum wage, and readjusted pay scales throughout the nation. These reforms required the reassignment of many working men and women to rural locations of the island in an attempt to rejuvenate Cuba's declining agricultural production.[9]

Perhaps by historical accident, the years 1978 and 1979 also saw Cuba's greatest advancement in secondary education for children who lived in those rural areas. Despite the tremendous strides made in Cuban education, many of the newly educated became discontented when the only jobs they could find were picking coffee beans, fruits, and vegetables in relocation camps at an average wage of 127 pesos per month (approximately $155 in 1979).[10]

The economic reforms of 1979 also upset previous systems of worker seniority and autonomy which, in turn, led to a slowdown in construction and aggravated the existing housing shortage. These problems had their greatest impact on the newly relocated, freshly educated farm worker.[11] In short, the Cuban reform of 1979 was supposed to enable citizens to overcome their economic crisis and lay the foundation for future stability in the country. However, the most immediate impact was to increase the burden on individual workers. Because of rising aspirations associated with advances in education, the reform created a disjunction between what many Cubans were led to expect and what they were actually given in terms of economic opportunity; hence, many of those employed in the agricultural relocation camps during 1979 did not fully embrace the economic reform policies of their government. There began a rapid increase in worker absenteeism, pilfering, and black-marketeering in the relocation camps.[12]

Last—and a major reason for their debt crisis—the latter half of the 1970s was also a time of renewed Cuban support for the exportation of communism, including the deployment of thousands of troops and civilians to Africa.[13] The growth of this military activity came at the expense of food imports, which decreased about 8 percent during the 1970s.[14] An increase in the Cuban military budget from 33.8 pesos per capita in 1962 to 85.7 pesos per capita in 1979 reinforces this conclusion.[15] Yet these figures may actually underestimate the cost of the Cuban military buildup. For instance, a hidden cost of this policy was that revenues from fishing decreased 14 percent in 1975, when the Cuban government directed its fishing fleet to transport troops to Angola. Similarly, fishing revenues fell 6 percent in 1977 when fishing boats were used to transport troops to Ethiopia.[16] Of the nearly ten million people who lived on the island of Cuba from 1975 to 1979, approximately two hundred thousand—2 percent of the total population—were involved in military interventions in Africa.[17]

Social Forces

In addition to economic forces operating in Cuba during the late 1970s, at least three social conditions contributed to the emigration of 1980. First, those Cubans who refused to fight in the African wars, those who participated in the black market, those who were caught stealing, and those who failed to work in relocation camps were branded by the government as "anti-socials," or "non-supportive, non-participative elements" of the regime.[18] Many of these "anti-socials" were arrested and interned in Combinado del Este Prison in Havana. By the late 1970s, Combinado del Este held as many as 3,500 of these political prisoners.[19] One of them, Armando Valladares, later wrote,

> There, political prisoners from Havana province were executed by firing squads against an execution wall. . . . Night after night the firing was punctuated with cries of "Long Live Christ the King!" and "Down with Communism!" from prisoners who went to their deaths. From 1963 on, they were gagged.[20]

Valladares also writes of a time when political prisoners were deprived of food for forty-six days; of "punishment cells" where "the walls and ceilings were painted dazzling white, [with] ten neon tubes which were kept on all the time, throwing off a blinding light"; and of beatings, rapes, and "political rehabilitation."[21]

Second, in early 1979, 115,000 members of the *Communidad* (exiled Cubans living in Miami) visited family and friends in Cuba as part of a political dialogue established by Presidents Castro and Carter. Foreign policy analyst Barry Sklar described the results of this dialogue:

> The success stories of members of the Cuban exile community in Miami told to their brethren in Cuba's cities, towns, and rural villages were underscored by photographs of the houses, the businesses, and cars, stylish quality clothing, expensive jewelry, calculators, tape recorders, and cameras. The exiles brought other symbols of affluence for their Cuban relatives and friends to see. A typical city scene in Havana of teenagers sporting Levis and T-shirts from Disney World and with slogans familiar to the United States such as "Better in the Bahamas," "Marlboro,"and "Adidas" was evidence of the change since the influx of the thousands of visitors from the exile community.[22]

It has been estimated that these Cuban-American tourists spent as much as $100 million during their 1979 visit.[23] After the *Communidad* visit, durable goods became increasingly available to the Cuban people.[24] In retrospect, the *Communidad* was a significant "pull factor" in the decision of many Cubans to come to America. Not only did the visits revive feelings of loss of family, they also demoralized many Cubans who could not understand why, while they had to struggle to make a living in Cuba, exiles thrived in the United States. Latin American scholar Peter Winn has gone so far as to suggest that it was not *communism* but *consumerism* that actually explains the wave of Cuban exiles to America in 1980. "Most Cubans," concludes Winn, were "not fleeing dictatorship but austerity, and their goal was not the land of liberty but the lap of luxury that they expected to find on the other side of the Florida Straits."[25]

In December 1979, for the first time since the 1958 revolution, anti-Castro posters and leaflets began to appear on the streets of Havana, representing a growing dissatisfaction with economic and social conditions in Cuba. In turn, Castro waged a crackdown against *blandengueria, negligencia, burocratismo,* and *acomodamiento*—spinelessness, negligence, cover-ups, bureaucracy, and complacency. Castro's get-tough campaign produced a flurry of arrests and increased imprisonment for black-marketeering, petty crimes, and other "anti-social" behavior.[26]

Political Forces

Finally, in early 1980, quiet discussions began between U.S. and Cuban officials that focused on the application of the recently passed United States Refugee Act of 1980 to the question of permitting a large number of Cubans—including political prisoners—to emigrate to America.[27] Cuba could obviously gain certain short-term economic and social benefits from such a policy. The decision to open the gates to all who wanted to leave permitted the government to free Cuba of both the segment of the population that was extremely unhappy under the Castro regime and those who were unemployed and unproductive. Such a policy would "thin out" the population dependent on precious Cuban resources and at the same time get rid of those who criticized Cuban's system of distribution and justice.[28]

These discussions eventually cleared the way for the single largest Cuban exodus in history. The mass emigration began on April 20, when the Cuban government announced that evacuation of those who wanted to leave would be permitted by boats arriving from Florida.[29] Between April and October 1980, a total of 146,965 people (approximately 1 percent of the nation's population) left their homes in Cuba on shrimp and lobster boats via the port of Mariel in search of better lives in Spain, Ecuador, Argentina, Canada, Belgium, and the United States.[30] Of this number, 120,737 refugees came to the United States.[31]

While it is cavalier to make generalizations, accounts indicate that some of the refugees were "anti-socials," former political prisoners, and petty criminals. However, the same accounts of the Freedom Flotilla reveal that the vast majority of Cubans passing through Mariel were upstanding family members who were students, government employees, professionals, or laborers. They were farmers, mechanics, fishermen, truck drivers, seamstresses, accountants, construction workers, plumbers, carpenters, and professional baseball players.[32] It is estimated that 75 percent of the refugees were of working age and, of those, 57 percent were men.[33]

U.S. Reaction

During the second week of the "boatlift," an event occurred that would later play a significant role in the resettlement of the Mariel people in America. On May 1, American INS officials at the Key West marina began to notice Cuban men who were "more hardened and rougher in appearance" than earlier arrivals.[34] Because of their appearance, the INS concluded that the Cuban government was taking advantage of the immigration accords by emptying the nation's prison system of hard-core criminals. The Carter White House endorsed this line of reasoning, and on May 14 accused the Cuban government of "taking hardened criminals out of prison and mental patients out of hospitals and forcing boat captains to take them to the United States."[35] The Cuban government denied such a deliberate policy, and on May 19 Fidel Castro characterized the refugees as simply "anti-social lumpen" (socially displaced individuals) and "anti-government reactionaries" who had decided to leave Cuba on their own accord. Castro further explained that mentally ill persons on the boatlift were there because family members in the United States had requested their passage through Mariel.[36] Beyond this, Castro made no further official comment about the Mariel people during 1980.

Yet analysts in the United States would overlook Castro's characterization of the Mariels in favor of the description offered by the Carter administration. Articles began appearing in the U.S. media accusing Castro of characterizing the Mariels as "murderers, vagrants, homosexuals, and scum."[37] Castro was trying to discredit the refugees, asserted the media, by intentionally adding to the boatlift a number of mental patients and prisoners taken directly from psychiatric hospitals and jails. In the months to come, official INS resettlement figures would show this characterization of the Mariel Cubans to be wrong. Unfortunately for the refugees, however, the damage had already been done. The collective

imagination of the Carter administration and the U.S. press inspired the belief that a number of Mariel Cubans were "dangerous" people who could not be trusted in this or any other land.[38]

This popular conception served a purpose for the Carter administration. By making Castro look as if he were trying to dump his
severe social misfits on the United States, the administration
could then blame Castro for diverting attention from the "real
cause" of the mass exodus—the moral failure of his totalitarian
system of government. Under such a strategy, communism became an easy target for criticism and was sure to be an issue in
the forthcoming presidential race with the conservative Ronald
Reagan.[39]

Characteristic of his administration, Jimmy Carter balanced a
mistrust of communism with an extraordinary compassion for the
human suffering of those who lived under totalitarian rule. At a
press conference held on May 5, 1980, President Carter was asked
about the first wave of Mariels then crossing into Key West. He
replied,

> Literally tens of thousands of Cubans will be received in our coun-
> try, as safely as possible on their journey across the ninety miles of
> ocean, and processed in accordance with the law. . . . We'll continue
> to provide an open heart and open arms to refugees seeking free-
> dom from Communist domination, brought about primarily by
> Fidel Castro and his government.[40]

Instead of "open hearts and open arms," however, many Cuban
refugees soon found themselves in what has been described as
"an Orwellian purgatory with little chance of escape in which the
United States government took the position that as a matter of
law, the Mariel Cubans were not really here."[41]

Chapter 5
The Resettlement

Despite Jimmy Carter's humanitarian interest in the Mariel people, the U.S. State Department, under the direction of Secretary of State Cyrus Vance, held that the Mariel boatlift was unlawful, and that refugees were technically illegal aliens. Under the terms of the Refugee Act of 1980, illegal aliens fleeing political, racial, religious, or other persecution could, however, be provisionally admitted to the United States. As applied to the Freedom Flotilla, this meant that the Mariel boat people were technically excludable from the United States because they did not have valid passports or visas. Because they lacked the necessary documentation, the Refugee Act stipulated that all excludable entrants be processed and screened by government officials before they would be allowed actually to relocate in America.[1]

The Relocation Camps

In April 1980, the INS set up two large relocation facilities in south Florida to process the Mariels in accordance with the law. The first, Campamento del Rio (River Camp), was established beneath an elevated interstate overpass off I-95 in Key West. The second camp was set up on the football field of the Orange Bowl in Miami.[2] Yet the massive influx of Cubans to the U.S.—which approached nearly sixty thousand during the week of May 20

alone—demanded supplemental receiving and processing facilities beyond these two camps.[3]

Accordingly, the INS established additional relocation facilities
at Elgin Air Force Base and Fort Walton Beach, Florida; Fort
McCoy, Wisconsin; Fort Indiantown Gap, Pennsylvania; and Fort
Chaffee, Arkansas. The Refugee Act required that each Cuban undergo a medical examination (complete with X-rays and lab tests)
and interviews with agents of the INS, the FBI, the Pentagon, and
the CIA. If it was determined that an alien posed no threat to the
safety of the general public, then he or she was placed on "parole"
by the INS with the understanding that if there was no violation
of the law, he or she would become eligible for permanent U.S.
residence after seven years. But if convicted of a crime during that
seven years, an alien would be deported.[4]

The tremendous daily flow of Cubans into the relocation camps
made the policy of case-by-case review nearly impossible, however. By June 1, 1980, more than seventy thousand Mariels were
in the camps waiting to be relocated. Many who had arrived in
the U.S. tired, seasick, and with no personal possessions beyond
the clothes on their backs began to complain about weeks of bore-
dom waiting for release, under conditions that were far worse
than those they had left behind in Cuba. Naturally, they also
began to complain about their "burning impatience" to be re-
united with relatives in the United States.[5] At this point, veteran
INS officials working directly with the resettlement problem argued that the meticulous screening process and continued detention of Cubans was becoming a serious threat to the security of
the agency. The Carter administration provided no short-term resolution to their plight. Instead, the White House directed the INS
to continue its processing of the Cubans in strict adherence to the
provisions of the Refugee Act of 1980. In protest of Carter's policy,
several top-level INS officials quit their jobs, and in so doing, they
captured the attention of both houses of Congress.[6]

The Senate leader of the Cuban-Haitian Refugee Committee
and presidential candidate Edward Kennedy argued that the Refugee Act of 1980 allowed the president to declare the Mariels "refugees"—as opposed to "excludable entrants." By giving a blanket
declaration of refugee status to all Mariel Cubans, the Senator

argued, INS could simplify its review process by allowing private organizations and state and local agencies to receive a variety of federal benefits if they participated in the Cuban relocation effort. A number of political leaders supported Kennedy's simplification plan, including Pennsylvania Governor Richard Thornburgh and presidential candidates George Bush and Ronald Reagan.[7]

The House of Representatives opposed this view. As Mariels began to fill the relocation camps, Representative Elizabeth Holtzman of New York, head of the House Subcommittee on INS activities, argued that extreme caution was needed in handling the exiled Cubans because, she said, "as many as 700 ex-convicts had been rounded up by the Cuban Government and given a choice of going to the United States or back to jail." In addition to the seven hundred criminals, Holtzman also was concerned about "a disturbingly high rate of venereal disease and tuberculosis" among the Mariel people.[8]

The Carter administration sided with Holtzman and the House of Representatives in their interpretation of the Refugee Act of 1980, employing a strict constructionist interpretation of the act, which required the case-by-case review of excludable entrants in order to ensure public safety. "No one," said White House Press Secretary Jody Powell during the fourth week of the Freedom Flotilla, "who does not meet the refugee definition [under current law] should be granted refugee status."[9] Again, this policy was based on a strong belief that a number of Mariels were dangerous. Ironically, this approach to the relocation of the Mariel people would ultimately produce its own simplification plan. The means to the Carter simplification strategy were, however, vastly different from the means envisioned by Kennedy and his colleagues in the U.S. Senate.

The Fort Chaffee Incident

On the evening of May 26, 1980, about two hundred Mariel Cubans peacefully walked through an unlocked gate at the Fort Chaffee camp in protest of their continued detention by the INS. Military guards immediately captured all the protesters without incident and returned them to their living areas. At about the same time, approximately sixty detainees at the Fort Walton Beach camp began throwing rocks at military guards while dozens of others scaled a barbed-wire fence and ran for their freedom.[10]

During the following week, the bureaucratic bottleneck in the camps narrowed. On June 6, nearly a thousand Mariels, weary of sitting in tents and barracks waiting to be processed, went on a rampage at Fort Chaffee, burning five wooden army buildings and storming the front gates of the military base toward a confrontation with the Arkansas State Police. State troopers opened fire over the heads of the Mariels and the Cubans retaliated by hurling rocks and bottles at the troopers. After about two hours, troopers dispersed the rioting Cubans with clubs and tear gas. The Fort Chaffee incident left one Cuban dead, forty Cubans seriously wounded, and fifteen Arkansas State troopers injured.[11]

Consistent with the Carter/Holtzman position, Jody Powell said on June 7 that the Fort Chaffee incident was caused by "some hardened criminals exported to the United States by Fidel Castro."[12] Meanwhile, an INS official boldly stated to *People* magazine that as many as "85 percent of the refugees are convicts, robbers, murderers, homosexuals and prostitutes."[13] The Fort Chaffee incident and the subsequent public reaction expanded prejudice against the Mariels beyond the federal bureaucracy. In June, Arkansas Governor Bill Clinton sent 140 National Guardsmen to the camp, because "people around Fort Chaffee are exhausted, irate, and afraid."[14] Arkansas Senator Dale Bumpers reported that residents living near Fort Chaffee "were armed to the teeth" following the riot.[15] Predictably, these developments brought the demonstration of bigotry and xenophobia into full and ugly view. Throughout the summer of 1980, the Ku Klux Klan turned up regularly near Fort Chaffee, Fort Elgin, and Fort Walton Beach, resounding the alarm that Mariel Cubans were dangerous criminals.[16]

Yet the Fort Chaffee riot spurred two major changes in the government's relocation policy. First, security was tightened at all the relocation camps. Two days after the Fort Chaffee incident, President Carter ordered expulsion proceedings against the riot's ringleaders, and then sent 3,700 troopers of the 82d Airborne Division to stand guard over the Mariels at Fort Chaffee and Fort Indian-

town Gap.[17] Increased security measures included the establishment of Cuban "security forces" within the camps. For example,
authorities at Fort McCoy set up the "Warhawks" to help keep
order at their facility. These were a group of Cuban detainees who
were given purple jackets donated by the nearby University of
Wisconsin at Whitewater, which were emblazoned with the
school's nickname on the back—"Warhawks." They were allowed
to carry broom handles, tree limbs, billy clubs, and knives in their
job of maintaining camp order.[18]

Second, after the Fort Chaffee incident the government began
streamlining its relocation policy. The INS dispensed with full
medical examinations, and FBI, Pentagon, and CIA officials limited their questioning to only those Mariels who admitted to a
criminal history in Cuba. These procedures rapidly accelerated the
movement of Mariels out of the camps, often allowing the release
of as many as five hundred restless Cubans in a single day.[19] By
October 1980, nearly all the Mariels had been released into the
community and the relocation camps were closed.

A Scorecard on the Freedom Flotilla

In retrospect, several important lessons were learned from the
Freedom Flotilla. To begin with, there were obvious problems with
the implementation of the Refugee Act of 1980. As interpreted by
the government, this legislation did not contemplate the kind of
situation faced by the INS during the massive Cuban influx of
1980. The procedures for dealing with excludable entrants into
the United States demanded lengthy examinations on a case-by-
case basis that left many Cubans in limbo status for long periods.
In turn, this condition created an intolerable situation for many
Cuban entrants and was a tremendous source of stress on INS and
military personnel responsible for receiving and processing them.

Compounding this problem, the times simply were not right for
President Carter's "open arms" policy. In 1980, Americans were
drifting into a recession. Many were troubled by the oil crisis, and
plant closings were beginning to become common as American
industries started to change. Americans were not especially dis-
posed toward inviting an additional 120,000 people into their

country during 1980.[20] Finally, it was clear that Mariel Cubans did not hold up well under indefinite terms of confinement. In less than one month, they had incurred the wrath of the president of the United States, who had been forced to use the army and air force to bring stability to the relocation camps. As such, the internment of Mariel Cubans had become a serious concern among high-ranking military officers, INS officials, and administrators within the Federal Bureau of Prisons.[21]

The Relocation Figures
Of the 120,737 illegal Cuban aliens processed by the INS in 1980, 119,081 were placed on parole and passed along to their families or to private relief groups in Miami, Los Angeles, Phoenix, Chicago, New York City, Rochester, and West New York and Union City, New Jersey.[22] The INS also identified 1,306 aliens who had questionable backgrounds and classified them as "potentially excludable" from relocation.[23] These aliens were sent to various minimum-security federal correctional institutions around the country for further observation and eventual parole. The remaining 350—*fewer than one-half of 1 percent of the total number of Cubans who came to the United States via the port of Mariel*—were found by the INS to have serious criminal backgrounds and were transferred to the United States Penitentiary at Talladega, Alabama, to serve an indefinite period of confinement.[24] On being processed into the Talladega facility, the Cubans were told their release "would be determined by their behavior in prison over the course of the next several months"—a theme that would later cause great anguish among thousands of Mariels who were unable to follow the conditions of their parole.

The Criminalization Process: "Overeager Warriors"

It has become an established principle that what criminals do and how criminal careers develop are strongly influenced by the agents of criminal justice.[25] Criminologist Daniel Glaser crisply summarizes the axiom:

> In trying to clear crimes for which they have no clues, or as a crime-prevention measure, some *overeager warriors* against lawbreaking

harass large numbers of persons known or alleged to have committed offenses in the past. They frequently detain them for questioning, and threaten or arrest them with little justification. Such
"busywork" tactics violate the spirit and often the letter of the Bill
of Rights, contribute little to the solution of puzzling crimes, and
cause many former offenders trying to "go straight" to lose jobs
and be stigmatized again, thus often fostering recidivism. [Empha-
sis added.][26]

This truth provides a useful tool for understanding what happened to many of the Freedom Flotilla Cubans once they had been
processed through the relocation camps. The evidence shows that
the refugees were a heterogeneous group of people whose incarceration followed from four distinct avenues of criminalization.

The Original Cohort: The Criminals of Cuba

First, there were those immigrants whose incarceration came as a
direct result of a stigma caused by the public's unwarranted hyste-
ria over the Freedom Flotilla. Once again, official INS relocation
figures indicate that fewer than one-half of 1 percent of the total
number of Cubans who came to the United States via the port of
Mariel in 1980 were found to have significant criminal histories.
Of the 120,737 immigrants admitted into the country, only 350
were found to have serious criminal backgrounds. By comparison,
in the same year approximately 6,000 out of every 100,000 U.S.
residents committed a major-index crime, as reported in the *Uniform Crime Reports*.[27] Criminality within the general U.S. population was roughly seventeen times greater than that among members of the Mariel boatlift.

Hence, it was a relatively small group of highly stigmatized offenders who made up the first cohort of prisoners who would
eventually occupy the cell houses and housing units of Oakdale
and Atlanta. They were characterized as "vagrants, murderers, homosexuals, and scum" who had been forced aboard the Freedom
Flotilla by Fidel Castro and dumped on America's doorstep to di-
vert attention from Cuba's severe economic, social, and political
problems. "Although most of the emigrants were good citizens,"
recalls Jimmy Carter in his memoir, "we were soon to discover

that some were mental patients and criminals."[28] To the extent that their criminality later influenced their propensity toward collective violence, the criminal records of these 350 individuals constitute an important chapter in the Oakdale-Atlanta story.

Yet within the entire corpus of academic, legal, and popular literature on the Mariel Cubans, little is revealed about this original group of detainees. We are left with an obvious question: How dangerous, in fact, were these émigrés to the safety and security of the American public?

I have identified thirteen of the original 350 immigrants classified by the INS as having had criminal backgrounds in Cuba. Their case files show that none of them had been charged with violent crimes, although one man allegedly had killed a fellow prisoner while incarcerated in a Cuban prison. To the extent that these thirteen cases represent the larger group of 350 (and there is no reason to assume otherwise until evidence is presented to that effect), their stories reveal a fundamental lesson about the power of criminal justice agents to criminalize a group of decent and law-abiding people. Among the thirteen cases, nowhere was this lesson more vivid than in the case of an Atlanta prisoner named Alberto Herrera. Some stories in the Mariel saga are so moving that they demand a brief digression.

The Tragic Case of Alberto Herrera

Alberto Herrera, the eldest of seven children, was born in Havana on November 21, 1952. Alberto's father was a mason and his mother was a seamstress. Alberto attended Havana's Sierra Maestra grammar school and received his sixth grade diploma in May 1965. When he was fourteen years old, he went to work for his father as a mason's apprentice, but the elder Herrera soon fell on hard times and closed the masonry service to take a job as a construction worker. This left Alberto out of work, and his parents, because of the newly implemented food rationing program, were unable to put enough food on the table for their family. Alberto decided to do something about this.

On October 24, 1971, eighteen-year-old Alberto Herrera walked into a government grocery store in Havana and hid a two-pound package of goat cheese under his jacket. He walked out of the store and began running down the street toward home. As he rounded the corner to his house, the Cuban militia stopped him with machine guns pointed at his head. Alberto dropped the cheese and surrendered.

Alberto was convicted of theft and sent to La Cabaña Prison, where he spent the next seven years of his life. During his internment, Alberto learned little about surviving in Cuban society. Because he already had his grammar school diploma, he was given no further education. Long, idle hours were spent in his cell. Any human in such a forlorn situation adapts by creating his own diversions. Some will turn to violence; others will turn to drink, drugs, or the prison rackets. Alberto found solace in the Santeria religion and its ritual of body tattooing.

Alberto was paroled from La Cabaña on May 1, 1979. Seven years of unproductive imprisonment had left him ill-prepared to meet the requirements of Cuba's ever-demanding society. Besides that, he now displayed no fewer than fourteen extravagant tattoos on his arms and hands. Most of them represented Catholic saints. Down the length of his back, he bore a large, colorful portrayal of Saint Lazaro.

Unable to find employment, Alberto quickly ran afoul of the law again. On September 21, 1979, he was caught trying to steal two pairs of pants from a Havana clothing store. Convicted for theft a second time, on January 2, 1980, Alberto received a thirteen-year sentence at the Combinado del Este Prison.

On June 24, 1980, a guard came to Alberto's cell and told him to gather his belongings; he was being deported to the United States aboard something called the "Freedom Flotilla." He knew almost nothing about the United States and had never heard of the Freedom Flotilla. The next day, along with some twenty other Combinado del Este prisoners, he was escorted under security to the port of Mariel and ordered onto an already overcrowded fishing boat.

During the two-day voyage, Alberto mixed with the civilians on board who incessantly talked about expensive cars, swimming pools, sportswear, Disneyland, and other forms of American mass culture that awaited them beyond the straits of South Florida. Because of these discussions, Alberto thought that he too would soon be given a chance to start his life anew and maybe one day to enjoy these fantastic material luxuries himself. No one had told him differently, and Alberto's excitement soared. About the voyage, he later recalled (in Spanish):

> That was the best time of my life.
> *Question:* Did you know where you were going once you got to the U.S.?
> *Answer:* No. I thought I would be free. I would work and be free.

On the morning of June 27, the fishing boat anchored at the public marina in Key West. Alberto was full of hope as he joined hundreds of other refugees for processing at the Fort Walton camp. Among these refugees, however, Alberto stuck out like a sore thumb. Wild-eyed with the excitement of the voyage and heavily tattooed, he became one of the young Cubans the INS would later describe as "more hardened and rougher in appearance" than men who had come on earlier boats.

A week later, Alberto was processed through the camp. Because of his prison record, he was assigned to the U.S. Detainee Facility in Talledega for further observation and was told that his release would depend on his behavior over the next several months.

Alberto's Talledega record was exemplary. Between July 1980 and January 1981, he received no prison write-ups and was involved in no acts of violence. Nevertheless, he was not released. Unable to locate a Cuban-American family to "sponsor" Alberto's resettlement, INS officials transferred him to the U.S. Penitentiary in Atlanta on February 14, 1981. He would not leave the Atlanta prison until December 4, 1987, after more than a thousand of his fellow prisoners nearly destroyed the institution by fire.

If his days on the Freedom Flotilla were the brightest of Alberto's life, his days in Atlanta were the darkest. There, he was confined to a cramped cell with seven other Mariel Cubans. The cell contained four bunkbeds, a sink, and an open toilet. Poorly ventilated, the cell was often without air-conditioning for weeks on end during the brutal Atlanta summers. Starting in 1984, Alberto and his cellmates were forced to remain inside this hideous cage for twenty-three hours a day. Like his cellmates, he was given little assistance or encouragement to escape his plight. And his plight was formidable.

Alberto was being "indefinitely detained" under these savage conditions because he did not have an "appropriate community support apparatus" (that is, a sponsor) to permit his release to the community. He did not have a sponsor because he did not know of one. He did not know of one because he had never been to the "community" and knew almost nothing about it. He did not have the social skills to recruit a sponsor because such skill development was unavailable at the prison. He was forced into this absurd existence and given no avenue of escape. When faced with absurdity, people can react in dramatic ways.

Alberto reacted with suicide attempts. On six different occasions between 1983 and 1987, Alberto tried to kill himself by strangulation with a rope, twice by overdosing on pharmaceutical drugs, by drinking gasoline, and by violently beating his head against a cement wall until he bled from the ears. Finally, on his last attempt, Alberto refused to eat for thirteen days. Near death, he dictated a statement dedicating his suicide to President Ronald Reagan in an effort to focus public attention on the plight of all incarcerated Cubans from Mariel.

On September 7, 1987, a month before the riot, Alberto borrowed a shank from another detainee in Cell House B. Despondent and weak from his suicide attempts, he made a feeble attempt to stab a guard in the neck; the knife glanced off of the guard's shoulder blade, leaving a superficial cut.

Question: Why did you try to hit that guard, Alberto?
Answer: I wanted to go home to Cuba. At least there I am given a chance. Here I am treated like an animal. I am not an animal. I am a man.

Because of the attack, Alberto was locked in the Cuban Segregation Unit (Cell House E) during the Atlanta riot, and he played no role whatever in the revolt. By that time he had become so physically depleted by the federal prison system that he was too weak to participate in its overthrow.

In 1991, Alberto Herrera was still incarcerated in a federal prison. Barely forty, he looked like an eighty-year-old man: He was sick, his hair was gray, most of his teeth were missing from the severe physical impacts of half a dozen suicide attempts, and he walked with a slow, sad shuffle. His eyes were flat from years of lithium used to treat his "behavior problems." He had been defeated and the life kicked out of him. He was no threat to anyone. More than forty tattoos festooned his body, with icons of Saint Lazaro and Saint Michael running like spiderwebs up the veins of his skinny neck. After more than a decade of incarceration in federal prisons, Alberto still could not speak one word of English. He knew nothing of mathematics, culture, or philosophy. He had no job skills. He had never made love to a woman and had no conception of what it meant to care for a family. He knew nothing about music, nature, or dreams of a better tomorrow.

Simply put, Alberto Herrera was a pathetic specimen of humanity and not an obvious candidate for parole. Who made him this way? Certainly, Alberto cannot be blamed. His record shows that he took five short minutes out of forty years to engage in two failed attempts at theft. The first one involved two pounds of cheese and the second involved two pairs of pants. For committing these offenses, he had spent nearly a quarter of his life behind the bars of one maximum-security prison after another.

As Glaser predicted, Alberto's criminalization was the work of "overeager warriors" of the criminal justice system. And fighting these warriors represented a challenge akin to the formidable problems Alberto struggled with in his darkest hours at the Atlanta Penitentiary. After the riots, I represented Alberto in his hearing before the INS panel set up to provide "full, fair, and equitable" reviews of each detainee case.

> *MH:* This man, Alberto Herrera, should be released at once. He has spent more than twenty years in prison for the theft of two pounds of goat cheese and two pairs of pants. This man is not a criminal. Look at him. Have you ever seen a more pathetic sight? Two pounds of goat cheese and two pairs of pants. For this, he gets twenty years in maximum security prison? Are you going to tell me this is fair? If so, I'm ashamed to say this happened in America.
>
> *INS Panel* (after a long silence): Maybe this is something that could be pursued by people like you who care for the Cubans. Maybe you could help him find a sponsor.

MH: We are attempting to locate a sponsor for Mr. Herrera. But as you can imagine, this is not an easy task. What about the role of the state in this affair? Don't you think the INS at least has the responsibility to do no harm to Mr. Herrera? This man tried to kill himself six different times and nothing was done about it. When someone makes that many suicide attempts, it is clear that something is terribly wrong with the correctional institution which has interned him. Don't you think the INS has some responsibility for the way Mr. Herrera has turned out? Because the way he has turned out directly affects our ability to locate a community sponsor. Look at him! Who would want this poor soul?

INS Panel: Our responsibility is to process Mr. Herrera in accordance with the rules of INS. . . . We will consider your statements on his behalf.

My attempt to gain release of Alberto failed because I was unable to locate an "appropriate" community sponsor. Frustrated by the wanton cruelty of the INS's "full, fair, and equitable" review process, I can do nothing more than give Alberto the final word and hope that it rings true in the heart of someone who has the authority to help him and others who face a similar situation:

> Life was not good in Cuba. Life was difficult for a laborer. I came to the United States looking for liberty. I found prison. . . . I will not steal again.

The Second Cohort: The Disadvantaged

The overwhelming majority of Mariel Cubans handled their adjustment to life in the United States quite well. In a news conference held on December 11, 1987, U.S. Deputy Attorney General Arnold I. Burns stated that approximately 117,400 Cuban refugees (nearly 97 percent of the boatlift population) had become "productive, law-abiding members of their communities." On the other hand, Burns reported that "7,600 Cubans had violated the conditions of parole and had been placed in prisons or detention facilities supervised by federal or state authorities."[29] The second, third, and fourth segments of Oakdale and Atlanta detainees would come from this population of parole violators. But like the first group, their criminalization was not the product of their own behavior; rather, it came through the actions of overeager warriors of the state.

Because of their status as "excludable entrants," these 7,600 Cubans also were excluded from their constitutional right to due process of law. This meant that paroles could be revoked at the pleasure of the INS and "parolees" were not entitled to a hearing of the charges against them.[30] Numerous accounts indicate that paroles were revoked and Cubans were incarcerated because they had no visible means of support or fixed address, or because they did not have an appropriate sponsor. Other Cubans ended up in prison for violating curfew or travel restrictions, or for failure to participate in government relocation programs. The case of Pedro Prior Rodriguez is an example.

While living in a halfway house in Rochester, New York, in 1983, Prior was mugged on the street and taken to a local hospital for treatment of an eye injury. The INS revoked Prior's parole on the grounds that he could not afford specialized eye care. INS officials then transferred Prior not to an eye specialist but to a mental hospital. There he was judged to be sane. The INS then sent him to the Atlanta Penitentiary, where he was treated and given a glass eye in November 1983. Remarkably, however, Prior was not released back to the Rochester halfway house. Instead, the INS left him in the Atlanta prison. Having committed no crime in the United States, Prior remained locked up in Atlanta until the 1987 riot.[31]

The Third Cohort: The Petty Criminals

Other Cubans were sent to Oakdale and Atlanta because of petty crimes. Between 1981 and 1987, the INS revoked Cuban paroles for such minor infractions as driving without a license, shoplifting, or possession of small amounts of marijuana and cocaine.

For example, Rafael Ferrer arrived at the Atlanta prison on March 19, 1984, after pleading guilty to possession of three grams of cocaine. Ferrer was "indefinitely detained" by the INS until his prison behavior would warrant his release. He was still being "indefinitely detained" when the riot broke out three years later.[32]

The Fourth Cohort: The Doubly Punished

The United States Constitution guarantees the right to be punished only once for a criminal offense. Because the "excludable entrants" from the Freedom Flotilla were not afforded this guarantee, they could be punished twice on charges arising from the same offense. Through this strategy of double punishment, the INS created a fourth avenue of criminalization by which other Cuban men were sent to Oakdale and Atlanta.

The strategy worked like this: After a Cuban had completed his sentence in a state prison or city jail, the INS would "re-arrest" him for violating the conditions of his federal parole. Then he would be "indefinitely detained" in a federal prison. This is what happened to Guzman Gonzalez. In September 1984, Gonzalez was convicted of armed robbery by a Miami city court. He received a one-year sentence for this crime and was incarcerated in the Miami City Jail. Upon his release in September 1985, Gonzalez was immediately re-arrested by INS agents and transported to Atlanta to await placement in a BOP halfway house. Gonzalez was still awaiting his halfway house placement when the riot began two years later.[33]

The Disinformation Campaign: "Warehousing Human Rabble"

Through these four avenues, then, by 1987 the overeager warriors of the U.S. Immigration and Nationalization Service had criminalized enough Cuban men to fill the federal prisons at Oakdale and Atlanta to overflowing. As a group, these men had long ago paid their debt to society for their criminal transgressions. The historic Oakdale and Atlanta revolts were not waged by violent criminals, but were fought in guerrilla fashion by dedicated collectives of leftover nonviolent offenders from Cuba, the disadvantaged, petty criminals, and the doubly punished. These are the people that penologist John Irwin refers to as society's "rabble."[34]

Of all the facts presented in this book, this may be the hardest for readers to comprehend. We have been led to believe that maximum-security prisons exist to punish society's most dangerous criminals. The maximum-security prison at Atlanta, however, was used to warehouse human rabble. The stereotypical image of the prison rioter is of a raging, half-mad convict who destroys and defiles everything in his path. Yet, as evidenced by the way they managed their revolt, Oakdale-Atlanta was waged by a group of relatively peaceful men.

These conclusions are supported by the most exhaustive study conducted on the conditions of confinement afforded detainees in the years preceding the revolt. In February 1986, the U.S. House of Representatives conducted an oversight inspection of the Atlanta Penitentiary. Their report indicated that *absolutely none* of the nearly 1,900 Cuban detainees housed in Atlanta was serving a criminal sentence.[35] Instead, they were all being "indefinitely detained" for reasons that had nothing to do with their propensity for violence. This conclusion is supported by the fact that the Justice Department opened the medium-security Oakdale prison in 1986 for the express purpose of housing the overflow of nonviolent Cubans from the Atlanta Penitentiary.[36]

This does not mean that the Mariel Cubans were incapable of violence. On the contrary, after the riots, I represented several Cubans who were responsible for a drive-by shooting that left four dead in Las Vegas. I represented others who were involved in a homicide in New York City. And I represented one detainee who had been captured by New York City police on the George Washington Bridge with a cache of automatic assault rifles and grenades. He was involved in an international plot to assassinate Fidel Castro. But none of them came from Oakdale or Atlanta; these violent offenders had been transferred from federal prisons on the west coast (such as Lompoc) or the midwest (such as Marion). The Cubans at Oakdale and Atlanta were on a different track. They were *the Abandoned Ones*.

How was the federal government able to continue to widen the net around an ever-growing group of nonviolent men and incarcerate them under deplorable conditions, bypassing our adversarial system of justice? There are two reasons: The first is that few U.S. citizens knew about the injustice and even fewer cared. The second reason can be traced to a darker force. From the early days of the Mariel resettlement, officials within the Justice Department, together with their political allies, engaged in a deliberate disinformation campaign to justify their continued harassment and abuse of Cuban men.

For example, on December 11, 1987, Deputy Attorney General

Burns claimed that about one-fourth of the Cuban detainees in-carcerated at Oakdale and Atlanta during the revolt "had been convicted of crimes of violence including murder, kidnapping, sexual assault, robbery, and arson."[37] Of these six hundred alleg-edly violent offenders, Georgia Representative Pat Swindall (the ranking Republican on the Immigration Subcommittee in the House) argued during the November riots that "Cubans at the Atlanta prison are a hard-core lot and 500 of them are convicted murderers."[38]

Setting aside the fact that these two statements are statistically impossible, the claims belie the aforementioned House of Repre-sentatives report that none of the Atlanta Cubans were serving criminal sentences as of February 1986. They also ignore the fact that, by its own admission, the BOP constructed the Oakdale facil-ity for the sole purpose of housing the overflow of nonviolent Cubans.

Conclusions

The information presented in this chapter raises three compelling questions, the answers to which may shed light on the underlying causes of the Oakdale and Atlanta revolts. First, their criminality notwithstanding, the very fact that the Cubans were found to be in violation of the conditions of their paroles made all of them subject to deportation to Cuba, in accordance with the Refugee Act of 1980. Why weren't these illegal aliens immediately repatri-ated once they had violated their paroles?

Second, why did the INS continue to lock up so many Cubans for nonviolent offenses or for being disadvantaged? Finally, there is the issue of the disinformation campaign. What did officials of the Reagan administration stand to gain from deceiving the American public?

Chapter 6
The Moral Crusade

The deportation of Mariels back to Cuba proved to be an empty threat. Between 1981 and 1984, the Cuban government refused to acknowledge the right of the United States to enforce deportation procedures against any Cuban.[1] This immigration discord took shape largely as a result of foreign policy initiatives of the Reagan administration. Cuba's revolutionary imperative in the 1980s stated that Cuba had the right and duty to support revolutionary and national liberation movements throughout the world. It was Cuba's striving, with support from the Soviet Union, to introduce Marxist-Leninist governments into Central America that was at the heart of the Reagan-Castro discord[2]—which reached a tumultuous and bitter peak with President Reagan's intervention into Grenada in October 1983.

Grenada represented the first direct, non-covert military conflict between the United States and Cuba in history.[3] Although this conflict lasted only a matter of days, it led to the surrender of 784 Cuban soldiers and civilians who had been expected to fight to their deaths to preserve several critical projects. These included the training and organizing of Grenada's armed forces, the establishment of ground-based communication networks linked to the Soviet Sputnik Satellite System, the construction of a new airport, and the development of an air defense system to protect the country against foreign invasion.[4] The deployment of American troops to Grenada effectively terminated all these projects.

As a consequence, President Castro became deeply angered with President Reagan. Castro called the U.S. invasion "a cheap, political, opportunistic operation" that amounted to "a cowardly and ridiculous act." "Ronald Reagan," said Castro, "has proven that he cares little for reason and law; . . . he's a total liar." Castro concluded that "there is no hope for [U.S.–Cuban] dialogue as long as Mr. Reagan keeps on thinking that what is happening in Central America is the result of malevolent orchestrations by the Soviet Union and Cuba."[5]

Then, on December 14, 1984, representatives of the State Department and the INS reached an agreement with Cuban officials that restored limited diplomatic relations between the two governments. Suddenly, Cuba agreed to take back 2,746 "excludable entrants" from the United States, starting with 1,500 Mariels who were then confined to the Atlanta Penitentiary. In exchange the U.S. would open its borders to the legal migration of some twenty thousand Cubans, including three thousand political prisoners, who had recently applied for exit visas to the United States.[6]

Both Reagan and Castro stood to gain certain short-term political benefits from these normalized migration accords. The White House could display its get-tough stance toward crime in America by disencumbering the nation of what the president called "some 2,700 common criminals"—a feat which had not been accomplished by the Democratic administration of Jimmy Carter or 1984 presidential hopeful Walter Mondale.[7] By opening U.S. borders to those who were attempting to flee Castro's regime, Reagan could also demonstrate to the American public his distrust and hatred for communism. Castro stood to benefit, much as he had in 1980, from normalized migration by ridding Cuba of three thousand new political prisoners who had become unproductive members of his regime. Castro was also likely to receive an influx of much-needed hard currency in the arrangement through a newly enacted Cuban law that placed high charges on the emigration of Cubans to the United States.[8]

Between January and April 1985, 201 Mariel detainees from the

Atlanta prison were deported to Cuba by plane. According to an official Cuban news release, at least seventy-three of these prisoners were immediately reimprisoned.[9] These events set in motion a series of legal battles over whom the U.S. could deport, as attorneys for the Cubans in Atlanta began to make a desperate bid to keep the detainees in America—even if that meant their staying in prison.

These cases were initially heard in Atlanta by U.S. District Judge Charles A. Moye, Jr., between January and May 1985. During the proceedings, Moye became outraged at the INS for its "unseemly haste" in trying to deport Cubans who had pending court challenges to their deportations. In turn, Moye began ordering that Cubans be kept off deportation planes from Atlanta until they could receive fair hearings. However, one by one, Moye's decisions were reversed by the 11th U.S. Circuit Court. The appellate court held, moreover, that the INS had the right to deport virtually any illegal alien it wanted.[10] Yet, just as the INS was winning its right to deport Mariels from Atlanta, President Castro unexpectedly suspended the immigration accord on May 10, 1985. Most sources suggest that Castro had become outraged by the CIA-operated Voice of America radio program, which started to beam aggressively anticommunist propaganda to Cuba (including statements made by President Reagan) on Radio Marti in the spring of 1985.[11]

The Struggle for Due Process

Meanwhile, the indefinite imprisonment of Cubans at Atlanta was also being challenged in the courts. Since 1981, attorneys for the Cubans had been trying to win due process rights for their clients and were often successful in the U.S. District Court of Atlanta. Between 1981 and 1986, three hundred Cubans were released from the prison when the INS conceded that it could find no evidence of criminal records for the detainees. Another 2,500 Cubans won release from the Atlanta prison because of a probation system set up by the INS under threat of a court order from U.S. District Judge Marvin Shoob.[12]

In a series of orders issued over six years of litigation—1980 to 1985—in the Atlanta District Courts, Judge Shoob would rule time and again that Mariel Cubans at Atlanta *did* have certain constitutional rights, such as the right to know why they were being confined to a maximum security prison. Shoob granted Mariel inmates a limited right to counsel, a "presumption of releasability," and the right to prior written notice of factual allegations supporting continued detention.[13] In short, Shoob held that the INS had to either prove their cases against the Mariels or set them free.

However, as it had reacted to the Moye rulings in 1985, the 11th Circuit Court often reversed Shoob's decisions. By January 1985, Judge Robert S. Vance of the 11th Circuit began to complain that Shoob was exceeding his "very, very narrow" authority and had "poached on the prerogatives of the executive branch."[14] As Vance explained to an attorney for the Mariels, "the government can keep them in the Atlanta pen until they die." By October 1985, an 11th Circuit ruling reversing Shoob on the question of rights for the Cubans reached the U.S. Supreme Court. By an overwhelming majority the high court denied certiorari. Vance's word had become law: Mariel detainees were not entitled to due process rights afforded by the Constitution. In defense of its position, the Supreme Court held that "physical detention of aliens is now the exception, not the rule, and is generally employed as to security risks for those likely to abscond. . . . Certainly this policy reflects the humane qualities of an enlightened civilization."[15]

This left some five thousand Cuban detainees stuck in federal prisons without legal rights to due process. Furthermore, they were unwanted by either the United States or Cuban government. Hence, the application of law in the case of the Mariel detainees allowed indefinite imprisonment until diplomatic accords could be reached between the U.S. and Cuba. And so the waiting began. Meanwhile, the INS continued to assert its legal authority as investigator, prosecutor, and paroling agent of the Mariel people. Official records indicate that the INS increased the number of Mariel violators it brought into the federal prison system after the Supreme Court decision of October 1985.[16] As a result, by the end of 1985 the Atlanta prison was filled far beyond capacity with nearly 1,950 Mariels. But why was the INS continuing to incarcerate such a large number of low-risk offenders?

The Dangerous Marielito: Image, Ideology, and Moral Panic

Following the Supreme Court ruling, INS officials moved beyond their criminalization campaign to a larger task: the reconfiguration of the general public's perception of all Mariel Cubans. This manipulation of perception constituted the basis for what Israeli criminologist Stanley Cohen refers to as a "moral panic."[17] Cohen argues that any attempt to criminalize groups and their activities must be waged at the level of a moral crusade. Moral crusaders must not only attack their targeted groups, they must also attack the public's limited awareness of those groups if they are to create legitimacy and public support for their criminalization campaigns.

There is nothing novel about moral crusades waged by agents of the state against Hispanics living on American soil. In the years following World War II, for example, public officials and the media crusaded against the Mexican-American "zoot-suiters" of East Los Angeles, culminating in one of the worst street riots in California history. "Overt hostile crowd behavior against the zoot suiters," recall two historians of the period, "was preceded by the development of an unambiguously unfavorable symbol [of the zoot-suiters] in Los Angeles newspapers."[18] Similarly, during the 1980s an increasingly intrusive and authoritarian "War on Drugs" was legitimated by the Reagan administration by stories about Hispanic gangs linked to Mexican and Latin American drug cartels.[19]

In much the same way, INS crusaders employed an array of threatening images, factual distortions, and symbolic references to create a specific picture of the Mariel Cubans. As with the zoot-suiters and the Hispanic drug gangs, this ideological attack was essential to the creation of moral panic around the Mariels. Once successfully constructed, moral panic served as a source of crusade support and the legitimation of the campaign of criminalization, and it was successful because the tides of history were in its favor. These historical forces can be traced to severe cultural conflict experienced in those communities that became home to the Mariels in the years after the boatlift.

Cultural Conflict

The majority of Mariel Cubans resettled in four large urban areas: New York City, Los Angeles, Las Vegas, and, of course, Miami.

Miami, in fact, became home to approximately seventy thousand Mariels in 1980, or about 35 percent of the Freedom Flotilla population. Despite emergency relief efforts provided by the Carter administration in the early days of resettlement, the massive influx of Cubans caused the rate of unemployment in Miami to nearly double, from 6.5 to an astounding 12 percent.[20] Any time more than one out of ten persons is without work in a metropolis the size and complexity of Miami, cultural conflict is likely to follow.

The conflict manifested itself at several different levels of social interaction, all at once. First, the massive influx of immigrants overwhelmed the city's ability to provide shelter, health care, and education: the Mariels were competing with other Miami residents for access to public housing, hospitals, and schools. Second, the Mariels began to compete for jobs with Miami blacks, Haitians, and Colombians, primarily in the city's construction, restaurant, and hotel industries.[21]

Third, not only did the Mariels find themselves in conflict with other minority groups over jobs, but they were also seen as social outcasts by the established professional class of Miami's large Cuban-American community, who differed from the Mariels by socioeconomic status and race. Those who had resettled in Miami in the wake of Castro's revolution were primarily doctors, lawyers, engineers, architects, publishers, accountants, manufacturers, and importers, and they were predominantly Hispanic.[22] By contrast, the Mariels were construction workers, mechanics, farmers, carpenters, seamstresses, and athletes, and nearly half of them were black.[23] Social psychologist Marvin Dunn aptly describes this aspect of Miami's cultural conflict:

> The black [Mariels] might just as well be Polish or Soviet Jews as far as identity with native black Americans is concerned. In Miami they live in a world isolated from the black community and only peripheral to the Cuban community. Within the racial context of this country their blackness carries a double burden: they not only get it from whites who discriminate against them but also from the Cubans who don't want to be identified with them.[24]

And fourth, as a result of this cultural conflict Miami's crime rate increased a spectacular 30 percent in the first three months following the resettlement.[25]

Because of the unexpected strain on the city's infrastructure, rising unemployment, antagonisms within the black and Cuban communities, and unprecedented crime rates—because of cultural conflict—the Mariels became an easy target for racism. This racism flourished not only in Miami's expansive multicultural communities but also at the highest levels of Miami's political order. At the height of the conflict, Miami Mayor Maurice Ferre said of the Mariels: "While many refugees are good and decent people, we're also getting the dregs of society. Castro is sending his worst element here. My God, I've never seen people like some of these. Hard-core thugs."[26]

When a public official of Ferre's stature labels an entire subgroup of people as "the dregs of society" and "hard-core thugs," cultural conflict will escalate, eliciting an onslaught from overeager warriors of the criminal justice system. And this is precisely what happened. On the heels of Mayor Ferre's statement, Miami was rocked by four days of bloody street rioting, which brought to the fore a festering racial hatred for the Mariels.[27] The Miami Police Department subsequently adopted a new word to identify the target of the city's most important problem: "Marielito" became a synonym for thief, drug dealer, rapist, and murderer, and analogous to such racist terms as "nigger," "spic," and "kike."[28]

The Contagion

In the years following the Miami riot, the term "Marielito" came to refer to one of the most despised immigrations in the history of the United States. This came about primarily through the efforts of overeager warriors of the American criminal justice system during the Reagan era, and it would later come to play a crucial role in the INS's construction of a moral crusade against all Cuban men from the port of Mariel.

At mid-decade, five years after the Freedom Flotilla and the Miami riot, criminal justice "experts" had emerged to make wild generalizations and blanket condemnations of the Mariels:

> Approximately 30% of the total population of Cubans arriving in the United States displayed one of the following behaviors: habitual alcohol intoxication, drug addiction, pandering, prostitution,

engaging in sexually reprehensible activities, habitual vagrancy, and general anti-social behavior. . . . The extreme violence of their behavior, accompanied by cultural and religious sanctioning of this behavior, makes the Marielitos a tremendous threat to even the private citizens of our country.[29]

Never mind the fact that the U.S. House of Representatives found that none of the Cubans detained at the Atlanta Penitentiary in 1986 were serving criminal sentences. Never mind the fact that the Bureau of Prisons constructed Oakdale for the express purpose of housing the overflow of nonviolent "detainees." And never mind the fact that nearly 97 percent of the Mariel Cubans became upstanding, law-abiding citizens after resettlement. These facts were not an issue. Here is another example of the myopic ethnic insensitivity and disregard for truth echoed by American criminal justice administrators during the Reagan era:

> We offer a descriptive profile of the Marielito [to] provide valuable insight in aiding criminal justice agencies identify and process Cuban offenders. The profile consists of five characteristics.
> First, the Cubans believe that physical confrontation and religious rites are a necessary practice for survival.
> Second is that of machismo in which violence is a dominant factor. This trait inspired Hollywood to produce a movie entitled *Scarface,* which portrayed the tremendously violent behavior exhibited by these Cubans.
> Third is vengeful activities of the religious cult of Santeria. Fourth is the fact that every Marielito has a tattoo. And last, the average Marielito is in his early 30s and has poor hygiene and body scars and a good strong physique.[30]

This sort of twaddle soon spewed forth from every criminal justice agency that had anything to do with the resettlement of the Mariels. By the time Ronald Reagan squared off against Walter Mondale in the 1984 presidential elections, police administrators in Miami, New York City, Las Vegas, and Los Angeles estimated that as many as forty thousand of the Mariel exiles in America were veterans of Castro's prison system[31] (ignoring the fact that official INS resettlement figures indicated that only 350 were previously locked up in Cuba). According to congressional testimony recorded in 1984, at least three thousand Mariel Cubans were thought to be "secret agents of Castro who had been spying on fellow exiles and running a vast underground network for addicting Americans to cocaine in a Castro inspired plot to spread social decay among the people of the United States."[32]

Never mind the fact that most Mariels despised Fidel Castro, which was why they had escaped from the island in the first place.[33] Again, facts were not an issue. By 1985, the New York City Police Department claimed to have made "7,000 arrests of Marielitos" since 1981.[34] Between August 1980 and April 1983, the Miami Police Department "charged 3,232 Mariel Cubans with 14,035 felonies, misdemeanors or criminal traffic violations."[35] In 1984, police administrators in Las Vegas said that "there are approximately 3,000 Marielitos in the City, of whom 550 are career criminals. Out of our last 100 homicides, 22 or 23 of them were committed by Mariel Cubans."[36] And in just one Los Angeles police precinct during 1983, officers arrested "183 Marielitos for 38 robberies, 44 burglaries, 37 narcotics offenses, 9 murders or attempted murders, 19 assaults with a deadly weapon, 17 auto thefts, 1 rape and 5 weapons violations."[37]

These official reports indicated that the "Marielitos" had proudly begun to call themselves *banditos*. According to one L.A. police administrator, the banditos were "absolutely the meanest, most vicious criminals we have ever encountered. . . . Even hardened American criminals are terrified of them."[38]

The Moral Crusade
This disregard for the truth about the Mariel Cubans set the stage for the INS's moral crusade. Unlike previous attacks waged at the local level, however, this crusade was a national affair, and there was reason for this.

Following the diplomatic discord surrounding the disrupted U.S.–Cuban immigration treaty of 1984 and 1985, the Cuban immigrants attained high-profile status in the international political arena.[39] The INS capitalized on this status to further enhance its own importance. In terms of public exposure and political recognition, it is in fact safe to conclude that the Mariels were the best thing that ever happened to the INS.

Accordingly, any parole infraction committed by a Mariel Cuban became a matter of serious concern for the INS and an opportunity to further legitimate the agency's authority within the Justice Department. The official approach used by the INS during the latter half of the 1980s was to exaggerate the criminal propensity of those Mariels already in custody, thereby justifying the continued criminalization of hundreds more. The INS had successfully created a moral panic around the Cubans.

Though examples of this strategy abound, the INS's moral crusade reached its height in the months and weeks preceding the Oakdale and Atlanta riots. Speaking on ABC's "Nightline" on July 3, 1987, INS general counsel Mike Inman informed the American public that

> Some 2,700 Marielitos have been found to have been guilty of committing serious crimes. We are trying to protect the citizens of this country by preventing [these] people from being released into society. We have a decision to make whether to detain someone who we think is violent or to let that person on the street and subject the citizens of this country to violence. And between the two alternatives, I think it's appropriate to take the conservative approach rather than put the citizens of this country at risk.

This overly cautious, "conservative" approach served as the ideological basis of the moral crusade and was manifest in INS decisions to release Mariels from Oakdale and Atlanta. On March 29, 1987, Louis Richard, INS district director of the Atlanta office, told reporters from the *Boston Globe*,

> We're trying to find ways to get the releasable types out [of prison], the ones who understand that their machismoism [sic] is not the way here. It's a slow horse, but the horse is going to get there. . . . If I'm going to err, I'm going to err in favor of the safety of the American public.[40]

By this time, Atlanta was filled to overflowing with the original cohort of nonviolent offenders, the disadvantaged, petty criminals, and the doubly punished. Few of them, however, were

"releasable types" under the strict guidelines used by District Director Richard. Instead, the Mariels were treated as human rabble
and sacrificed on the altar of the INS's moral crusade. Later in the
summer of 1987, INS rhetoric became outright vicious. On July
13, Richard described the Atlanta detainees:

> We've got everything from skyjackers, arsonists, rapists, murderers,
> aggravated assaults, crimes of virtually every type you can think of.
> A couple hundred are hard-core deviates that do strange things.
> They are psycho cases. I would be for keeping these people in jail
> for the rest of their lives before I would take a chance of letting one
> harm your child.[41]

The moral crusade was waged at every level of the agency. On
August 23, Craig Raynsford, associate general counsel for the INS
in the Washington office, told reporters from the *Minneapolis Star
and Tribune* that "the Bureau of Prisons has seen these groups of
Mariel criminals as being the worst group of criminals they've
ever had."[42] Meanwhile, Thomas Schiltgen, the INS official in
charge of paroling Mariels from Oakdale, referred to the detainees
as "career criminals . . . who aren't the nicest people in the
world."[43] Crusade rhetoric also was well received by allies of the
INS. When asked to describe the Mariels detained in Atlanta,
Roger Conner, executive director of the Federation for American
Immigration Reform, replied that they were "the worst criminals
the nation has ever seen."[44]

Not surprisingly, then, the moral crusade influenced the administrators and guards within the Bureau of Prisons who were
responsible for carrying out the INS policy of indefinite detention.
Said an Oakdale security administrator after the riot,

> We were given special training on how to handle the Marielitos.
> We learned about their religious beliefs in Santeria and how it leads
> to violence. Everybody learned to keep their back up.
> *Question:* You were told that they were dangerous then?
> *Answer:* Oh hell yes!
> *Question:* Did you personally ever have a problem with them? Were
> you ever attacked or threatened by one of them?
> *Answer:* No, I always got along with them.

Benefits and Costs of the Moral Crusade

Two primary benefits accrued to the INS as a result of their moral crusade. First, it produced its expected results, legitimating the campaign of criminalization and increasing the perceived importance of the INS within the administrative branch of government. The overflowing populations at Oakdale and Atlanta were testament to the success of the criminalization campaign and increased budget allocations stand as testimony to the increased importance of the INS.

Before the Freedom Flotilla, the INS was a relatively obscure subdivision of the Justice Department that operated on a yearly budget of roughly $900 million. In 1983, the INS broke the billion dollar mark with a budget of $1,076,000,000. This figure remained constant during 1984 and 1985. Then, in 1986, the agency requested a significant increase over previous years: nearly $1.6 billion. The reason for this unprecedented increase, according to the *Budget of the United States,* was to "support the construction of the alien detention facility in Oakdale, Louisiana."

Then came the moral crusade, and with it the most exorbitant budgets in the history of the United States Immigration and Naturalization Service. In 1987, Congress approved the spending of $1.9 billion by the INS, and in 1988, the budget soared to $2.2 billion—more than a 100 percent increase over six years.[45] In terms of national priorities, President Reagan considered what he called some 2,700 "common criminals" from the port of Mariel more of a problem than the socioeconomic factors that were then beginning to rip American urban areas apart at the seams. As the INS budget more than doubled, President Reagan successfully passed through Congress legislation slashing billions of dollars from welfare, health care, and educational enhancement programs for the poor.[46] Reagan did not rob Peter to pay Paul; he robbed Peter to pay for something much less altruistic.

This cannot be said of Reagan's successor, George Bush. In 1989 and 1990, President Bush reduced the INS budget to a pre-crusade level of $1.1 billion—a 50 percent reduction. Any time that the successive budgets of a relatively small branch of the federal government fluctuate by more than 100 percent, it is a fairly good indicator that something excellently foolish is going on in the halls of government.

The Ethics of Edwin Meese III

The second benefit of the INS's moral crusade was not as detectable as the first. In fact, the benefit was perceived and understood only by a few.

The central office of the Immigration and Naturalization Service is located in a giant building at 425 I Street NW in Washington, D.C. In March 1985, a real estate magnate named Howard Bender bought the building from the Department of Justice for $37 million. He then leased it back to the INS from 1985 through 1987 at a profit. On or about May 13, 1987, at the height the moral crusade, Bender sold the building to another private investor for $60 million—a 60 percent return on his initial investment in less than two years. With a net worth of more than $60 million, Howard Bender became an influential figure inside the Beltway.

Bender then funded a high-paying executive-level position for Ursula Meese at the national Multiple Sclerosis Society.[47] Ursula was married to the attorney general of the United States, the titular head of the INS and the BOP. Though no evidence of a bribe was ever discovered, the impropriety of the event was obvious.

The moral crusade against the Cubans, then, effectively served to deflect public attention from the corruption inherent in the U.S. Justice Department under Edwin Meese III. And there was, to be sure, much deflecting to be done.

During July and August 1987, Attorney General Meese appeared before a Senate investigating panel to answer questions about his involvement in the infamous Wedtech scandal (to be covered in greater detail later). The Senate found that Meese had failed to identify his holdings in the Wedtech Corporation as required by law and that he had failed to seek approval from the Office of Government Ethics before making a financial investment in the company.[48] In summarizing Meese's failures, Representative Gerry Sikorski, chairman of the Subcommittee on Human Resources, Post Office, and Civil Service, charged that

> The American people have good reason to be disheartened, perhaps even angered by [these] failures. . . . Mr. Meese is not some middle-

level functionary; he holds a very important position in our government and his personal history should make him extraordinarily
sensitive to disclosure issues. . . . The ethics buck stops at his desk.[49]

Following the Wedtech hearings, the Justice Department, once
the premier administrative agency of the federal government,
began to hit new lows in public esteem and confidence. Justice
Department officials began to flee for reasons both bureaucratic
and philosophical. Several of these, including the deputy attorney
general and the associate attorney general in charge of the Criminal Division, charged that the Justice Department under Meese
was ready to collapse owing to the attorney general's inability to
recognize the potential criminality of his own conduct. At the
same time, protesters began appearing on the steps of the Justice
Department with banners proclaiming, "Meese Is a Pig!" and local
curio shops responded by producing a line of T-shirts depicting the
attorney general as a pig.[50] Edwin Meese had become a mockery of
the Reagan administration's tough law-and-order rhetoric. Some
of this damage was stanched, however, by the moral crusade
against the Mariel Cubans. At least on that score, the Justice Department seemed to have its house in order.

Yet just when it seemed that nothing else could go wrong for
the embattled attorney general, Meese was dealt the most devas-
tating blow of his career. On November 17, 1987, four days before
the Oakdale riot, the 690-page Iran-Contra Committee Report was
released suggesting that the attorney general had failed to give
the president sound legal advice, had not fully investigated the
scandal, and may have participated in a cover-up. The report further conveyed the message that Meese had contributed to an over-
all "disdain for the law" which had become characteristic of the
Reagan administration.[51]

While the moral panic legitimated the authority of the INS and
deflected public attention from the general corruption of the Justice Department, the Bureau of Prisons would ultimately pick up
the tab for its excesses. In the early days of October 1987, prison
guards working behind the walls of Oakdale and Atlanta began
to hear a strange new cry echo through the cellblocks: *Somos los
Abandonados!*

Chapter 7

The Pains of Imprisonment: Atlanta, 1984–1987

Anyone who has ever spent time inside the Atlanta Federal Penitentiary knows of its deplorable history. The institution once held the great socialist and humanitarian Eugene V. Debs, who waged a presidential campaign from his cell against Warren G. Harding back in 1920. "I was caged in a cell with five other men," recalled Debs in his prison memoir. No stranger to incarceration, Debs had spent time in penitentiaries and city lockups from Chicago to San Francisco. But Atlanta was the worst. "The Atlanta Penitentiary," he wrote, "was a sepulchre in which the living dead had been sequestered by society."[1]

Its history of violence began in the early 1930s when an inmate "industrial foreman" named Al Capone set up an elaborate prison contraband market supported by a system of violence he called "success through extortion."[2] After Capone's time, physical intimidation and graft became a way of life for thousands of convicts who passed through the maximum-security penitentiary. Because of its age and its legacy of corruption and violence (there had been a series of killings at Atlanta during the late 1970s), the Bureau of Prisons planned to demolish the prison in 1981, when bed space was suddenly needed to incarcerate the first shipment of rabble washed ashore from the port of Mariel.[3] Public attention was not drawn to the Mariel plight, however, until nearly five years later.

The Protests of 1984: "Libertad"

On the afternoon of October 14, 1984, fifty detainees gathered peacefully on the Atlanta recreation field and held up two bed sheets inscribed with the word "Libertad."[4] They were protesting their "indefinite detention" in the squalid old prison. Fifteen minutes later, they walked to the Administration Building carrying their sign. Guards stopped them and ordered them to go stand by the dining room entrance and wait. The detainees complied.

More than two dozen guards then entered the Administration Building and returned to the yard ten minutes later dressed in full riot gear, including batons. They descended on the Cubans and easily put them up against the dining room exterior wall. The detainees were handcuffed and escorted to the Cuban Segregation Unit (Cell House E).

For the next two days, administrators placed the institution on emergency lockdown, cutting off water, movement, and communication with the outside world. More than 1,500 Mariels were forced to stay in their cells twenty-four hours a day without running water, making the use of toilets and sinks impossible. To make clear their message about who controlled the institution, administrators also deprived the Cubans of toilet paper.

On the second day of the lockdown, a group of detainees started several small fires outside their cells. The fires immediately burned themselves out; they did not spread to other parts of the prison nor was anyone hurt by them. Simultaneously, detainees in Cell House A started breaking the Plexiglas windows in their cells. Another group of detainees in Cell House B passed a "kite" (a letter) to a guard for delivery to the warden that read:

> These acts were committed due to the fact that the entire Cuban population had been placed on lockdown status for the protest of a relatively small number of detainees in the yard on the previous Sunday.

The lockdown ended the next morning. But before the Cubans were allowed to leave their cells, administrators ordered guards to enter each cell to remove every item of personal property, and to throw it in piles outside the cells. This included photographs, Bibles, letters, and other small personal mementos of the detainees' lives before they were incarcerated. Operating against BOP procedures, American prisoners from the Atlanta work release camp were used as quasi-guards to strip the cells and destroy these personal items in front of the detainees' eyes. The massive piles of shredded pictures, Bibles, and memorabilia were then swept into garbage bags and removed. This administrative action had only one goal: to break the will of the Mariel detainees. For the most part, it did not work.

About two weeks later, on November 1, 1984, a detainee named José Hernandez Mesa got into an argument with a guard in Cell House B. Hernandez told the guard that he "didn't feel like taking such treatment anymore." For this, he was escorted to Cell House E. On the way, Hernandez began pleading with the guards to return him to his cell so he might retrieve some items of personal property acquired since the October 17 shakedown. The guards agreed. But as he entered his cell, Hernandez shouted, "I'm being set up!" The guards charged into the cell and put Hernandez up against the wall. One guard began to choke Hernandez with his baton as three others grabbed his hands and cuffed him. At this point, a small group of detainees began milling around outside the cell.

The guards marched Hernandez to the Segregation Unit, locked him in a cell, and returned to the Administration Building to don riot gear. This time they armed themselves with tear gas canisters. The guards returned to Cell House B and saturated it with tear gas. Wearing bandanas soaked in toilet bowl water, the Mariels retaliated by starting fires and breaking windows. Once the tear gas had filled the air, the cells were opened and the detainees were ordered to leave the cell house and to gather together on the recreation field.

Obviously, the Cubans had not yet gotten the message. Once assembled on the recreation field, the Mariels were hog-tied, with hands and ankles bound together behind their backs, and left to lie on the cold ground for six hours. As they lay there, guards circulated among them with batons, ruthlessly beating them on the legs, buttocks, and feet (so as not to leave visible marks). The detainees were returned to Cell House B on the morning of November 2.

Later in the day, Atlanta Warden Jack Hanberry told a group of journalists that "no improprieties had occurred" at the prison the night before. Yet because of "unrest among the Marielitos," Hanberry had decided to "play it safe" and resume the lockdown. In this case, "lockdown" meant that all detainees were confined to their cells (though with running water) for twenty-three hours a day. Cell House A was locked down for nearly a year, until September 1, 1985. Cell Houses B, C, and E would remain locked-down for more than three years—that is, until the historic riot of November 1987.

Aftermath
In January 1986, two detainees were brought to trial in the U.S. District Court in Atlanta to answer for the 1984 disturbance. Both were immediately acquitted of all criminal charges. According to the *Atlanta Constitution,* "the jurors believed that there were no real leaders of the disturbance, and that the living situation of the detainees was shameful."

This shameful situation subsequently became the focus of a class-action lawsuit filed on behalf of the detainees by Atlanta attorney Gary Leshaw (who, together with Bishop Roman, would come to witness the signing of the agreement ending the riot in 1987). In *Owens v. Hanberry,* Leshaw argued that the Mariels in Atlanta were being denied adequate lighting, recreational facilities, access to personal property, and privacy. They frequently were offered poor and unsanitary food, limited medical care, only weekly access to showers, and no air ventilation during the brutally hot Atlanta summers. Since the 1984 disturbance, Leshaw had also tenaciously worked to bring the Mariel story to the attention of Congress. By February 1986, he had succeeded.

The House of Representatives Report: "Brutal and Inhumane"

On February 3, 1986, a congressional subcommittee led by Representative Robert W. Kastenmeier, Chairman of the Subcommittee on Courts, Civil Liberties, and the Administration of Justice, conducted an oversight inspection of the Atlanta Penitentiary. The purpose of the inspection was to assess the conditions of confinement afforded the Mariel detainees and to determine the appropriate congressional response. Based on their inspection and on supporting documents, Kastenmeier's subcommittee drew the following conclusions:[5]

1. Of the 1,869 Mariel detainees incarcerated at the prison, none was serving criminal sentences. That is, the detainees had already served their sentences for criminal transgressions, or they had committed no crimes at all.

2. The prison was estimated to be 45 percent overcrowded—the worst crowding conditions among the fifty-nine institutions in the federal prison system. Detainees in Cell Houses A and B were being housed eight to a cell, with an average space of seven feet by four feet per inmate. Each cell included a toilet without a partition, a sink, and four bunk beds. Detainees in Cell Houses B, C, and E were confined to their cells twenty-three hours a day. Warden Hanberry acknowledged to Kastenmeier that these conditions were far below those set out in the American Correctional Association's current *Manual of Standards*.

3. Violence was considered a "significant problem." From January 1982 through February 1986, there had been seven suicides among the detainees; the total would rise to nine by November 1987. There had also been 158 serious suicide attempts, more than two thousand serious incidents of self-mutilation, nine homicides, and at least ten deaths from heart attacks and other "natural causes." The inmate-on-inmate assault rate among the detainees averaged fifteen per month, more than half the total for the entire Bureau of Prisons population. The number of inmate-on-staff assaults ranged from eleven to forty-one per month, accounting for about one-third of the Bureau total. In 1984 and 1985, the number of inmate-on-staff assaults referred by Atlanta officials to the U.S. District Attorney had increased from five to fifty.

4. Approximately two hundred detainees (about 11 percent of the total population) were classified as mentally retarded, mentally disordered, or psychotic. Another 587 detainees (31 percent

of the total) had medical problems of some kind. Most of these infirm detainees were locked in Cell House C, where they were administered daily doses of psychotropic medication (either lithium or Haldon).

5. Of the 518 employees of the Atlanta prison, only about a hundred (fewer than 20 percent) spoke Spanish.

6. The average staff turnover rate was one of the highest in the federal prison system. Atlanta staff also had the highest rate of sick leave and the highest disciplinary rate of any staff in the system. Hanberry attributed these problems to the severe conditions of employment and the increased level of stress brought on by the 1984 disturbance.

7. Since the 1984 disturbance, all staff had been put on mandatory twelve-hour shifts and,

8. The cost of housing Mariel detainees at the prison was estimated at $40 million per year—roughly $240 million during the period 1981 to 1986.

Kastenmeier's committee concluded their report with these words:

> The measure of a nation can be seen in the way it treats the least advantaged among us. By this measure our country has failed to meet any minimal standard of decency in our treatment of the Cuban detainees at Atlanta. . . .
>
> The current living situation for Cubans at the Atlanta Federal Penitentiary is intolerable considering even the most minimal correctional standards. These detainees—who are virtually without legal rights—are worse off than virtually all other Federal sentenced inmates. They are required to live in conditions which are brutal and inhumane. They are confined without any practical hope of ever being released. These conditions . . . present a strong possibility of future violent confrontations. For these reasons alone, Congress and the Administration should be motivated to seek out a constructive solution.[6]

Equilibrium and Administrative Action: "The Pains of Imprisonment"

Thirty years before Kastenmeier's committee made its prophetic statement, a wave of prison riots had spread across the United

States, prompting penologist Gresham Sykes to undertake what many consider to be the premiere scholarly attempt to explain prison rioting. According to penologist John Conrad, the publication of Sykes's *The Society of Captives* was

> a sociological *tour de force*. . . . The basic questions Sykes tried to answer were, *How is control possible in the maximum security prison?* and the related question: *What is the basis for an equilibrium in the prison community?* [emphasis in original][7]

To answer these questions, Sykes expounded an indigenous origin theory of prisoner societies. This theory began with a typology of deprivations that equally affected all prisoners living in maximum security custody. For Sykes, these significant deprivations had to do with losses of liberty, goods and services, heterosexual relationships, autonomy, and personal security. Together, these deprivations formed what Sykes called the *pains of imprisonment*.

Though rarely discussed in penology literature, Sykes's theory also included an important recommendation for administrative action to stop prison riots before they begin. Sykes argues that riots in maximum-security institutions can be traced to the pains of imprisonment. Even the smallest uprising is both a warning siren for administrators to pay attention to the deprivations, and an opportunity to correct them before things get worse. In other words, prison disturbances can serve as a "self-correcting mechanism in that [they] . . . set in motion forces which bring [the deprivations] to an end."[8] According to Sykes,

> Riots do not suddenly come into being but are a long time in the making. They are the culmination of a series of minor crises, each of which sets in motion forces for creation of a new and more serious crisis. In other words, riots are not an "accident." . . . Instead, riots [are the] most obvious, startling expressions of disorder . . . a logical step in a pattern of repeated social change.[9]

At every point in this pattern of repeated social change, administrators are afforded an opportunity to take action that will reestablish equilibrium by correcting the pains of imprisonment, thus heading off a potentially more serious crisis in the future.

The Pains of Imprisonment Reconsidered:
Human Rights and Moral Panic

While the indigenous origin theory of prisoner societies appears to provide a powerful exegetic tool for explaining what eventually would happen at Atlanta, Sykes did not contemplate the sort of abyss into which the Mariel detainees had fallen by 1986. Not only were they deprived of liberty, goods and services, heterosexual relationships, autonomy, and personal security, but the Mariel Cubans also were deprived of fundamental human rights. According to standards established by the United Nations, penological consensus, the application of common sense, and prevailing notions of plain decency in human affairs, when persons are confined to maximum-security prisons for any other reason than serious criminal offenses—or when they are confined for years beyond the sentences imposed on them by the criminal courts—then a violation of human rights has occurred. To then institutionalize these individuals in deplorable and inhumane conditions "without any practical hope of ever being released" is universally recognized as perhaps the most egregious of all human rights violations, despite their embodiment in law by the nation's highest legal authority—an authority that views its policy as reflecting "the humane qualities of an enlightened civilization."[10]

For example, the Universal Declaration of Human Rights, adopted by the United States in alliance with forty-eight of the member countries of the United Nations in 1948, states:

> All human beings are born free and equal in dignity and rights.
> They are endowed with reason and conscience and should act
> towards one another in a spirit of brotherhood. . . . No one shall be
> subjected to arbitrary arrest, detention, or exile. . . . Everyone is
> entitled in full equality to a fair and public hearing by an indepen-
> dent and impartial tribunal, in the determination of his rights and
> obligations and of any criminal charge against him.[11]

Yet, the Mariel Cubans of Atlanta were subjected to a repeated pattern of arbitrary arrest and detention in maximum-security custody for indefinite periods. Some were arbitrarily arrested and indefinitely detained once they stepped off the Freedom Flotilla.

Some were arbitrarily arrested and indefinitely detained because they were disadvantaged or were petty criminals. And still others were arbitrarily "re-arrested" and indefinitely detained after they had served sentences for more serious offenses. Some of them still faced arbitrary exile in the form of deportation to Cuba. Equally important, none of the Atlanta detainees was offered what could be considered a "fair and public hearing by an independent and impartial tribunal." Instead, they were systematically deprived of an adversarial system of justice and deliberately criminalized by an extremely partial tribunal of INS officials, not by neutral judges.

Because of these institutionalized violations of fundamental human rights, the pain experienced by the Atlanta detainees had taken a far greater toll on their spirits than anything Sykes could have envisioned. Sykes developed his classic theory from observations made in the mid-1950s, before people of color represented nearly one-half of the U.S. maximum-security prison population, and long before the pains of imprisonment made suicide attempts and self-mutilation a daily occurrence for some groups of prisoners.[12] Such was the case of Atlanta, where most of the detainees were black.[13]

Furthermore, Sykes did not contemplate the kind of rapacious abuse of power that characterized the administration of justice during the years that Edwin Meese III held sway over the Immigration and Naturalization Service and the Federal Bureau of Prisons. Sykes viewed the prison riot as the tumultuous climax of a "series of minor crises" that took place inside the maximum-security prison itself. He did not consider the possibilities, and the consequences, of a successful moral panic engineered by state agents outside the correctional arena, specifically designed to influence parole decisions concerning the time of release from custody.

It was, then, the confluence of these two mighty forces—institutionalized violations of human rights and state-organized moral panic—that transformed the Atlanta Federal Penitentiary into a living powder keg. Attorney Gary Leshaw has aptly summarized the problem:

We shall probably never know all of what took place during those years at the Atlanta pen. The detainees had descended from purgatory into hell. And Mephistopheles was on the loose, but the government didn't want to find him. Why? Because he was one of them.[14]

These problems were witnessed not only by Representative Kastenmeier and Leshaw, but also by other legal representatives for the Cubans, prison staff members, more than a dozen congressmen, a federal judge, and the mayor of Miami. Their denouncements of the Mariel crisis were made public countless times by the print media.

The Reverend Russ Maby, chaplain of the Atlanta Federal Penitentiary in 1986 and one of the hostages taken during the riot, described the plight of an Atlanta detainee:

> I had never before confronted that much pain. American inmates know why they're in prison, how much time they have and about when they'll get out. This Cuban didn't know when he was getting out or—if he got out—whether he would go live with his wife and kids or be deported. Underneath his pleasantness there was real rage. He had no control over his life.[15]

Similarly, in April 1987, an Atlanta guard told a local journalist, "You know they're renovating the place, trying to make it a better place. But if the Cubans continue to feel they have no hope of freedom, sooner or later they will burn it down."[16]

This was, of course, the theme echoed time and again by Judge Marvin Shoob in his series of decisions on the federal policy of indefinite detention. In 1986, Shoob warned, "After some years pass and we can view this more dispassionately, there will be some real criticism of the decision to detain these people in a maximum security prison without a trial for up to six years." A year later, Judge Shoop commented further on the seriousness of the Atlanta situation. "Until I went on the federal bench," he said, "I think I was with the vast majority of people in this country who felt that the government could do no wrong. . . . The moral of the Cuban situation is that it *can* happen here . . . and it is a disgrace."[17]

The dual themes of human rights violations and the benefits accruing from a well-organized moral panic were clearly pointed out by Sally Sandidge, legal representative for the Mariels in numerous cases before the INS in the deep South before the riots. She recalls that

> Often, the detainees were viewed as chattel. The impoverished rural areas of Louisiana and Mississippi used the Cubans in detention to make money, collecting federal dollars to house them and supplement their own budgets. I remember one small town in Louisiana where the local lawyers [representing the INS] had just paid the light bill for the courthouse as the lights had been turned off for nonpayment. Through the policy of indefinite detention, these small local jails were generating money and jobs for their communities.[18]

In May 1986, the American Civil Liberties Union filed an appeal with the United Nations, charging that "the arbitrary and prolonged indefinite detention and cruel, inhumane, and degrading treatment of the [Mariel Cubans] amount to a consistent pattern of gross violations of human rights . . . and warrants an independent investigation . . . by the competent United Nations authorities."[19] A month later, the *Washington Post,* among other widely circulated newspapers, reported that the Atlanta Penitentiary "cages 1,857 Cuban prisoners who are not serving time for crimes and have almost no legal rights and few hopes of ever being released."[20]

And on July 1, 1987 (four months before the riots), the debate on human rights and moral panic reached the highest level of the American democratic order. In a two-page letter to INS Commissioner Alan Nelson, thirteen members of Congress (including John Lewis, Ronald Dellums, Kweisi Mfume, John Conyers, Barney Frank, and Mike Espy) declared:

> As members of Congress, we are concerned about the indefinite detention of approximately 3,400 Mariel Cubans in prisons, jails, and detention centers across the United States. These individuals are not serving prison terms, but are being held for deportation to Cuba, a deportation process closed by Fidel Castro. We believe that

detention of this type serves no useful purpose. The indefinite detention of these Cubans is justified only if they pose a clear risk to our national security, or present a significant threat to persons and property.[21]

Not only were the congressmen willing to point out the problems of indefinite detention to Commissioner Allen, they also went on record in voicing their commitment to doing something about the problem. Concerning the detainees, the congressmen concluded that

Fundamental fairness, one of the most cherished principles of American government, argues against the indefinite detention of any individual. We urge you to act immediately and decisively on these concerns. We will certainly support you in this effort.[22]

Because of this public outcry, the detainees briefly caught the attention of the Reagan White House. Shortly before the federal government began implementing its reforms to correct the problems at Atlanta, Vice President George Bush wrote to Miami Mayor Xavier L. Suarez "regarding the current situation of some Mariel Cubans." About the policy of indefinite detention, the vice president said,

The Immigration and Naturalization Service will soon implement a comprehensive review plan that will respond to the legitimate concerns you identify. Pursuant to the plan . . . senior INS officers will begin a process whereby individual determination will be made for suitability of placing certain Cuban entrants into appropriate Community Relations Service or Public Health Service–contracted halfway house projects. In these projects, the Mariel Cubans are provided appropriate vocational and educational training to facilitate their assimilation into society. . . . Hope this is helpful. . . .[23]

The Constructive Solution: "Pocket Freedom"

The pivotal years for administrators, guards, and detainees behind the walls of the Atlanta Federal Penitentiary were 1986 and 1987. Because of Kastenmeier's report and its subsequent support, administrators finally had the political power to alleviate some of the deprivations that had been going on for years. And in the summer of 1986, the Oakdale facility was opened, which meant an immediate reduction in crowding at Atlanta. Said an Atlanta detainee of the time, "When it [Oakdale] opened, I thought it was my chance for liberty. But when I got there, the only thing I got was pocket freedom."

The INS reforms would come to little. Few detainees would ever realize the Reagan administration's promise of "appropriate vocational and educational training to facilitate their assimilation into society." According to Sykes, such a failure should not be surprising because "such a solution is far from perfect . . . if only on the grounds that the transfer of [the reforms] from paper to reality is beset by problems."[24]

The Reagan Reforms

The House of Representatives Report recommended the implementation of a structured review plan that would give "careful consideration to releasing those detainees who can be sent into the community without endangering community safety." The Cuban Review Plan was designed by the INS in 1987 to fulfill this recommendation. The new plan was a crucial point in Sykes's pattern of potentially correctable events that might lead to a prison riot. Under the plan, each detainee was to be interviewed by a panel of two INS agents to determine the detainee's appropriateness for release based on five factors:

1. The nature and number of prison discipline infractions.
2. Past criminal behavior.
3. Psychiatric and psychological reports by the INS and the BOP.
4. Prison program participation.
5. "Any other information that would assist the [INS] panel in making a prediction of parole success."[25]

The plan called for the two-member panel to recommend either release to "contracted halfway houses" or continued incarceration. In the former case, the recommendation was to be forwarded to Washington where "Senior INS officers" would issue a final decision within thirty days. In the latter case, of course, the inmate would remain indefinitely under prison conditions that were brutal and inhumane.

In addition to the usual problems in transferring reforms from paper to reality, the Cuban Review Plan suffered from a more fundamental shortcoming. While the new criteria outlined by the INS were an improvement over the blind whimsy that had characterized previous release decisions, the plan did not offer the detainees basic constitutional protections. For example, requests for release from maximum-security custody were to be considered by INS agents, not by neutral judges. Hearsay evidence against the detainees was to be considered admissible. The detainees were not to be given the right to legal representation. Nor were they to be allowed the right to challenge the word of hostile witnesses or to compel attendance of their own witnesses. And the reviews were to be conducted at the leisure of the INS, so that detainees would not be given sufficient time to examine the evidence against them.

In addition to this seriously flawed reform, the 99th Congress in 1987 approved the emergency expenditure of $42 million for the BOP's renovation of the Atlanta prison to further ease the crowding problem.[26] But before these reforms got off the ground, an event occurred that would ultimately mitigate against any chance of their success. Explaining this event demands another brief digression.

The Birth of a Martyr: "Definitely a Bad Ass"

Although few individual leaders emerged among the Atlanta detainees in the years before the riot, Santiago Peralta Ocana certainly was one of them. Peralta, in fact, became a source of inspiration for many detainees struggling with almost crippling adversity during their long years of internment. Not one to succumb to the pains of imprisonment by committing suicide, and definitely not one to allow his spirit to be broken by guards, Santiago Peralta would ultimately emerge in the Atlanta story as the Cuban equivalent of George Jackson, the infamous "Soledad brother." For this he was greatly respected by fellow detainees and absolutely feared by guards. As one officer recalled, "Peralta was definitely a bad ass. The macho of the macho." And as a detainee responded, "Peralta? Yes, everyone knew him."

Santiago Peralta was born in 1957 in the rugged Escambray Mountains of central Cuba. His parents were *campesinos,* or peasants, and their skin was black as coal. It is unknown how young Santiago ran afoul of the law, but his record shows that he was sentenced to a Cuban prison where he allegedly killed another prisoner during the late 1970s.

Like Alberto Herrera and some 350 others, in 1980 the twenty-three-year-old Cuban prisoner was forced aboard the Freedom Flotilla and exiled to the United States. He was immediately detained in Talledega and later sent to Atlanta for an indefinite period of incarceration.

By 1987, Peralta had grown into a startling physical specimen. Hours of strenuous exercise had given him an extremely muscular physique. Though only five feet seven inches tall, Peralta weighed 252 pounds, hardly any of which was fat. He had also transformed himself into a prison fighter of historic proportions; more than forty knife and club wounds from his numerous battles covered his enormous arms and torso. Because of this, Peralta was usually confined to Cell House E, where he was caged in an eight-by-eight-foot cell behind a three-inch thick steel door with a small food trap in the center. Peralta was strong enough to kick this massive door off its hinges and had done so on at least two occasions.

Then, on February 18, 1987, Peralta got into an argument with a guard in Cell House E while the Cubans were being served lunch. He claimed that he was intentionally being served cold food. The guard ignored his protest, and Peralta began kicking the cell door off its hinges. Fellow detainees cheered him on. The guard radioed for help and within minutes the assistant warden of the penitentiary and some twenty guards came to Peralta's cell to appraise the situation. At this show of force, Peralta became docile, recognizing that he was seriously outnumbered. Assuming that the situation was under control, the assistant warden left the scene and returned to the Administration Building.

Following BOP procedures, an officer then told Peralta to back up to his food slot, put his arms behind his back, and stick them through to be cuffed. Once he was handcuffed, guards opened the door and took him outside. He was then asked to explain. In Spanish, Peralta said, "A guard was messing with my food."

The accused guard stepped forward and called Peralta "a liar." Peralta reacted by spitting in the guard's face and the guard retaliated by kicking the handcuffed Cuban with savage force between the legs with his steel-toed boot. Then he kicked him again and again. Peralta fell to the floor in excruciating pain and screamed *"Ayudeme, por favor, ayudeme"* (Help me, please, help me).

They were the last words he ever spoke. Three guards then descended on Santiago Peralta and choked him to death in full view of six other detainees and perhaps as many as seventeen guards of the Atlanta Penitentiary.[27]

The following morning, newly appointed Atlanta Warden Joseph F. Petrovsky issued a press release reporting that Peralta had died of a heart attack. But the Cubans, Gary Leshaw, and the media quickly recognized this statement for the sham it was. Leshaw immediately entered a motion to compel discovery in his pending case on prisons conditions, arguing that "a Justice Department cover-up" was being committed by agents of the INS and the BOP in their handling of Peralta's death.[28] Autopsy reports later confirmed the fact that the extremely physically fit Cuban prisoner had not died of a heart attack. Each autopsy report included evidence of "a large purplish bruise" around Peralta's powerful neck, indicating that he had died of asphyxiation: Santiago Peralta had been strangled to death.

> *MH:* Tell me about Peralta. How did he die?
> *Atlanta detainee from Cell House E* (in English): The guards they choke him. You know, they kill him. Oh! it was very bad.

A month after the incident, the DeKalb County medical examiner who had conducted one of the autopsies on Peralta's body testified,

> I didn't know of anybody involved in this investigation who does not believe this man died while he was being moved or restrained because he was choked. I've convinced everybody that one of the guards, either intentionally or unintentionally, did something that caused this fellow's death.[29]

Stories about Peralta's murder circulated among the Mariels, and in late February Petrovsky received a kite from a detainee spokesman:

> We all know it was a brutal crime and we all are witness of that crime. And you know that any crime is neither legal or justifiable. And although Santiago Peralta Ocana has been a bad Cuban detainee, his death will not be justified.[30]

Petrovsky told the detainees that the FBI would investigate the Peralta case and that the Bureau of Prisons would reach a decision on the incident as soon as possible. After a month of waiting, however, there was still no decision and the detainees grew restless. On April 4, an officer was stabbed in the back by a detainee wielding a double-edged homemade knife as the guard was trying to break up a fight between two Cubans in Cell House A. In response, Petrovsky ordered a massive shakedown. Between April 4 and April 19, guards uncovered thirty-nine homemade machetes, as well as ropes, clubs, saw blades, and several gallons of homemade liquor.[31]

Meanwhile, the suicides and self-mutilations continued unabated. On February 23, twenty-six-year-old Alberto Arma Castillo was found hanging from a rope in Cell House C—the eighth suicide in five years.[32] A week later, thirty-one-year-old Oscar Bermudez Dominguez was found dead on the catwalk outside his cell, a victim of either suicide or foul play. "At this sad juncture," wrote the Reverend Joseph A. Fahy in the *Atlanta Constitution*, "it is important to remember that the majority of Mariel detainees are not guilty of violent crimes. Many have already served their sentences for lesser crimes, such as driving under the influence. Others had their paroles revoked for simply being charged with a minor crime or for parole violations that are non-criminal."[33] It was within this context that the Reagan administration enacted its "constructive solution" to the extraordinary problems facing the Atlanta Federal Penitentiary.

The Cuban Review Plan: "A Major Problem"

The INS implemented its Cuban Review Plan on June 22, 1987 (five months before the riots). By early November, approximately

1,300 Atlanta detainees had come before INS panels.[34] Of this number, only eighty were released.[35] It was, after all, the height of the INS's moral crusade, and to release more than 6 percent of the detainee population would have compromised the effectiveness of the growing moral panic around the Mariels.

Eight hundred detainees were, however, eventually approved for release pending placements in halfway houses or with community sponsors.[36] The fact that 880 of 1,300 detainees—roughly 68 percent of the Atlanta population—were approved for release under the strict and highly subjective criteria used by the INS stands as testimony to the fact that the detainees were not a threat to public safety. Hence, hundreds of millions of dollars were squandered on the maximum-security confinement of men who could have been handled in a less restrictive and more humane fashion. As a result of these decisions, the term "pocket freedom" took its place alongside "the abandoned ones" in the prison argot of the detainees. Sykes argued that "the critical function of prison argot [is] . . . its utility in ordering and classifying experience within the walls in terms which deal specifically with the major problems of prison life."[37]

Recognizing the symbolic import of new forms of prison argot represents yet another potential opportunity for administrators to stem the tide of "major problems" leading to more serious crises. The epistemological and aesthetic signification of pocket freedom was this: In the minds of detainees, the constructive solution of 1987 was a monumental failure.

Chapter 8
The Adaptation and Equilibrium

An important and extremely obvious question is: Why didn't the Atlanta Federal Penitentiary and its receiving institution, Oakdale, erupt in rioting sooner than they did? Sykes's theory offers an answer: Because prisoners adapted to their deprivations and this adaptation, in turn, created a social equilibrium between inmates and guards that stemmed the progression toward more serious crises. On this aspect of Sykes's theory, John Conrad commented, "Human beings are resilient creatures, capable of adaptation to appalling adversities." Through this adaptation, Conrad suggested, inmates could overcome "exposure to prison conditions that are generally regarded as horrifying."[1]

In Sykes's formulation, the problem common to all prisoners is to reduce as far as possible the impact of the pains of imprisonment caused by loss of liberty, goods and services, heterosexuality, autonomy, and security. Prisoners adapt to these deprivations through one of two channels.

On one hand, "prisoners can bind themselves together with ties of mutual aid, loyalty, and respect, presenting a united opposition to the officials."[2] This united opposition gives rise to an inmate code of conduct that prizes inmate cohesion above all else. "The more inmates stick together," Sykes asserted, "the better able they are to alleviate the frustrating circumstances of prison life."[3] Sykes further argued that the degree of inmate cohesion may be influenced "by the nature of the culture from which the inmate population is drawn."[4] It then becomes possible for inmates to "develop a source of solidarity in ethnic militancy,"[5] and this adaptation takes on a political character.

The other way that prisoners are able to adapt to their pains of imprisonment is through collusion with guards and officials.

> There is strong pressure on the officials to compromise—to overlook a number of infractions that are considered relatively trivial in exchange for compliance in areas considered significant. Inmates may be allowed to remain out of their cells without authorization, to cook food stolen from the institution's kitchen, to pass letters back and forth—and in return they are expected to refrain from violence . . . and to maintain some degree of civility toward one another and the guards.[6]

In this collusion, Sykes reasoned, "guards come to see those they guard as something other than enemies of society, to be suppressed at any cost. Bonds of friendship are established."[7]

To the extent that these two channels are kept open, Sykes theorized, equilibrium between prisoners and guards can be maintained. The pains of imprisonment are assuaged by an informal system of social control in which both guards and prisoners play an important role. If both channels are closed, however, a riot is likely.

For the most part, these two channels were kept open at Oakdale and Atlanta. But in addition to the deprivations common to all maximum-security prisoners, the Mariel detainees faced a special kind of pain. In most nations of the world, maximum-security prisons exist for the explicit purpose of punishing persons for serious violations of criminal law or for grave infractions against the state. The Cuban detainees were guilty of neither. They were put in maximum-security custody and punished by the deprivation of human rights to further the self-serving goals of a state-organized moral crusade against them. Because the deprivations, and the forces causing them, were so uncommon, the adaptations employed by the detainees were equally uncommon. And these adaptations provided the equilibrium necessary to contain social arrangements at Oakdale and Atlanta in the period preceding

November 21, 1987. The first adaptation was spiritual, and it was supported through collusion with guards and administrators. The second adaptation was political, but instead of supporting it, prison authorities tried to stop it—not because the adaptation threatened prison security, but because it caused great anguish among nearly everyone associated with the Mariel story.

Santeria: "The Way of the Saints"

There is almost overwhelming consensus among those familiar with the situation that the detainees adapted to their predicament by relying on the religious principles and rituals of Santeria, and this created the basis for detainee cohesion and a code of conduct—which, in turn, created the social equilibrium necessary to avoid rioting. The practice of Santeria flourished behind the walls of Oakdale and Atlanta, because guards and administrators allowed it to flourish by overlooking a pattern of relatively "trivial infractions" of prison rules. For this important reason, then, Santeria deserves a careful explanation and analysis.

Background[8]

Santeria began in the early 1800s, when hundreds of thousands of the Yoruba people (those from the areas of Africa that now make up the nations of Nigeria and Benin) were brought to the Caribbean as slaves to work in the booming sugar, coffee, and mining industries. During this period Cuba was a colony of Spain, and the Spanish treated the Yoruba slaves much as slaves were treated in the United States. They were forced to work long hours in the tropical climate; they were treated as property, poorly fed and uneducated, and they were brutally punished and sexually exploited.

Because their masters were Spanish, Yoruba slaves also were expected to become Catholics. But the Catholic influence was slow to take hold because it did not offer the Yoruba salvation from the pitiless conditions of slavery. Though outwardly accepting the symbols of Roman Catholicism, the Yoruba slaves began to reconstruct their religious lives by fusing the traditions remembered from their homeland with the folk piety of the Catholic church in

Cuba. This blend of ancient African ancestor-reverence and European Catholicism became known by the Spanish word *Santeria*—"the way of the saints"—and devotees became known as "Santeros." Because Santeria was really one religion concealed in another, a tradition of secrecy emerged among the Yoruba in order to survive the oppression of slavery. Hence, little was known about Santeria beyond the stories and practices of living devotees.

In order to worship the Yoruba spirits, called *orishas,* under the guise of Catholicism, later generations of Santeros began to construct elaborate systems of correspondence between the *orisha* spirits and Catholic saints. Despite the presence of Catholic symbols in Santeria rites, however, the Santeria religion remains to this day, an African way of worship.

Santeros believe that every person is given a destiny, or "road in life." Each person therefore has the responsibility to understand this "road" and to grow and benefit from it rather than becoming its victim. Santeria, in other words, is a religion of survival. The complete fulfillment of people's destinies (ultimately, escape from slavery and oppression) can be accomplished only through deep devotion to the *orishas,* which promises both worldly success and heavenly wisdom and which takes four principle forms: divination, sacrifice, spiritual mediumship, and initiation.

Divination
For the ordinary devotee, Santeria provides a means for resolving everyday problems. Through the *orisha* spirits, the Santeros receive assistance in hexing and killing enemies, protecting themselves against physical and spiritual abuse, outwitting the law, bringing luck in financial matters, and attracting and keeping lovers.

Sacrifice
Divination can be achieved only by deepening the Santero's relationship with the *orishas.* The truest way for a devotee to develop such a relationship is to share with the *orishas* the devotee's most important substance: food. That is, divination can be accomplished only through sacrifice.

Each devotee has a particular *orisha* that is worshipped above all others. Each *orisha* has a number as well as its favorite group of foods, favorite colors, animals, and objects, and an appropriate day of the week for its worship. Each *orisha* also has a corresponding array of Catholic saints. Because Santeria is African in origin, it views spirituality as an integral part of everyday life and its sacrifices are offered as household acts (instead of acts performed in a church). The sacrifices, together with pictures of the appropriate saints, are placed on an altar and a candle is lit in honor of the saint. The altar also has an appropriate location for worship in the home.

Spiritual Mediumship

Although sacrifices are necessary for divination, offerings of food and icons of Catholic saints are regarded as empty unless they are accompanied by various rituals. Foremost among these is the placing of stones, or *piedras,* behind a curtain in the lower part of the altar. Without these stones, no Santeria shrine can exist. The *piedras* are referred to as the "Stones of the Saints" and are believed to have life; some stones can walk and grow, and others can have children. *Piedras* are precious to the Santero; the most powerful are said to have been brought to Cuba from Africa by the original Yoruba slaves, who smuggled them in their stomachs by swallowing them.

The power of the *piedras* is conceived as an invisible fluid, the force of which can be felt by the Santero and which protects the devotee and his or her family. It is through this power that the saints, or "guardian angels," manifest their divination. This miraculous power is given to the stones by treating them with two other essentials of the Santeria religion, blood and herbs, which is known as the *bautismo,* or baptism. Stones that have not been baptized are curiously called *judia* (Jewish) and are regarded as completely powerless.

The blood used to baptize the stones must come from a sacrificial animal, such as a chicken, lamb, or pig. According to ritual, the slaughter must be performed by a Santero designated by others as a *matador.* The killing must be done swiftly and cleanly, and the flesh is to be immediately cooked and consumed by devotees as part of the *bautismo* ritual. When the stones are baptized, the blood must be *caliente,* or warm, so that the invisible fluid within the stones may be brought to life.

Though blood is viewed as the major animator of the invisible fluid, the stones also are treated with herbs and are kept safe by *resguardos,* or protective charms. Before and after the *bautismo,* the stones are washed in a mixture containing the herbs, water, blood, and baptismal solutions saved from previous ceremonies. As in the system of sacrifice outlined above, each *orisha* has its own particular set of herbs and charms, its own type of stone, and a special animal from whom the blood must come for the *bautismo.*

Because Santeros believe that all people have a responsibility to understand their "road in life," they believe that a knowledge of the properties and uses of herbs, charms, blood, and stones is every bit as important as knowledge of the system of sacrifice and the promise of divination.

Initiation

As the Santero grows in devotion, one particular *orisha* may begin to assert itself as the devotee's true patron. In other words, the sincere devotee may one day be given divine and everlasting protection from the cruel adversities of everyday life. The profound love of this true *orisha* will then provide its devotee with his or her basic orientation throughout life.

When the *orisha* calls for it, the devotee undergoes a demanding initiation into the study of the patron spirit. The initiation ceremony, conducted in the home of an initiate of long experience, requires lengthy period of isolation and learning. During this period, the *orisha* is "enthroned in the head" of the Santero and the devotee is reborn as the spiritual child of the blessed spirit.

Worship Behind the Walls: "Lighting the Candles"

It is unknown how many detainees at Oakdale and Atlanta were devotees of Santeria, though it is safe to conclude that most of them were. History teaches that the majority of Cubans (especially the *campesinos*) are deeply religious people,[9] and that most Cubans were excluded from full participation in the rituals and practices of the Catholic church in Cuba. In 1959, Fidel Castro closed the churches, but he did not outlaw Santeria. According to Fidel, even his own mother is "one who lights the candles."[10] There was a good reason for this: Because Santeria was a religion born of survival against the brutal powers of colonial exploitation, it coincided perfectly with the revolutionary goals of Cuban nationalism and independence.

But the Santeros of Oakdale and Atlanta were confined in conditions that dispossessed them of their sacrificial foods, spiritual mediumship to the heavenly *orishas,* and opportunities for initiation. In other words, the detainees suffered yet another deprivation: Not only were they denied fundamental human rights, but, at least indirectly, they also lost their right to worship. And there was a good reason for this as well.

It is ludicrous, for example, to envision animal sacrifices taking place in an American correctional institution. It is equally strange to imagine baptism ceremonies, spiritual possession, and a governmental source of supply for the long list of esoteric herbs, charms, and foods needed to fully practice the religion. But like their Yoruba forebears, the Cuban detainees, in collusion with sympathetic guards and administrators, adapted to the situation by improvising elaborate rituals to achieve spiritual divination in a hostile environment.

The impact of religion on human behavior is best understood phenomenologically. Yet there is absolutely no way to construct a body of recollections of Santeria's impact on social equilibrium behind the walls of Oakdale and Atlanta before the riots—if for no other reason than that nothing has ever been written on the subject. We may estimate Santeria's influence, however, by paying attention to the ethnographic particulars of the rituals and customs used by the Santeros of Oakdale and Atlanta *since* the riots, and then applying these findings "backward" in an attempt to understand their effect on equilibrium.

The Study[11]

Although the practice of Santeria was not officially sanctioned at Oakdale and Atlanta, it was allowed to exist in clandestine form. Said an Atlanta guard:

Yeah, I saw it all the time. At first we thought it was some kind of voodoo! You know, all those charms and things. But once you watched it, it was something else man [laughs]. It reminded me of some of those old stories my grandmother used to tell me about African slaves.

Question: Did you ever do anything to stop it?

Answer: No. . . . There wasn't anything illegal about it.

My study of incarcerated Santeros took place over eight months. The first phase lasted four months and was concerned only with observations of Santero prisoners. During this phase, I was assisted by a correctional officer (a student of mine), who was assigned to work the Cuban cellblock of the maximum-security Federal Penitentiary at Terre Haute. The officer worked forty hours per week in the Cuban cellblock, where he took notes on Santeria practices in a journal. Like guards at Oakdale and Atlanta, Terre Haute guards were familiar with the practice of Santeria and allowed it to continue. The officer also familiarized himself with the limited body of scholarly research on the Santeria religion. His reflections were based on nearly a thousand hours of observation, study, and academic mentoring.

The second four-month phase included interviews with twenty-three devotees of the Santeria religion. All these detainees had spent time in Oakdale or Atlanta before the riots. All interviews were conducted in Spanish either by myself (through a translator) or by the officer/criminology student.

The results of this study are reported in terms of the four primary aspects of Santeria: *divination, sacrifice, spiritual mediumship,* and *initiation.*

Divination
All twenty-three detainees said their worship was conducted to resolve their most immediate problem at this point on the road in life: imprisonment. None of the detainees were seeking any kind of profound "spiritual awakening," nor were they seeking to hex or kill their enemies, to protect themselves against abuse, to outwit the law, or to attract luck in matters of finance and love. Instead, the detainees were using their religion in an attempt to

adapt to conditions that were, by all definitions (save those of the Justice Department and the Supreme Court), considered to be unfair and oppressive. Moreover, the Santeros believed that their devotion to the *orishas* could get them out of a maximum-security prison and back to the difficult task of resettling in America. That was the sole purpose of Santeria and the basis of the detainee code of conduct. A single quote suffices:

> *Question:* Why do you light the candles, Alberto?
> *Answer:* To get out of prison. To be a free man and get out of prison.

Sacrifice

As indicated, the *orishas* are believed to be hungry and choosy spirits. We observed twenty-three altars during the research and found that the altars shifted from the corner of the cell nearest the doorway, to the sink, to the windowsill of the cell. The altars were usually constructed from discarded cereal boxes. All together, we counted about four hundred cereal boxes used in this fashion. Although security rules dictated that cereal boxes be removed from the cells once detainees had finished their breakfasts, the guards allowed these boxes to stay in the cells. They were usually covered with a white piece of cloth or a white T-shirt. Altars were not observed in any other areas of the cells. However, even when the altar was placed nearest the door or beneath the sink, we also observed Catholic holy cards mounted on the Plexiglas windows of the cell.

All the altars displayed icons of Roman Catholic saints connected with Santeria; holy cards often appeared in basket-weave picture frames made from cigarette wrappers and colored paper. Seventeen devotees were tattooed with images of the various saints. Some of the tattoos (like those of Alberto Herrera) were quite dramatic. For example, three prisoners had the image of the Lady of Caridad del Cobré tattooed across the full width of their backs, and several others had the mark of St. Lazaro painstakingly tattooed from the shoulder to the hand. Tattooing needles and ink also were contraband items, but guards allowed prisoners access to them.

All the altars had some form of makeshift candle as well. Usually, these candles were made from matchsticks set in rancid milk that had hardened in milk cartons pilfered from the prison mess hall. Once again, guards who inspected the Cuban cells—sometimes as many as twenty times per day—overlooked these stolen milk cartons (which also should have been collected after each meal). They ignored as well the fact that each altar contained at least one of the following: apples, oranges, coffee, cigars, or pigeon feathers. Some of these items also were pilfered from the mess hall. Pigeon feathers, gathered during weekly visits to the prison's recreation yard, were a sad and pathetic Santeria invention born from the pains of imprisonment; nowhere do pigeon feathers appear in the Santeria system of sacrifice and worship. The interviews revealed that these contraband items were intended as offerings to the saints.

Spiritual Mediumship

Some form of rock candy was regularly present at sixteen of the altars. The interviews revealed that the candy signified the "Stones of the Saints," the most important part of a Santeria altar. We found that these precious pieces of rock candy were often smuggled into the prison by guards or were sent by family members. We observed no other ritual connected to the elaborate system of spiritual mediumship.

Initiation

Likewise, we found that none of the devotees had advanced in the Santeria religion to the point where he had been "enthroned in the head" by a special *orisha*.

The Case of Antonio García Pérez

These findings can be best summarized in a brief case study that elucidates the phenomenology of Santeria in federal prisons. Like Santiago Peralta, Antonio García Pérez was born in 1957 in the Escambray Mountains of central Cuba.[12] His parents were *campesinos* and had lived their lives as devotees of the Santeria religion. Although they worshiped the icons of Roman Catholic saints, they had never seen a Catholic priest in their lives, much less attended church, and the legacy of secret devotion to the *orisha* spirits was deeply ingrained in young Antonio from an early age.

In 1979, García and two companions were caught stealing chickens and rice from a rural relocation camp and, in time, they were imprisoned. In the summer of 1980, García was put aboard the Freedom Flotilla, exiled to the United States, and incarcerated at Talledega. He was later transferred to Atlanta, where he shared a cramped cell with Alberto Herrera during the darkest days of Alberto's life. García remained in Atlanta until the riot and then was transferred to Terre Haute, where he became a subject in this study. Antonio's primary spirit was Oshun and his religious life was lived improvisationally.

Because of the Oakdale and Atlanta riots, the Cubans at Terre Haute were on permanent lockdown status, spending twenty-three hours a day in their cells, which meant they were deprived of education, vocational training, counseling, and other rehabilitative services. García was confined to a cell with three other detainees, all of whom were Santeros.

Naturally, García had no *ochin-chin* (a plant indigenous to the Cuban highlands) to offer Oshun, and no honey, cinnamon, or pumpkins. Therefore, he would routinely save oranges from his meal tray and hide them under his bunk. Each day he would tear an orange in half and place it on an altar built from cereal boxes and covered with one of his white T-shirts. He couldn't find a candle in the Terre Haute prison, so he made his own from a match and butter turned sour in milk containers, which he also kept under his bed. Antonio also had ripped sections of yellow and green from the top of one of his athletic socks and placed these pieces of cloth on the altar, as well. And because he had no access to quails, vultures, parrots, peacocks, gold, bells, fans, mirrors, or scallop shells, Antonio offered up pigeon feathers to his beloved *orisha*.

To make up for his meager offerings, García also placed a cup of cold coffee and a half-smoked cigar on the altar. Before these offerings he set a postcard image of the Lady of Caridad del Cobré. Behind the altar, Antonio put a piece of strawberry rock candy. His altar was set to the right of the cell door, and it smelled horrible.

Conclusions

Two major findings result from our study. First, when confined to conditions of incarceration similar to those at the Atlanta Penitentiary, Santeria provided the major path to adaptation for the detainees. Historically, the Santeria goal of day-by-day survival has been the central premise of the religion since Yoruba slaves fashioned it two centuries ago to survive the savage conditions of slavery. The religion allowed devotees to undergo the brutality of slavery with increased hope, dignity, and personal betterment; if it had not, Santeria would have disappeared quickly. In the same way, a highly improvisational form of Santeria, aided and abetted by friendly guards, helped the detainees to withstand the experience of confinement in a maximum-security prison.

Second, Santeria provided the detainees with the emotional impetus necessary for a clearly identifiable code of conduct, an attempt to metaphysically renegotiate the forces that had abrogated their human rights by indefinitely detaining them in maximum-security custody. The code of conduct was natural: *Behave in a way that is most likely to get you out of prison.* For detainees, that meant survival until "the Immigration and Naturalization Service can find a way to give these immigrants justice," to quote Jimmy Carter in 1993.[13]

Regarding their personal adaptations to the pains of imprisonment in maximum-security penitentiaries, Sykes argued that "reactions of inmates are not a grab bag of idiosyncratic responses but constitute a coherent whole that is remarkably similar from one institution to another."[14] Following Sykes's path, we may deduce that the discoveries made at the U.S. Penitentiary at Terre Haute after the riots are applicable to the inmate arrangements at Oakdale and Atlanta before the riots. That is, detainees adapted to their deprivations by relying on the religious principles and practices of Santeria. This spiritual adaptation, in turn, created a social equilibrium between prisoners and guards that headed off a more serious crisis. But just as the detainees created an extraordinary new spiritual culture, one that had been lost and found within the confines of the American maximum-security prison, they also improvised on Sykes's theme of political adaptation to create a human tragedy that is unparalleled in the annals of American penology.

Mass Suicide Attempts: The Unified Opposition

Since the historic Attica rebellion, there has been nothing unique about the display of ethnic militancy among inmates incarcerated in maximum-security prisons. Moreover, this militancy has been an exercise in "group think" designed to call public attention to the pains of imprisonment. And, as Sykes noted, it is typically expressed through political manifestos, work strikes, and other methods of activism intended to show solidarity with relatively powerless left-wing groups in the community.[15] The Abandoned Ones, however, expressed their militancy in a remarkable new way. Instead of written or verbal activism designed to align themselves with leftist causes, the detainees dramatically acted out their code of conduct to capture the attention of a powerful and extremely conservative force residing in 1600 Pennsylvania Avenue, Washington, D.C. They did so through mass suicide.

As pointed out in the previous chapter, records show that there were ten official suicides among the Atlanta detainees between 1982 and 1987. Kastenmeier's inspection of the penitentiary further revealed that there had been 158 serious suicide attempts and more than two thousand serious incidents of self-mutilation at Atlanta. As with other official statistics, these figures vastly underreport the extent and dimensions of the problem. There is evidence to show that suicide at Atlanta was far more prevalent than was reported by officials of the Justice Department under the direction of Edwin Meese III.

Denny McLain, a former pitcher for the Detroit Tigers and two-time winner of baseball's Cy Young Award, was incarcerated at the Atlanta Penitentiary during 1986 following a drug conviction. In his prison memoir, McLain writes, "Representative Kastenmeier didn't even see the worst of it. One time there were as many as 300 Cubans refusing to eat for days on end, hoping to bring attention to their plight."[16]

McLain, who worked as a "dietary specialist" for the prison and witnessed these events with his own eyes, describes how Atlanta officials responded to the hunger strikes with mass force-feeding administered not by medical professionals, but by sympathetic guards.

> The cops [guards] cuffed a guy to a hospital bed, hands to the top and feet to the bottom, and held his arm while someone shoved a needle in it to feed him intravenously. Less fortunate guys got fed through tubes in their noses. Milk was poured through the tubes which were oversized and gave the Cubans bloody noses. Their blood mixed with the milk and drained into their stomachs. Some guys almost drowned in their own blood.[17]

Together with official statistics, these observations suggest that in the months preceding the riot perhaps as many as one-third of the detainees at the Atlanta Penitentiary made serious attempts to kill themselves. At no other time in the nearly 220-year history of American penology has this happened. It does not require a penologist to understand that when one of three prisoners is trying to kill himself, there is something monumentally wrong with the criminal justice system. In Sykes's view, suicide among the detainees was not some "idiosyncratic response" to the pains of imprisonment. Rather, each suicide attempt constituted part of a "coherent whole" used as an adaptation to deprivations caused by a broad violation of human rights, state-organized moral panic, and spiritual oppression.

Like spirituality, death and dying are best discussed in phenomenological terms. And here there is no need to reconstruct recollections. From the hundreds of Atlanta detainees who attempted suicide in the months before the riots, I have gathered and examined the last wills and testaments of seven. All seven Mariel Cubans attempted to kill themselves through the long and painful process of self-starvation. Two of these are examined below.

The Case of Antonio Pi Montalvo

I don't know where Cuban detainee Antonio Pi Montalvo came from. And I don't know why he was incarcerated at the Atlanta Penitentiary. But I do know that he tried to kill himself sometime during August 1986 by refusing to eat for nearly a month.

Essentially, Antonio lay on his bunk bed in an overcrowded,

unair-conditioned cell at the Atlanta Penitentiary during the hot Georgia summer of 1986 and attempted to slowly and deliberately starve himself to death for a political cause. That is, he decided to end his life as part of the collective struggle to be released from maximum-security custody.

As Sykes would have predicted, Antonio's suicide attempt could have been avoided if INS and BOP officials had intervened to correct his pains of imprisonment. But they did not, despite the fact that they had sufficient time to do so. Officials ignored the problem and Antonio ended up strapped to a hospital gurney, where he was intravenously force-fed by guards who tried to save his life. On the day that he began his hunger strike, Antonio sent this letter to President Ronald Reagan.

To All Chiefs of States
All Presidents and Prime Ministers of All Member Countries And To Everyone Who Cares About Justice
My name is Antonio Pi Montalvo. I am 37 years old of Cuban origin and one of the refugees who arrived in the United States from the Port of Mariel in 1980. I am making this petition in order to de-nounce the crime that is being committed against more than 5,500 Cubans in this country, who fled from the Port of Mariel, like myself. Most of us are now in prison in Atlanta and other "correctional institutions" all over the United States. More than 3,000 of us have already terminated our sentences and ought to be released, but in fact we are kept indefinitely imprisoned under all sorts of legal pretexts. All of which in reality violate any acceptable human rights standard. Now, I am announcing my decision to go on a hunger-strike to the end. My action is taken in conscience of those who would like to help remedy this gross violation of human rights. I am starting my hun-ger-strike on July 18, 1986, the day my term in prison is officially coming to an end, but in fact the end of my term is only another date in the continuous struggle for freedom which I started back in Cuba.
If I do not survive my hunger strike, I hereby wish that my body be donated for medical investigations. . . . I put my life in the custody and good will of:
   (a) God Almighty

*(b)   The Democratic, Humanitarian and Love of Justice of the
      People of the United States.*

*Y [sic] prayer my petition, in my own name (Antonio Pi Montalvo)
and in the name of all the Mariel refugees who have become pawns
in the United States and Cuba, would move the conscience of the
world so that human beings in the USA would be treated as decently
as in any other country according to the United Nations.*

The Case of Rafael Cruz Hernández

The detainee code of conduct also was played out "to the end" by
detainee Rafael Cruz Hernández, who attempted to slowly starve
himself to death at Atlanta sometime in the fall of 1986. Here is
his last testament:

Dear President Reagan:

*There has been much written regarding the Cuban refugees that
arrived in this country in the Freedom Flotilla of 1980, accusing
them of being criminals, killers and mentally ill. But the public
judging from this evident propaganda, don't know the real truth
about us, "The Marielitos." Only those that have lived in the communist poverty know the truth of the Cuban refugees and why the
increases [in] discrimination that your Government has set up for
us that live in the Mariel exodus.*

*A person who is aware of Communist policy must know that
when a country suffers for more than a quarter of a century from
Marxist doctrine, anyone who is not convinced of that doctrine experiences constant persecution from the system, even coming to view
himself as outside the law. It is true that many Cuban refugees come
out of Communist prisons, brutalized by the misery, degradation and
torment of communism. They were not real delinquents but rather
made to be so. What Cuban didn't have to break the rules to provide
food for his children that were begging with starving and tearful eyes
for a piece of bread?*

El Exilio: "The Romanticism of Death"

President Reagan did not respond to Pi's or Cruz's letters of protest, nor did any official of the Justice Department. Perhaps

suicide attempts behind the walls of Atlanta had, in fact, become so frequent as to attract little attention. Perhaps officials of the Meese Justice Department simply did not care. After all, moral crusaders rarely show compassion for their victims. Whatever the case, political opposition expressed in the form of mass suicide attempts would contribute greatly to the well-developed inmate cohesion necessary to capture control of Oakdale and Atlanta in November 1987. Thus, three questions remain: Why were so many Mariels willing to lay down their lives for the detainee code of conduct? Why did they choose such an agonizing method of suicide? And why did they dedicate so many of their suicides to the president of the United States?

There are a number of reasons the mass suicide attempts should not be surprising. First, recent studies show that black suicide rates in the United States have increased steadily since the late 1960s; most of the Cuban detainees in Atlanta were black. Second, studies show that suicide is connected with immigration: in other words, suicides by immigrants have and continue to exceed significantly those of native-born Americans.[18]

In this context, the dilemma faced by the Mariel detainees was especially distressing. They came to the United States seeking a new life in a promised land. They migrated to escape the lean proletarianism of Marxist society. When the vision they sought fell far short of its promise, they became depressed and lethargic. Confined to a maximum-security prison under brutal and inhumane conditions, without any hope of ever being released, the detainees became anomic. Unable to return to a rejected past, they found in self-destruction a viable alternative.

Their preferred method of suicide—starvation—cannot be understood without reference to the cultural context in which it occurred. For example, in New York City, jumping from buildings accounts for an estimated fifty percent of suicides by blacks. "So much of the life in Harlem," writes suicide researcher Herbert Hendin, "is lived in and on top of these tenements that they occupy the unconscious life of their inhabitants and come to provide a tragic setting for black suicide."[19] The Cuban suicides at Atlanta can be understood in the same way. So much of the life in Atlanta was lived by the black Mariels in severely overcrowded cells where they routinely sacrificed food to the heavenly *orishas* as a spiritual ritual designed to cope with their extraordinary pains of imprisonment that sacrificing food had come to occupy much of their unconscious life. The sacrifice of food from their own bodies, then, was a logical extension of the cultural and religious practices of Santeria.

Finally, all suicides, successful as well as attempted, have fantasy aims, not the least of which involves the imagination of the reactions of others to their deaths. Some researchers have called this a "quest for the future" or a strategy "that seeks and finds a solution to an existential problem." Others have referred to it as a "romanticism of death" that moves the survivors rather than the departed to the center of mourning rituals.[20]

This seems to explain the mass suicide attempts at Atlanta. Essentially, the institution was held together by a delicate thread that had been constructed by detainees and guards. Abandoned by the United States government and left to suffer in brutal and inhumane conditions, the Mariels coped by turning to primitive religion and suicide in an attempt to elicit what is known in Spanish as the spirit of *el exilio*—a term referring to a bizarre, phantasmagorical state of mind—in which they actually believed that President Ronald Reagan would emerge as a champion of human rights and deliver them from the gates of Hell. It wasn't much, but it was enough to establish equilibrium and avoid rioting.

What happened, then, to upset this fragile equilibrium?

Chapter 9
The Human Rights
Offensive

To fully understand the event that toppled the delicate equilibrium and triggered the Oakdale and Atlanta riots, it is necessary to return to the earliest days of the Reagan administration and move forward from there. This exercise is important because, as we shall see, the triggering event was the culmination of a pattern of ethical transgressions by Edwin Meese III and his associates between 1981 and 1987. Contrary to Sykes's theory of prison riots, the event that triggered Oakdale and Atlanta had less to do with prison management than it did with another state-organized moral panic engineered outside the correctional arena, this one waged in the complex area of U.S. foreign policy. This second panic created the ultimate pain of imprisonment for the detainees. But consistent with Sykes's theory, there were, as we shall also see, many opportunities to avoid the precipitating event in the years and months preceding November 21, 1987. Unfortunately for the detainees, no public official had the compassion, courage, or power to step forth and take such an opportunity.

The Early Years: "The Man Deserved to Die"

The relationship between Ronald Reagan and Edwin Meese began in California during the turbulent 1960s. In May 1964, students and radicals at the University of California at Berkeley organized themselves around the celebrated "Free Speech Movement" intended to influence U.S. foreign policy in Vietnam. They did so by waging a demonstration not against the Johnson White House in Washington, which was actually fighting the war, but against the administrators at the University of California, who had little to do with foreign policy in Vietnam, or any place else, for that matter. Because their protest vandalized and destroyed property owned by the University of California, the Alameda County prosecutor had jurisdiction. The case was assigned to a young deputy district attorney and University of California law school graduate named Edwin Meese III.[1]

Over the next year, Deputy D.A. Meese successfully prosecuted 773 University of California students for their parts in the Berkeley uprisings. Because of his phenomenal success, Meese was invited to Washington in June 1966 to testify before the House Un-American Activities Committee. Meese stated that "the 800-member Berkeley Vietnam Day Committee which organized teach-ins and demonstrations against escalations of the war was affording aid and comfort to the enemy."[2]

In order to combat these forces more effectively, Meese began using undercover agents to infiltrate the Berkeley antiwar movement. And in the early days of August 1969—as tens of thousands of counterculture youth swarmed toward the historic music festival that would be called Woodstock—one of Meese's undercover agents shot and killed a young man during an antiwar demonstration at People's Park in Berkeley. Within hours of the killing, Meese coldly stated to a television reporter that "the man deserved to die."[3]

Shortly thereafter, Edwin Meese captured the attention of California Governor Ronald Reagan. Reagan had become impressed with Meese's no-nonsense law-and-order beliefs and his ability to translate them into action. And in December 1969, Reagan appointed Meese secretary of legal affairs for the State of California. Meese held this job until 1975, when Reagan promoted him to the position of executive assistant to the governor. During this period, Meese recalls that "an important part" of his responsibility was "to plan state support for the local police in the event of a riot or campus disturbance."[4] After Reagan's tenure as governor ended,

Meese left public service to become an attorney in the private sector.

The Wedtech Debacle: "Small Case Bob" and "The Second Most Powerful Man in America"

After his 1980 victory over Jimmy Carter, Ronald Reagan coaxed Edwin Meese back into public service by offering him the position of general counsel to the president. Meese accepted this prestigious appointment and, together with Chief of Staff James A. Baker III and Deputy Chief of Staff Michael K. Deaver, Meese became part of the troika that would run the Reagan White House during the administration's first term in office.[5]

In May 1981, General Counsel Meese began receiving memoranda from his personal attorney and law school friend, E. Robert Wallach, informing him of an obscure tool and die company called the Welbilt Corporation, located in New York City's South Bronx.[6] Wallach's memoranda would ultimately ensnare Meese in the second-largest government scandal since Watergate, after the Iran-Contra affair.

Robert Wallach was a successful San Francisco attorney who specialized in representing the victims of auto accidents, airplane crashes, and medical malpractice. By all outer appearances, he was a reform-minded liberal. In 1975, Wallach was elected president of the San Francisco Bar Association on a platform advancing the interests of women and minorities and improving aid to indigents. A year later, he ran unsuccessfully for the U.S. Senate, promising to decriminalize marijuana and to eliminate nuclear arms. But investigative journalists William Sternberg and Matthew Harrison argue that Wallach "was so ostentatious about his do-gooderism . . . that some colleagues found the man obnoxious."[7] They further note that:

> Even by California standards, Wallach was something of an odd
> duck, a man who seemed to cultivate eccentricities. Like the poet
> e. e. cummings, he spelled his name entirely in lower-case letters
> . . . associates called him "small case bob." He was a health fanatic,
> a vegetarian, . . . a modish dresser [who] wore a fresh yellow rose

in his lapel each day, had hair transplants, tooled about town in a vintage Jaguar, and was trailed seemingly everywhere by a golden-haired dog.[8]

Wallach would later move from San Francisco to the nation's capital, where other analysts also found him to be "something of an odd duck"—even by Washington standards in the Reagan era. For example, Suzanne Garment of the conservative American Enterprise Institute went so far as to suggest that nuances of life-style lie at the very heart of individual political deviance:

> Wallach, born in the Bronx and raised in California, was in no way a Washington type. Indeed, he was the sort of person that most of politically active Washington could not even look at without being overwhelmed by sinister vibrations. They objected . . . to his name . . . spelled . . . in lower case letters. They also objected to his appearance. He was rail-thin from following the diet of a longtime client, Dr. Nathan Pritikin, and his bushy eyebrows and the eyes under them stood out in relief. He sported what seemed to Washington a strange wardrobe, which looked as if it had come out of a cross between a Giorgio Armani menswear boutique and a Sausalito weaving and knitting workshop. Bobbing in a sea of dark suits, white shirts, and the ever-present Adam Smith neckties, these outfits of Wallach's made a statement, and they did not say "solid citizen."[9]

In November 1980, on the eve of Reagan's election victory, the *San Francisco Examiner* described Wallach as one of the city's "elite, big-bucks, hot-shot superlawyers" in an article ranking him among the Bay Area's top five private attorneys. In a caustic indicator of things to come, the *Examiner* asked, "Want to have some influence in the Reagan administration? Can't bear the thought of talking to a Republican? Then see e. robert wallach, a Democrat with ties to people in both parties, including Ed Meese."[10]

In 1981, Wallach began cashing in on what he called his "notoriety as a friend of Ed Meese."[11] It was then that he was hired by the Welbilt Corporation specifically for his personal and professional contact with the general counsel. Not only did Wallach promote Welbilt to Meese as proof of the Reagan administration's belief in the powers of free enterprise, he also began sending Meese extensive memoranda on topics ranging from Meese's personal fitness to U.S. foreign policy—a subject about which he had little expertise. Sternberg and Harrison show that Wallach sent Meese memos advising the general counsel on Soviet-Polish relations, on the Pacific Basin, on Afghanistan, on how to settle the conflict in the Falklands, and other international affairs. "In his memos," they write, "Wallach would suggest to Meese at various times that he (Wallach) be appointed the ambassador to the United Nations, a Middle East negotiator, or solicitor general of the United States."[12] About these memoranda, Wallach would later lament, "They were written in the form of advice from one friend to another. Whether they were good, intelligent or naive, I can't tell you. But they were helpful to him, I think, in performing his duties and living his life."[13]

• • •

In the winter of 1982, Welbilt officials responded to a federal request for proposals on a U.S. Army engine contract. It was actually a request for extended funding on a Defense Department contract awarded to the corporation in 1981. Welbilt was seeking an extension because they had been "slow and inefficient" on their previous contract.[14] Wallach's job was to smooth all this over with his friend and client, the general counsel to the president of the United States.

When Welbilt filed the proposal, Wallach sent Meese a memo asking him to help the corporation get "a fair hearing." In response, Meese directed a Justice Department aide to prepare a favorable report on Welbilt, which led to a $32 million "no bid" Army engine contract being awarded to the corporation in September 1982.[15]

A year later, the company went public with a stock offering under the new name of Wedtech Corporation.[16] Wallach then relocated from the West Coast to Washington, where he promoted himself as the "right-hand man" to Edwin Meese. To showcase his powerful contacts within the Washington Beltway, on May 26, 1983, Wallach hosted a luncheon banquet for a group of influential attorneys and judges at an upscale restaurant, where he told

his guests, "I meet Ed Meese daily—he's the second most powerful man in America—or maybe in the world. . . . Through me, you
can send messages to this man."[17]

After this, things began to go swimmingly for "lower case bob"
and his two principal clients: Wedtech and Edwin Meese III. Between 1984 and 1986, Wedtech received another $218 million in
government contracts, most of them no-bid awards through the
Small Business Administration.[18] In total, the Wallach-Meese
partnership sank more than $250 million in taxpayer money into
this "slow and inefficient" tool and die company in the South
Bronx. Yet, despite this massive infusion of government resources,
by 1987 the corporation was bankrupt. Wedtech, as it later turned
out, was being managed by a group of men who were systematically stealing the company blind.[19]

The Attorney General Hearings: "A Question of Character"

In late 1983, Attorney General William French Smith told his
longtime friend Ronald Reagan that he would be stepping down
from his post at the end of the president's first term. As a replacement for Smith, Reagan selected Edwin Meese to be the next attorney general of the United States.

Hearings on the nomination and confirmation of Edwin Meese
began in the Senate Judiciary Committee on March 1, 1984. They
would not end until January 31, 1985. These proceedings were
beyond doubt the longest and most vociferously debated in the
history of nominating and confirming appointments to the administrative branch of government. They produced 1,597 pages of
testimony, rendering perhaps the most critical evaluation of a
public official in American history. In a move that would later
become richly ironic, Meese was represented by Robert Wallach,
who was paid more than half a million dollars by Wedtech to serve
as legal counsel for Meese during the confirmation hearings.[20]

During the hearings, Wallach not only continued his lobbying
efforts on behalf of Wedtech, but also began to draw parallels between his responsibility to represent Meese before the U.S. Senate
and his responsibility to Wedtech. For example, on March 2, 1984,
Wallach sent Wedtech executives a memo noting that they and

Meese were "my two major East Coast clients." Then, in reference to a $134 million navy contract about to be awarded to Wedtech by the Small Business Administration, an optimistic Wallach proclaimed

> I see much more than our victory. . . . I see a whole new attitude
> and philosophy for the company emerging. As with Ed, our only
> refrain during the course of his excellent performance during yes-
> terday's hearing was to urge him: "Don't get cocky—stay humble."
> The same advice applies to us [Wedtech].[21]

Similarly, Wallach continued to promote Wedtech to Meese as Meese was being represented by Wallach for Meese's nomination to the highest law enforcement office in the land. And Meese continued to be comfortable with this arrangement, pushing for one Wedtech financial "victory" after another. In a memo to Meese in October 1984, a copy of which was sent to Wedtech, Wallach suggested that President Reagan "make an appropriate campaign stop" at Wedtech's plant in the South Bronx.[22] A month later, Ronald Reagan did just that.[23]

Given the fact that this sort of opportunistic and politically immature behavior was displayed at the highest level of the American legal order with such brash conspicuousness, it is not surprising that in April 1984 the Senate produced evidence indicating that Edwin Meese had been unethical since first coming to Washington three years earlier. According to the Senate Judiciary Committee, the specific charges against him were as follows:

1) He provided presidential nominations of two public servants who had recently made loans to the bank account of Edwin and Ursula Meese.

2) The job as deputy under secretary of the interior was given to an attorney named Thomas J. Barrack, Jr., who had helped the Meeses sell their California home when they were already in deep financial trouble.

3) Meese had received an irregular promotion to colonel in the Army Reserves, allowing him a higher pension.

4) Three loans had been made to the Meeses—with a "general tolerance" of their failure to repay on time—by the Great Ameri-

can Bank of California. Four officials of this bank were subsequently given presidential appointments.

5) Ursula Meese had received a loan from a man named Edwin W. Thomas. After this, Edwin Thomas's wife and son ended up on the federal payroll.

6) Edwin Meese accepted certain "moving expenses" when he moved to Washington to which he was not entitled—and then lied about this fact on his tax return by claiming the revenue as "consulting fees."

7) During the 1980 presidential race, Edwin Meese allegedly stole and destroyed an important speech written by Jimmy Carter.[24]

Concomitant with the Senate's filing of these charges, the Reagan White House released a statement that Meese, after a recent trip to Korea, had kept a set of jade cuff links given to him by the South Korean head of state. At the time, government rules stipulated that a federal official could accept only gifts worth less than $140. According to the White House, Meese's cuff links were valued at nearly $400.[25] Beyond its cuff link report, the Reagan administration made no further comment on Edwin Meese's qualifications to become the next attorney general.

In response to this litany of charges, Meese called for an independent counsel to clear him of what he called "the false allegations" against him.[26] In accordance with the Ethics in Government Act of 1978, the Senate appointed Jacob A. Stein as special counsel to investigate the allegations—and if necessary, to prosecute Edwin Meese. Stein's investigation lasted five months and produced interviews with more than two hundred persons about the charges against Meese.[27] For their part, Meese and Wallach sent Stein letters and supporting documents indicating that as general counsel to the president Meese had "thousands of important matters" on his mind, and that personal finances were the last on his list of priorities. Meese conceded that he was a poor money manager and that the subject of money was generally of little interest to him.[28]

Meanwhile, the national press mounted a vigorous campaign against Meese, sounding an alarm over the importance of high ethics in the administration of justice. For example, the *St. Louis Post-Dispatch* said this about Meese on December 23, 1984: "The issues of judgment, ethics and sensitivity to priority—in short, the question of character—remain unsettled. The nation's highest law enforcement officer must have impeccable credentials on these matters."

On January 31, 1984, the *Los Angeles Times* called Meeses actions "ethically indefensible; . . . an ethical blind spot is a major infirmity in an Attorney General." And on the same day, the *Cleveland Plain-Dealer* boldly stated that "If the Attorney General of the United States should be a person whose credentials should be above reproach—then Meese is the wrong individual for the post."

Despite this broad assault on Meese's character, special counsel Stein concluded on September 20, 1984, that while Meese exhibited an "amazing sloppiness" about his personal finances, a "casual disregard" for financial disclosure laws, and a "curious blindness" to the way such dealings would appear to the American public, no criminal prosecution was warranted.[29] "Nowhere in the statute or the order [appointing me] is there a directive," Stein wrote, "to investigate and report on the propriety or the ethics of [Meese's] conduct."[30] Stein therefore had produced no indictment of criminal behavior, but no verdict of ethical innocence either, and no findings were presented on Meese's qualifications for the post of attorney general.

On January 29, 1985, the U.S. Senate resumed its confirmation hearings. In that morning's edition of the *Washington Post,* the editors warned that

> None of us knows if Mr. Meese yet even realizes that he made
> many mistakes of judgment—one after the other—and that his re-
> peated failure to maintain a strict wall between his personal and
> private interests and his public powers and duties was wrong.

For the next three days, testimony on the floor of the Senate ranged from rancorous diatribes denouncing Meese as an "ethical pygmy" to Wallach's languid support of Meese as "fit for high office."[31] These were the extremes of the Meese nomination. On one hand, Edwin Meese was perceived as a "major infirmity" to good government; on the other, he was simply "fit" for service. But the partisan politics that dominated the Reagan era quickly resolved this cognitive dissonance. On February 5, 1985, Edwin Meese III was confirmed as the 77th attorney general of the United States of America.

Meese's acceptance speech was symbolic of the culture of self-interest that had by then pervaded political Washington. Instead of setting forth a progressive administrative vision for American criminal justice, Meese simply pledged that from that day forward he *himself* would not break the law. With his "hot-shot" California lawyer at his side, fifty-three-year-old Edwin Meese III, a bloated ex-D.A. from California whose only major accomplishment was the prosecution of a rebellious and misguided group of college students twenty years earlier, promised the American public,

> I've learned a great deal from this experience, and if in the future a similar situation occurred, I would go overboard to avoid any appearance that might be construed, misconstrued or misinterpreted, or even distorted.[32]

Ethics, Wedtech, and Human Rights

Less than four months later, on May 23, 1985, Attorney General Meese entered into a personal business partnership with an investor named W. Franklyn Chinn, a member of the Wedtech board of directors. This partnership had been arranged by Robert Wallach, himself recently appointed to the Wedtech board of directors. From the sale of his California home, various loans, and a recent inheritance from Ursula's mother, Meese was able to scrape together approximately $55,000 for Chinn to invest in a "limited blind partnership" called Meese Partners.[33] A "limited blind partnership" meant that Chinn was able to invest Meese's money in financial projects that would be unknown to Meese himself—an arrangement that allowed Chinn to make investments in the Wedtech Corporation while keeping his client "blind" to such business dealings.[34]

These arrangements immediately paid great dividends to everyone involved. For Wedtech, the multimillion-dollar government contracts continued to flow from the Small Business Administration.[35] The arrangement helped Meese acquire more wealth than he had ever seen. Between 1985 and 1987, Chinn parlayed Meese's $55,000 into $100,000—an astounding 83 percent return on his initial investment in less than two years.[36] And for his part in arranging the Wedtech contracts and the Meese-Chinn partnership, Robert Wallach received two gifts. Wedtech rewarded him with more than $2 million in cash and stock,[37] and his client and friend, the attorney general, gave Wallach something he had always wanted: a nomination to the position of U.S. ambassador to the United Nations Commission on Human Rights.[38]

U.S.–Cuban Relations in 1987:
"Firing Squads" and "Institutionalized Torture"

With the attorney general's support, the Reagan administration appointed Wallach to the UN Human Rights Commission in April 1986.[39] At the time, the United States was waging a fierce diplomatic offensive against human rights abuses allegedly taking place in Vietnam, Cambodia, and especially Cuba. Indeed, U.S. Ambassador Vernon E. Walters had recently told the UN General Assembly, that "Since Castro took control, . . . this regime has become a brutal dictatorship . . . and operates a vast network of prisons, labor camps, and firing squads to keep itself in power."[40]

The U.S. human rights offensive against Cuba had in fact been launched by President Reagan two years earlier, shortly after his victory over Fidel Castro in Grenada. On January 5, 1984, the eve of the 25th anniversary of Castro's revolution, President Reagan delivered a radio address, translated into Spanish and broadcast to an estimated audience of twenty-two million people throughout south Florida, the Caribbean, and Latin America. Within the Florida segment of this audience were thousands of refugees from the port of Mariel, some of whom would eventually end up behind the walls of Oakdale and Atlanta.

In his speech, President Reagan was particularly harsh on the subject of what he called "prisoners of conscience convicted of their political activities" whom he said had been "languishing in Cuban prisons deprived of all freedom for nearly a quarter of a century. Some prisoners convicted in the last year," Reagan said, "can expect to be in prison well into the 21st century if the present system in Cuba survives that long."[41]

Following this diplomatic assault, Assistant Secretary of State Elliott Abrams asserted that Fidel Castro was "one of the most vicious tyrants of our time."[42] At length, the human rights offensive against Castro became enshrined in administrative policy. On January 6 (no doubt timed to coincide with Reagan's speech), the U.S. House of Representatives issued a report entitled *Human Rights in Cuba*, which claimed that "The Castro government actively engages in acts of torture and harassment, as well as other drastic steps to suppress all forms of political dissent."[43]

By 1986, the U.S. human rights offensive against Castro's Cuba had been elevated to the status of a state-organized moral panic. In that year's survey of human rights abuses around the world, the State Department charged that "repression of basic human rights is so pervasive that Cuba holds the dubious distinction of being the Western Hemisphere's most serious violator of human rights and fundamental freedoms."[44] On May 21, 1986, in a speech commemorating Cuban Independence Day, Vice President Bush spoke out against alleged abuses before the Cuban American Foundation in Miami. "It's a sad truth," said Bush, "but under Castro today Cuba has only two big exports—sugar and death of its young."[45] And on November 18, Elliott Abrams once again condemned Cuba's "brutal and methodical crackdown" on human rights.[46]

Because of these official statements, the U.S. media began asserting a one-sided and highly uncritical portrayal of Cuban prisons. Obviously, these media reports were followed with great interest by the Cuban detainees at Oakdale and Atlanta. Human rights abuse in Cuban prisons was in fact the most-covered Cuban topic reported by the U.S. media during the year preceding the riots. According to research conducted by Latin American scholars Flora Biancalana and Cecilia O'Leary, two-thirds of nearly four hundred U.S. news items about Cuba in 1986 referred to the plight of political prisoners, their "inhuman treatment" in Cuban prisons, and their efforts to emigrate to the United States. The other one-third focused on the Cuban dissident Armando Valladares.[47]

Valladares was released from a Cuban prison in 1982 after serving a twenty-two-year sentence. According to the Cuban Ministry of Justice, Valladares was a former member of dictator Fulgencio Batista's brutal police force and a terrorist who was fairly tried and imprisoned for grievous actions against the state. According to Valladares, he was nothing more than a postal clerk and an aspiring young poet who was unjustly imprisoned and tortured because he spoke out against the Castro regime. The truth of the matter is probably known only to Valladares himself, but the 1986 publication of his prison memoir, *Against All Hope*, became an event of major significance in U.S.–Cuban relations during the period leading up November 21, 1987.

In *Against All Hope*, Valladares writes of being savagely beaten as a matter of almost daily routine; of being deprived of sleep by guards wielding wooden prods called "Ho Chi Minh poles"; of being forced to go naked for weeks on end during the winter; of being doused with buckets of excrement and urine; of being submerged in a ditch filled with raw sewage; of being forbidden to wash for months at a time; of being denied medical attention for a serious illness caused by the brutality of his confinement; of being deprived of food for as long as forty-six days at a time; of punishment cells with "neon light torture"; and of being fed worms, cockroaches, dead rats, broken glass, and the waste-filled rectum of a cow's intestine. Finally, Valladares also claims to have witnessed "thousands and thousands" of executions during his twenty-two-year internment. Valladares describes these savage abuses as only "the merest sketch of the terrible reality of Cuban prisons."[48] The U.S. media bought this frightening description of Cuban prisons lock, stock, and barrel, without ever once looking into the matter for themselves.

On May 19, 1986, the *Wall Street Journal* reported that Valladares's book "chronicles more variations on cruelty than anyone should ever know." On June 3, the *New York Times* proclaimed that *Against All Hope* was "an important book that shattered all illusions" about the Cuban revolution. Five days later, the *New York Times Book Review* said, "It has taken us twenty-five years to find out the terrible reality—Mr. Castro has created a new despotism that has institutionalized torture as a mechanism of social control. . . . Valladares gives us . . . a picture on the hell that was the Cuba he lived in." And on July 26, the *Washington Post* went on record claiming that "Fidel Castro takes his place as yet another of this century's mass murderers." The moral panic had been completed.

• • •

On December 11, 1986, President Reagan hosted an internationally televised ceremony on the front steps of the White House commemorating "National Human Rights Day in America." At his side was the presidential guest of honor, Armando Valladares. Reagan expressed his "outrage" at the "horrors and sadism" of the Cuban prison system. "Throughout the communist world," proclaimed the president, "the cupboards are empty and the jails are full."[49]

With this speech, Ronald Reagan captured the hearts and minds of thousands of Mariel Cubans, like Alberto Herrera, who were being "indefinitely detained" in federal prisons under "brutal and inhumane" conditions of confinement. Soon, hundreds of detainees would send him letters pleading for his help. Others would kill themselves in vain attempts to win his mercy. Alas, the detainees were willing to lay down their lives for Ronald Reagan as a literal and imaginative expression of *el exilio*. This extraordinary spiritual devotion to President Reagan was motivated by one overarching reason: The detainees believed that if they were repatriated to Cuba, they would be classified as "political prisoners" and experience the horrific torture and death referred to with such clarity and passion by Mr. Reagan, Armando Valladares, and the American media. Ironically, the most immediate effect of the U.S. political offensive against human rights abuses in Cuban prisons was to politicize Cubans locked up in U.S. prisons.

It was against this explosive backdrop that the United States government dispatched not an expert on human rights and diplomacy, but a flamboyant personal-injury attorney and tool-and-die consultant—the eccentric E. Robert Wallach—as its "leader" to inject moral panic into the complex arena of international political affairs. Wallach's efforts were not only a monumental failure, they would ultimately trigger the riots at Oakdale and Atlanta.

The Geneva Human Rights Convention of 1987:
"A Lot of Embarrassment Around"

Wallach attempted to implement the moral panic at the United Nations Human Rights Convention held in Geneva between January 19 and March 11, 1987. Although Wallach was the leader of the U.S. delegation at Geneva, he was joined by the chief U.S. ambassador to the UN, Vernon Walters. They were indeed an odd couple to be addressing the subject of human rights in Cuba. Wallach was an amateur diplomat who did not speak Spanish and who knew next to nothing about Cuba. Walters was a former deputy director of the CIA who had planned a covert action to assassinate Fidel Castro in 1976.[50] Their singular purpose in Geneva was to gain the convention's endorsement of a formal resolution condemning Cuban violations of human rights. Although Walters and Wallach had never set foot inside a Cuban prison, their initial resolution expressed "deep concern" for more than "15,000 Cuban political prisoners" who were being routinely tortured and killed.[51]

Ambassador Wallach made these remarkable charges in a rambling, rattling speech delivered on January 19:

> What we [the United States] intend to do is bring evidence before the committee, people who have suffered abuse in Cuba. We want the committee to stand up and be counted on this subject and if it's not prepared to do that, then there's going to be a lot of embarrassment around. We want to resurrect some kind of evenhandedness in this committee. . . . We're not perfect in the U.S. But at least we're a free society and we're prepared to defend human rights.[52]

The most immediate effect of Wallach's speech was to cause the Cuban delegation to file a proposal of its own, accusing the United States of violating the human rights of Hispanics, Puerto Ricans, American Indians, and blacks—especially the three black males who recently had been clubbed to death by a gang of Italian youths in the Howard Beach section of Queens.[53] (The Cuban delegates did not, however, raise the issue of human rights violations against Cubans from the port of Mariel who were incarcerated in U.S. prisons. They truly were the Abandoned Ones—abandoned by officials in both Washington and Havana.)

The counterresolution was introduced by Cuban delegate Raul Roa Kouri. Unlike his U.S. counterpart, the diplomatically inexperienced Wallach, Roa was a skilled diplomat with a sharp understanding of human rights and U.S.–Cuban political affairs. And unlike the hot-shot Washington lobbyist, Roa had worked his way to Geneva by virtue of public service. By the time he squared off against Wallach, Raul Roa held the position of deputy minister of foreign affairs of the Republic of Cuba.[54]

Roa called Wallach's resolution a "deliberate smear" of Cuba by Washington. He then explained his reason with impeccable clarity: "Cuban exiles in the United States are an important constituency for the Republican Party and elections are coming up, so we understand the situation."[55]

Roa's counterresolution, however, had less to do with human rights abuses in the United States than with the two peculiar men dispatched to Geneva by the U.S. government to discuss the issue of human rights in an international forum. About Wallach, Roa was silent; perhaps he was baffled by Wallach or perhaps he knew nothing about Wallach's past. But against the credentials of Ambassador Walters, Roa leveled a stinging indictment. Vernon Walters, said Roa,

> is the worst possible person to be chosen to introduce a human rights resolution here. It is preposterous that somebody who was involved in the 1976 attempt to assassinate President Castro, as was proved by the [U.S. Senator Frank] Church committee, should be introducing an anti-Cuban resolution here.[56]

Because of this crisis in character, Roa proclaimed that "The U.S. government is not qualified to discuss human rights anywhere in the world."[57] By the time he left Geneva, more than half the world would agree with him.

• • •

For the next six weeks, the discussion of human rights moved through two acrimonious dimensions. For each charge leveled by Wallach, Roa offered a rebuttal to show that Cuba did not have a human rights problem. At the center of Roa's counteroffensive were the actual dimensions of the problem. While Wallach claimed that Cuba had some fifteen thousand "political prisoners" incarcerated because of their antisocialist beliefs, Roa provided evidence that there were only 468 Cubans imprisoned for being "counterrevolutionaries." Roa argued that "counterrevolutionary prisoners in Cuba are not imprisoned because they are against the ideas of socialism but because they have violated Cuban laws, either by planning to sabotage the economy or harm our leaders."[58]

Driven solely by the Reagan administration's obsession with the Communist presence in the Western Hemisphere, Wallach ignored this argument and forged ahead with a ferocious propaganda campaign designed to expose Cuba's "brutal treatment of thousands of political prisoners." To drive home his point, Wallach compared Castro's Cuba to Nazi Germany.[59] Because there is no worse comparison, a number of Geneva delegates viewed the U.S. resolution with great skepticism. At the height of Wallach's campaign, a *New York Times* reporter observed that

> The diplomats say they [are] puzzled by the timing of the United States' human-rights campaign against Cuba. The campaign does not come amid reports of new abuses. On the contrary, since last fall Cuba has released more than 90 prisoners.[60]

The diplomatic consensus was, of course, wasted on Robert Wallach. Instead, he insisted that the United States had the votes necessary to pass its resolution condemning Cuba for human rights violations. "Everybody got on board," Wallach incorrectly concluded about the resolution. "There was a deep sense of commitment to the cause."[61]

During the convention, Wallach flew eighteen ex-political prisoners (including Armando Valladares) from the United States to Geneva to testify about the torture they had endured in Cuban prisons.[62] One of the first ex-prisoners to testify dramatically removed a prosthesis on the convention floor, claiming to have lost his leg as a result of torture.[63] In a further attempt to win support for the U.S. resolution, Wallach threatened UN delegates from developing countries that the United States would halt delivery of precious aid, such as medicine and wheat shipments, should they not go along with the condemnation of Cuba.[64] As an additional incentive, Wallach promised delegates that if the U.S. won enough votes to pass the resolution, Washington might be willing to pay some of the $400 million in back dues it owed to the United Nations.[65]

Shortly before the vote was taken in Geneva, Ambassador Wallach pulled out all the stops in his indictment of the Castro regime. In the final hours of the convention, Wallach hosted a controversial "prayer breakfast" at which he asserted the highly ethnocentric belief that faith in God should be an integral component of human rights and sound prison management—subjects about which he knew utterly nothing.[66]

Meanwhile, back in Washington, the State Department prepared extensive portfolios documenting Cuba's human rights record as Elliott Abrams and other officials urged foreign ambassadors to accept Wallach's proposal.[67] Even President Reagan joined the offensive. Following the prosthesis incident, Wallach told a reporter that President Reagan had sent "very personalized messages" to President François Mitterand of France and President Abdou Diouf of Senegal pleading for their support.[68] During the first two weeks of March, Reagan stressed the urgency of the U.S. resolution in personal notes to other heads of states, and directed U.S. ambassadors in forty-two capitals around the world to call on foreign ministry officials for their votes. In total, Reagan officials sent out more than four hundred diplomatic cables urging support of the U.S. resolution.[69]

Yet Wallach's awkward, hard-sell campaign proved to be a colossal misadventure. Fewer than half the countries represented were "willing to step up and be counted" in the U.S. offensive against human rights abuses in Cuba. Not only did the delegates find Wallach's evidence on systematic torture and murder less than compelling, they also considered his diplomatic style highly abrasive. Said a veteran European delegate at the Convention, "It was an extraordinary effort, something that was never done before. The Americans deployed their forces so intensively that it was at times, let's say, not very diplomatic."[70]

Similarly, a Latin American delegate observed, "It was very difficult to understand why, all of a sudden, there was all this pressure for this issue this year and never before."[71] And a second

European delegate charged, "The Americans pushed people into corners and twisted arms wherever they could."[72]

The final text of Wallach's resolution called for the convention to express its "deep concern" about the alleged abuses in Cuba. It also called on Cuba to release all "political prisoners" and to allow free travel from the island. The final text, however, made no reference to numbers of political prisoners or systematic torture. Instead, it condemned deprivation of the rights to a fair trial, to freedom from arbitrary arrest and detention, and to freedom of expression.[73] The first two charges were, of course, the same human rights abuses being suffered by Mariel Cubans in Wallach's own country.

The votes on the U.S. resolution and on Cuba's counterresolution were counted on March 13, 1987. Despite Wallach's wild theatrics and intense pressure, the convention voted 19–18 against the U.S. resolution, with 6 abstentions. And despite Roa's countercharge that the rights of blacks, American Indians, Hispanics, and Puerto Ricans were being systematically violated in the United States, a similar majority rejected the Cuban counterresolution.[74] It was, on balance, a lose-lose situation for both the U.S. and Cuba. In Wallach's words, there was "a lot of embarrassment around." For Wallach, the embarrassment had only just begun.

Resistance to the U.S. resolution came from five countries that Wallach considered potential "swing votes" in Geneva: India, Mexico, Argentina, Colombia, and Venezuela. In the end, these delegates stood behind the word of Raul Roa and the Republic of Cuba. Yet these delegates also provided the necessary votes to defeat Roa's counterresolution. A delegate from India explained: "The rejection of both motions was an effort to avoid overly politicizing the Commission's debates."[75]

Wallach's reaction to his defeat was what might have been expected from an amateur diplomat sent into the complex arena of international political affairs to represent a foreign policy initiative about which he knew nothing. He first assailed the delegates from Colombia and Venezuela for "failing to support the United States position or from abstaining from voting."[76] Then he issued a warning to the convention in general that the convention should avoid "focusing attention" on the U.S. setback to condemn Cuban human rights policies. Instead, the delegates should look forward to new evidence that would be presented by the United States at the 1988 convention.[77] "Obviously," said Vernon Walters shortly after the votes were counted, "we didn't put enough energy into it this year."[78] And as he left Geneva, Robert Wallach told a reporter that his failure should be "thought of as a disappointment, not a defeat."[79] They were his last official words as Human Rights Ambassador for the United States. Nine months later, Wallach would be indicted by a federal grand jury on charges of racketeering, mail and wire fraud, and conspiring to defraud the United States in his work for Wedtech.

This serious error in judgment in international politics set in motion two "new" diplomatic strategies. The first was a counteroffensive waged by the Cuban government against the United States. The second was a diplomatic retaliation to that counteroffensive waged by the Reagan White House, a retaliation that would trigger the Oakdale and Atlanta riots.

The Counteroffensive: "All Kinds of Disgusting Lies"

When Fidel Castro learned about Wallach's bizarre performance at the Geneva convention, he became just as livid as he had been after the war in Grenada. On the heels of the U.S. setback, Castro delivered an impassioned speech before the Conference of American Jurists in Havana, charging: "They—Reagan—did incredible things over there in Geneva, incredible! They have made up their own characters . . . with all kinds of disgusting lies."[80]

About the issue of human rights afforded Cuba prisoners during the previous quarter-century, Fidel proclaimed: "Not a single prisoner was murdered, not a single prisoner was beaten, not a single prisoner was tortured or physically attacked. . . . To say people are tortured here is above all an insult to the people [of Cuba]."[81]

This had been, indeed, the position taken by Fidel Castro since the charge of "human rights abuses" was first hurled against him three months before the U.S. invasion of Grenada. On July 28, 1983, Castro had told a group of French and American journalists:

> From our point of view, we have no human rights problem—there
> have been no "disappeareds" here, there have been no tortures
> here, there have been no murders here. In twenty-five years of rev-
> olution, in spite of the difficulties and dangers we have passed
> through, torture has never been committed, a crime has never been
> committed.[82]

Wallach's ill-conceived diplomatic offensive led President Castro
to issue invitations to dozens of governments and independent
human rights organizations to visit the island and inspect Cuban
prisons for themselves. These delegations (which included busi-
nessmen, politicians, scholars, and human rights specialists from
all corners of the world) would, on balance, confirm Castro's
claims.

One of the first delegations to visit Cuba following the Geneva
convention came from the Washington-based Institute for Policy
Studies (IPS). The IPS visited six Cuban prisons between February
26 and March 5, 1988. The IPS delegation was led by Peter Ball,
president of the Edna McConnell Clark Foundation, in New York
City. He was accompanied by Dr. Howard Hiatt (former dean of
the Harvard School of Public Health), Aryeh Neier (vice-chairman
of Americas Watch), Herman Schwartz (professor of law at American University), and several IPS staff members. They drew eight
specific conclusions:

1) The great majority of Cuban prisoners worked a regular week
at productive jobs.

2) Almost all prisoners who worked were paid. They were re-
munerated for their labors at the same wage that could be earned
by civilians (less 35 percent for living expenses).

3) All Cuban prisons were clean and hygienic.

4) No Cuban prisoner had been the victim of an instrument of
torture, nor was any mention made by prisoners of extrajudicial
executions or disappearances. (This finding was based on confi-
dential interviews with prisoners conducted beyond earshot of
guards and prison officials.)

5) A system of conjugal visiting was well established in the
Cuban prison system.

6) Many prisoners acquired practical skills during their confinement.

7) Prisoner-against-prisoner violence was rare.

8) The outpatient, hospital, physical therapy, laboratory, and pharmacy areas of each Cuban prison were modern, hygienic, and well equipped. Each prison had a sufficient number of doctors, nurses, and assistants required for the prison populations.[83]

Moreover, the IPS asserted that there were a number of "humane and constructive features" in the Cuban prison system. These conclusions were corroborated by other experts in human rights and penology. In their 1987 report on Cuba, Amnesty International found "no credible reports of the death penalty having been carried out during 1985–86." In fact, Amnesty International was able to verify only twenty-nine cases of legal execution in the country between 1980 and 1986.[84] (By contrast, the United States carried out sixty-four executions during the same period.)[85]

Further evidence of the "humane and constructive" nature of Cuban prisons was documented by the 39th International Course in Criminology. Between July 6 and July 10, 1987, more than 250 penologists and human rights specialists from around the world were allowed to visit Cuban prisons and speak freely with prison officials and inmates. Following these visits, the international delegation issued this resolution:

> We were able to verify the respect for human rights demonstrated in the treatment of prisoners, resulting from a recognition of their human dignity and their inalienable rights to re-education and re-integration into the community. We also verified that important and valuable human and material resources are allocated to prisons and prisoners. We encourage the Cuban government and Cuban people to continue on the road to improving their penal system, using their present achievements as a starting point.[86]

Regarding inmates categorized as political prisoners, or *plantados* (meaning those who "stand firm" against the Castro regime—those whom Ronald Reagan referred to as "prisoners of conscience"), the IPS delegation concluded,

> Those who resist re-education or violate prison discipline—including passive violation such as hunger strikes—are confined

for extended periods, sometimes in extremely harsh punishment cells—bare, tiny, dark, cold . . . sometimes with insufficient food. . . . All but one of the prisoners we saw in punishment cells were common criminals, not those confined for politically motivated offenses.[87]

Similarly, those *plantados* identified by Amnesty International were believed to "have been denied visitation, correspondence, reading material, and regular exercise."[88]

During the Geneva Human Rights Convention of 1987, Robert Wallach had charged that there were as many as fifteen thousand political prisoners confined to Cuban penal institutions who, in the words of Ronald Reagan, "can expect to be in prison well into the 21st century." Yet Amnesty International estimated that while more than three thousand political prisoners were being held in Cuban prisons in 1978, nearly all of these inmates had been released by the end of 1979. As of 1988, Amnesty International and the IPS set the total at between four hundred and six hundred, and Amnesty International further estimated that the average length of incarceration for political prisoners was about three years (not the twenty years suggested by Reagan).[89] According to President Castro, this policy was "made possible by reducing their sentences and in other ways demonstrating the Revolution's generosity toward political prisoners."[90] These policies also have been documented by others. In 1987, Cuba scholar John Wallach concluded, "The record shows numerous examples of mothers and fathers who have been able to make [successful] personal appeals to Fidel Castro to free their sons from prison."[91]

• • •

These discoveries provided a second major setback for the United States in its international campaign against Cuban human rights policies. Although the Castro government acknowledged imprisoning people on charges of sabotage and trying to overthrow the state, neither the United Nations Human Rights Commission nor the international delegations that visited the country were able to corroborate the U.S. charge that Cuba was comparable to Nazi Germany. There was no evidence of "institutionalized torture," of

"Ho Chi Minh poles," of "firing squads," of "death of its young." There were not "thousands and thousands" of executions. Cuba was not the "tropical gulag" it was portrayed to be by the Reagan administration. All of that was nothing more than the hysterical and vitriolic language of moral panic, a message that was heard, unfortunately, with chilling clarity by the Mariel Cubans behind the walls of Oakdale and Atlanta.

Thus, by mid-1987, the preponderance of evidence seemed to point in the opposite direction from U.S. public opinion. In fact, the evidence suggested that human rights violations against imprisoned Mariel Cubans in the United States were far greater than anything being visited upon its own prisoners by the Republic of Cuba. But a third setback in the United States international offensive against Cuba was just around the corner.

Scandal: "A Pig" and "A Babe in the Woods"

Three months after the U.S. setback in Geneva—on July 20, 1987—front-page headlines in the San Francisco Examiner exclaimed: "Malpractice Suit Says SF Lawyers Cheated Little Girls." The story involved an out-of-court settlement in which two young, female burn victims received annuities amounting to $730,000, while their attorneys, E. Robert Wallach and David Baum, negotiated a $1 million legal fee for themselves.[92] Moreover, Wallach and his partner had violated a fundamental ethical principle of the legal profession that stipulates that counsel in accident injury cases is entitled to no more than one-third of the total settlement. After this, a close friend of Wallach's told a journalist that the ambassador had begun to "speak in despairing terms" about his life.[93]

Several weeks later, stories began circulating among Washington journalists about Wallach's and Meese's possible involvement in an unsuccessful 1985 effort by Wallach to obtain Defense Department support for a $1 billion Iraqi oil pipeline project. Essentially, Meese and Wallach were suspected of not only breaking U.S. racketeering laws (Wallach had allegedly accepted a bribe from an Israeli labor union official in the deal), but also of violating the Foreign Corrupt Practices Act signed into law by President Carter in 1977.[94]

All this happened before the American public had even heard of the famous Wedtech scandal.

• • •

In May of 1987 (as international human rights delegations were about to give Cuban penology a clean bill of health), federal grand jury investigations in Washington and New York City began examining the role played by Meese and Wallach in Wedtech's rise from an unheard-of tool and die company to a multimillion dollar defense contractor. These investigations led to three central discoveries:

First, Wedtech executives pled guilty to plundering the corporate treasury of more than $70 million for their personal gain. Despite federal contracts of more than $250 million awarded to the company over a five-year period (1981–1986), by 1987 Wedtech was bankrupt. Instead of contributing to the public good, these precious resources were consumed in a feeding frenzy of naked greed.[95] With sentencing in sight, the Wedtech executives began cooperating with federal prosecutors and providing names of others who they said were their partners in crime.

Second, and as a result, the Wedtech executives admitted to bribing local, state, and federal authorities in order to keep government contracts coming from the Small Business Administration.

And third, they admitted to hiring E. Robert Wallach solely because of his personal relationship with Edwin Meese III.[96]

Because of these discoveries, during July and August Meese and Wallach were ordered to appear before the Senate Subcommittee on Human Resources, Post Office, and Civil Service to answer questions about their involvement in the Wedtech affair. The subcommittee also identified three major failures of the attorney general.

First, he had not identified the holdings of "Meese Partners" as the law required. That is, Edwin Meese—through his personal attorney, Robert Wallach—did not list the various stock and cash transactions made by Franklyn Chinn in 1985, transactions that were, once again, arranged by Wallach himself.

Second, Meese did not seek advice or approval from the Office of Government Ethics (OGE) before establishing his "limited blind partnership" with Chinn. Therefore, Meese Partners was never approved by the OGE, as required by law.

And third, in his recent financial disclosure (prepared by Wallach) Meese did not report the true name of his largest and greatest source of income. On the advice of Wallach, the attorney general had deliberately withheld information about the 83 percent return on his initial investment with Chinn that had been arranged by Wallach—who by this time was a member of the Wedtech board of directors.[97]

Having violated at least three federal laws, Meese was then castigated by Gerry Sikorski, the House Chairman on Human Resources, Post Office, and Civil Service. "The American people have good reason to be disheartened, perhaps even angered," said the senator. "Mr. Meese is not some middle-level functionary; he holds a very important position in our government and his personal history should make him extraordinarily sensitive to disclosure issues."[98] In accordance with the Ethics in Government Act, Sikorski's committee then appointed Special Prosecutor James C. McKay to investigate Meese's connection to Wedtech and, if necessary, to prosecute him.[99]

As for Wallach, Sikorski's committee suspected that certain criminal charges could be brought against the ambassador. Accordingly, Wallach's case was turned over to a New York grand jury for possible prosecution by U.S. Attorney Rudolph W. Giuliani.[100] Wallach then became the subject of intense media interest. "Who am I in Washington if I'm not Ed Meese's friend?" asked a worried Wallach of a *Washington Post* reporter in July.[101]

A month later, Wallach moved back to San Francisco and attempted to rebuild his tarnished reputation. By this time, the ambassador had been publicly ridiculed for stealing money from two young girls, for conspiring to rob the U.S. government of more than $250 million, for taking a bribe in the Iraqi pipeline project, and for leading a delusive human rights offensive against Cuba. Working out of a cramped office in an aging downtown San

Francisco high-rise, Wallach attributed his hardships to his own naïveté and overloaded ambition.

On September 3, 1987, the ambassador told a *Washington Post* reporter,

> I have found I am such a babe in the woods. Even if they [Wedtech officials] were crooks, they worked endlessly. . . . It is very painful. If it were not for Wedtech, I would be at Meese's side helping him prepare his testimony for the Iran-Contra hearings. I would have been at his house, or having sherry with him at his office.[102]

Reflecting on the series of events that led to his problems, Wallach curiously said to a *Los Angeles Times* reporter, "It [1981 to 1986] was a moment in time, diminished by events."[103] And in an interview with the *California Business Journal,* Wallach said, "I worry that I'll be indicted. It really scares me."[104]

Ethics, Human Rights, and Criminal Justice
Both Meese and Wallach had plenty of reason to be afraid. Although Special Counsel McKay would eventually find that Meese had "probably" violated the law, there was insufficient evidence that Meese had "knowingly participated in criminal activity in connection with his Wedtech actions."[105] In any event, Attorney General Meese was driven out of office in 1988 for his involvement in the Wedtech affair.[106]

History would be more ruthless with E. Robert Wallach. He would eventually be indicted by U.S. Attorney Giuliani on charges of racketeering, mail and wire fraud, and conspiring to defraud the United States. According to Giuliani's eighteen-part indictment, "Wallach, in his capacity as advisor, consultant, and lobbyist for Wedtech, sought to influence Edwin Meese and other government officials on behalf of Wedtech, primarily in connection with the firm's efforts to obtain government contracts."[107]

Wallach was arrested by FBI agents, arraigned in federal court, and tried and convicted under the RICO statutes. He was eventually fined $3.8 million and sentenced to six years in federal prison.[108] In other words, Wallach was found guilty of committing greater crimes than all of the Cubans at Oakdale and Atlanta put together.

In September 1987 President Reagan stripped Robert Wallach of his ambassadorship to the United Nations Human Rights Commission.[109] As a replacement for Wallach, Reagan appointed the diplomatically inexperienced Armando Valladares to lead the U.S. human rights offensive against Cuba.[110]

The Triggering Event

This, then, was the state of federal criminal justice during the fall of 1987. The attorney general was devoting most of his time to the complex tasks of defending and covering up the actions of high-ranking officials of the Reagan administration who had become embroiled in the Iran-Contra scandal. About his involvement in the Iran-Contra affair, in 1992 Meese admitted, "Plenty of errors were made, both in substance and procedure, and their net impact was profoundly harmful to the Reagan government and the country."[111]

Yet the writing had been on the wall for years before this "profoundly harmful" event took place. Between 1981 and 1987, the man who in 1992 spoke with such authority on the subject of "substance and procedure" of public policy had himself been investigated twice by the United States Senate and twice by a special prosecutor for his own potential criminality. He had been accused of everything from owning a pair of illegal cuff links and consorting with the gang of thieves at Wedtech, to helping his personal attorney arrange an illegal foreign pipeline deal, to concealing information from Congress on the sales of military arms to Iran in exchange for hostages. Meese had also been accused of several questionable real estate deals, of selling presidential appointments, and of lying, stealing, and cheating.

Yet in November 1987, Edwin Meese was the executive administrator of a federal agency with seventy-two thousand employees, a yearly budget of $3.6 billion, and statutory responsibilities that included drug enforcement, civil rights, judicial selection, immigration, and the administration of federal prisons.[112] Because of the criminal nature of his own conduct, high-ranking Justice Department officials were fleeing the agency left and right and protesters began showing up on the steps of the Justice Department with signs proclaiming, "Meese Is a Pig."[113] Even young kids who were completely turned off by government were sporting "Meese Is a Pig" T-shirts on their nightly excursions to the street corners, rap concerts, video arcades, and nightclubs of Washington. In effect, Edwin Meese's criminal behavior had become a part of popular culture.

By November 1987, the United States government had been rocked by three setbacks in its attempt to inject moral panic into the arena of international politics regarding the issue of human rights in Cuba. First, there was Wallach's debacle in Geneva. Then came the exoneration of Cuban prisons by international delegations of penologists and human rights specialists. And, finally, there was Ambassador Wallach's arrest on racketeering charges and the subsequent "embarrassment" of the United States in the international discourse on human rights.

Meanwhile, several thousand Mariel Cubans were being "indefinitely detained" at Oakdale and Atlanta, where they had begun to hear about the firing squads and institutionalized torture that were (supposedly) taking place in their homeland. They became deeply frightened of the "horrors" and "sadism" of Fidel Castro's prison system—and of their possible return to those conditions.

The Mexico City Meetings
With Valladares now leading the way, Elliott Abrams and his associates at the State Department waged a two-pronged attack to make up for U.S. setbacks. First, they began gathering additional dossiers on men who said they had been abused in Cuban prisons. These were to be used by Valladares in his offensive against the formidable Raul Roa at the Geneva Human Rights Convention in 1988.[114]

The second plan ignited the Oakdale and Atlanta riots. In order to call worldwide attention to the "obvious" human rights violations occurring in Cuba, in November 1987 the State Department sought to reactivate the 1984 emigration treaty that had been suspended since May 1985, when President Castro had suddenly canceled all diplomatic relations between the two countries because of Ronald Reagan's antagonistic Spanish-language broadcast to twenty-two million people throughout the Caribbean Basin and

Latin America in 1984 ("Prisoners of conscience . . . can expect to be in prison well into the 21st century if the present system in Cuba survives that long").[115]

Reactivation of the 1984 U.S.–Cuban emigration accord would have allowed the United States to open its borders to some twenty thousand Cubans, including three thousand political prisoners. Such a migration from Cuba to the United States would have served two critical foreign policy objectives of the Reagan administration during 1987.

First, it would have offset Wallach's failure in Geneva by demonstrating to the United Nations, once and for all, that Cubans under Castro were "voting with their feet" in support of Ronald Reagan's style of democracy.

Second, by putting U.S.–Cuban relations on a more stable footing, the U.S. human rights offensive against Cuba would not be likely to interfere with the 1988 Reagan-Gorbachev summit. Such a normalization in U.S.–Cuban relations might, in fact, have been used by President Reagan to focus the superpower discussion on more urgent geopolitical issues of the day: Afghanistan, Angola, El Salvador, Nicaragua, Suriname, and perhaps even the real battlefield of international politics—the Middle East, with its vast oil fields, strategic military location, and rampant terrorism.

In exchange for the twenty thousand Cubans who would be permitted to leave the island, the accord called for Cuba to repatriate 2,543 Mariel Cubans who were classified as "excludable entrants" by the INS—beginning with those who were incarcerated at Oakdale and Atlanta.[116]

These low-level discussions blossomed to full diplomatic accord in a secret meeting held between U.S. and Cuban officials in Mexico City on the evening of November 19. The next day in New York City, a gentle snow began blowing in from the Atlantic as Tom Brokaw prepared his notes for the NBC "Nightly News" of November 20, 1987.

Part III

Action Theory for Administrative Reform

A little while later, the door opens and [the prisoner], immune and passive by now, waits for the blows. But instead a flashlight is trained on his bruised face and he is looked at sympathetically by two new recruits, who are appalled at what is happening within their own corps. "Horrible, isn't it?" one young voice asks. "Yes, it's terrible," replies the other. There is recognition here that what is being practiced is unfair, against . . . the whole body of civilized and humane behavior.

—*Kate Millett: The Politics of Cruelty*

Chapter 10
The Oakdale and Atlanta Riots Revisited

The snow that drifted over New York City on the evening of November 20 is an apt metaphorical starting point in puzzling out the Oakdale and Atlanta riots. Prison riots are like snowflakes because no two are ever the same. Each is the result of a unique set of historical, political, and social circumstances. Therefore, not only is a "general theory" of prison rioting of little heuristic value, such a theory is impossible to construct. Each riot has its own theory, and each theory has its own implications for public policy to prevent a similar crisis from occurring in the future.

Useem and Kimball recognized this when they offered four different theoretical explanations to account for the rebellions at Attica (1971), Joliet (1975), Sante Fe (1980), the State Prison of Southern Michigan (1981), and the West Virginia Penitentiary (1986). Each explanation, however, was based on a core of common assumptions that Useem and Kimball referred to as the breakdown/deprivation hypothesis. For Useem and Kimball, "breakdown" referred to:

> Social mechanisms which channel human desires and actions
> into "acceptable" paths. These mechanisms range from religion
> through law to the individual's socialization within the family set-
> ting. Riots, suicide, . . . and other disorderly behavior are signs that
> something has gone haywire with these mechanisms. . . . The only

important pre-existing sociological theory of prison riots, that of
Gresham Sykes, is a classical breakdown theory.[1]

"Deprivation," on the other hand, refers to "the commonsense
position that riots and protests come in response to bad conditions" of incarceration.[2] This concept also was at the core of
Sykes's meditations on the pains of imprisonment, adaptation,
and equilibrium. Putting these two concepts together, then,
Useem and Kimball created their four theoretical hybrids. One of
these they called the *liberal deprivation/breakdown theory,* in which
"the system normally keeps people well fed, employed, fulfilled,
and happy. When the system fails to do so, through greed on the
part of the elite or because of stupid policy choices, . . . the masses
revolt."[3] This Sykesian theory of prison rioting, emphasizing political "greed" and "stupid policy choices," appears supremely suited
to the tasks of both explaining the present case study, and, in the
tradition of Sykes, offering an administrative action plan to prevent its recurrence.

Imposing Order

If riots are analogous to snowflakes, a scholarly theory is like an
iron vise grip. A theory attempts to hold historical, political, and
social events firmly in place, where they can be dissected and analyzed in an effort either to confirm or to refute the theorist's ex-
pectations. This examination must be conducted in an orderly
fashion: Step by step, events are examined and findings are summarized in a coherent evaluation of the theory in question.

Scholars working in the Sykesian tradition of prison rioting,
from Vernon Fox in the early 1970s to Useem and Kimball in the
late 1980s, have distinguished several important stages in the loss
and re-establishment of control by the state. For Useem and Kimball, the first is called the *pre-riot stage*—"the period preceding the
riot during which prisoners and the forces of the state develop
those material and cognitive resources which will determine the
course of the riot event."[4] The end of this stage is the triggering
event.

The second stage is the *initiation,* where "the action by prisoners
. . . first crosses the line into open rebellion" and is followed by

the state's initial response.[5] The third stage is *expansion,* during which "prisoners most often try to take control of as many human, material, and spatial resources as possible against the resistance or non-resistance of the state."[6] The fourth is a *state of siege,* in which "the prisoners control some territory in the institution, the state assembles its forces and concentrates its options for recapture, and bargaining may (but need not) go on among the state, prisoners, and other parties."[7] The last stage is *termination* of the riot and recapture of the institution.

Useem and Kimball conclude that the "full value of the marriage [between breakdown and deprivation] is yet to be explored."[8] To that end, this study concludes with an analysis of the *liberal breakdown/deprivation theory* in terms of Useem and Kimball's five stages of prison rioting.

Pre-Riot: "A Conflict of Interest"—"No One Blinks An Eye"

Simply put, the Oakdale and Atlanta riots would have never occurred were it not for the U.S.–Cuban emigration treaty of November 19, 1987. Because of the state-organized moral panic around the issue, the accord promised to send the detainees back to a Cuban system of punishment where they could expect nothing less than firing squads and institutionalized torture. Not only was this the ultimate breakdown in social authority for the detainees, it also was, obviously, the ultimate deprivation of human rights. In the minds of the detainees, the breakdown/deprivation represented what Albert Camus referred to as *absurdity*—an existence that is totally out of harmony with reason. For Camus, revolt was a natural and altogether logical reaction to this condition.

When we take a close look at the treaty, we see that it was truly a "stupid policy choice." First, the accord called for the United States to open its borders to twenty thousand Cubans, but it made no mention of who those Cubans were or whether there were in fact twenty thousand individuals who wanted to leave the island in 1987 (two years before the collapse of the Soviet Union and the subsequent plummeting of the Cuban economy and standard of living). Second, it called for the United States to accept three thousand political prisoners, but the best estimates were that there were only four hundred to six hundred political prisoners in Cuba at the time. And third, the treaty called for Cuba to repatriate 2,543 Mariel Cubans, beginning with those confined at Oakdale and Atlanta. Once deported, they could expect to be in prison "well into the 21st century," if they survived that long.

Beyond these important problems, the treaty made no distinction between detainees who had been approved for release under the Cuban Review Plan of 1987 (about 70 percent of the Atlanta population), and those who had not. It made no distinction between those with families in the United States and those who had none, or between those considered dangerous and those who were not. Once more, the U.S. government had failed to deal with the detainees as individual human beings. Instead, they were treated as rabble.

The substance and procedure of the emigration accord were not based on the advancement of foreign affairs or the pursuit of public interest. Rather, it was the product of political corruption. Moreover, the treaty reflected the lack of moral vision that characterized government at the height of the Reagan era. Without a clear moral vision, U.S. foreign policy had been drawn backward into a political adolescence that allowed certain bad apples—like the arms smuggler Oliver North and the racketeer E. Robert Wallach—to emerge as important figures in global affairs. The 1987 emigration treaty was an attempt by the United States to make up for three diplomatic setbacks in their human rights offensive against Cuba, setbacks that can be traced to naked greed.

Ethics in Government
The most general provision of the United States Constitution, defining the authority of the president as Chief Executive, is in the clause "he shall take care that the laws be faithfully executed" (Article II, Section 3). The emphasis here is on the enforcement or execution of the law. The attorney general is the president's chief subordinate in this endeavor and the Justice Department exists for the single purpose of managing the resources necessary to carry out the constitutional requirement.

The framers of this article of the Constitution were Thomas Jefferson, Alexander Hamilton, and James Madison.[9] Yet, the framers never contemplated the possibility that a U.S. attorney general could use the powers of that high office for his own personal gain. Obviously, they never foresaw that such abuses of power could, in turn, actually shape the course of foreign and domestic policy.

Jefferson, Hamilton, and Madison were soon warned of such a possibility, however. Shortly after his election as the first president of the United States, George Washington was visited at Mount Vernon by a friend seeking a presidential appointment. In no uncertain terms, Washington told his friend, "You are welcome to my house, you are welcome to my heart. . . . My personal feelings have nothing to do with the present case. . . . As George Washington, I would do anything in my power for you. As President, I can do nothing."[10]

Washington's ethical position was later embedded in U.S. administrative policy by Franklin D. Roosevelt as part of the 1937 President's Committee on Administrative Management. Under Roosevelt's administration, public officials were required by oath to "avoid using power for its own sake."[11] In FDR's vision of government, public service must always be just that: service to the public. It must forever be a selfless task advancing the public good and never a selfish task advancing personal interests. These ideas held sway in the administrative branch for the next three decades. As a consequence, smugglers, racketeers, and other state-organized criminals were not allowed to conduct the affairs of government. Then came Watergate, and the line between personal and public interests became less clear.

In response to the perfidy of those involved in the Watergate scandal, Congress enacted the Ethics in Government Act of 1978. The act created explicit prohibitions against bribery or the making of any decision, especially of a policy nature, that might affect private interests. The Reagan White House was the first administrative unit to be subject to the act. The implementation of these important regulatory requirements was handed over to Edwin Meese III, who crafted the following policy:

> A conflict of interest may exist whenever a government official has a personal interest (financial or otherwise) in a matter which is related to his or her official duties. . . . For purposes of conflicts of

> interest, not only must you consider interests held in your own
> name but also those of your spouse . . . and other members of your
> immediate household. When considering whether an interest cre-
> ates a conflict it is important to avoid even the *appearance* of a con-
> flict as an actual conflict.[12]

Yet, as this study has shown, there was a problem with this mandate. The policy did not call for a strong moral commitment from
administrators to serve the public first and foremost, but simply
required them to avoid appearances of wrongdoing. There is a vast
difference. Meese's deliberate eschewal of his own mandate allowed for unprecedented abuses of power. Unforeseen were their
effects on foreign and domestic policy.

In the present case, the greediest and least intelligent policy
decision was that made by Edwin Meese himself to nominate his
personal attorney, investment counselor, and friend to the prestigious position of ambassador to the United Nations Human Rights
Commission. If Meese had not made the nomination, Robert Wallach would not have gone to Geneva and made a diplomatic fool
of himself. There would have been no "embarrassment all
around" in the U.S. human rights offensive against Cuba. There
would have been no counteroffensive by Fidel Castro, and no subsequent setback over the Wedtech affair. But most important,
there would have been no reason for the United States to initiate
the U.S.–Cuban emigration treaty of November 1987 and, hence,
no riots at Oakdale and Atlanta. In other words, the entire affair
could have been avoided if ethics had truly mattered.

Reflecting on his tenure as the 77th attorney general, Meese
has written that "what all of us were after, then and now, was,
quite simply, respect for the rule of law."[13] Yet within the entire
corpus of journalistic and academic literature on him, there is not
one scintilla of evidence to suggest that Edwin Meese will be
viewed by historians as one who contributed to a "respect for the
rule of law." Quite the opposite: He will no doubt go down in
history as one of the most villainous, corrupt public officials since
New York City's "Boss" Tweed engaged in monumental robberies
from the public treasury in the Civil War era.[14] Unlike Tweed,
however, who was, by all accounts, a highly effective public ad-

ministrator, Edwin Meese is not likely to be remembered as one who advanced intelligent public policies—at least not as far as the Bureau of Prisons and the Immigration and Naturalization Service were concerned.

These are more than the reckonings of a "liberal" penologist struggling to explain the theoretical roots of his own moral indignation. Indeed, there is an abundance of conservative evidence to indicate that Meese's affiliation with Robert Wallach was extremely naïve. There is, in fact, absolutely no evidence—conservative or liberal—to suggest that Meese's involvement with Wallach led to anything but "stupid policy choices."[15]

For example, between his confirmation as attorney general and his resignation following the Wedtech scandal, Meese also was represented in his numerous legal battles by the Justice Department's Office of Legal Counsel (OLC). Douglas Kmiec, director of the OLC between 1985 and 1989 and a strong supporter of Edwin Meese, suggests in his memoir that Meese violated his own conflict-of-interest policy:

> Meese would be constantly harangued and defamed with questions about the "Wedtech scandal." For the Attorney General, the so-called scandal amounted to . . . asking his White House deputy to ensure that Wedtech was getting a fair hearing.[16]

Then, in a blatant refutation of the high ethical standards advanced by George Washington and Franklin Roosevelt, the attorney general's lawyer sophomorically explains that

> Such "constituent referrals" are the constant diet of much of government. Congressmen incessantly contact government agencies about everything from housing projects to why Aunt Mabel didn't receive last month's social security check. No one blinks an eye. . . . That is not to say there was no one making the Attorney General look bad. E. Robert Wallach . . . received substantial monetary and stock benefits from Wedtech. . . . Mother always said, be careful what friends you keep. Mom would not like E. Robert Wallach.[17]

The Rubber Meets the Road, or Implementing a Stupid Policy
By the time the United States and Cuba signed their 1987 emigration treaty, Oakdale and Atlanta were filled to overflowing with

nearly four thousand prisoners who were being indefinitely detained for no other reason than that they were Cubans from the port of Mariel. Whereas most maximum-security prisons exist for the sole purpose of incapacitating violent criminals, Oakdale and Atlanta were warehouses for human rabble: nonviolent criminals from the Cuban penal system, the disadvantaged, petty criminals, and the doubly punished. These were the so-called "dangerous Marielitos" who had emerged onto the landscape of urban America as a result of a state-organized moral panic.

This transformation of the relatively benign Mariel Cuban into the dangerous Marielito did not come without considerable effort. INS officials in the Meese Justice Department first created an ideology that transcended customary law and substituted for it a higher cause and a greater necessity. Thus, the road to Oakdale and Atlanta was laid by extralegal methods—an entire series of special enabling legislation and the creation of special state powers. All this nullified the rule of U.S. criminal law on cruel and unusual punishment. It also usurped the tenets of constitutional democracy and fundamental human rights. The intended result of such an administrative plan should be profound human despair.

Once the moral panic had been completed, the INS was able to incarcerate most of these men in brutal and inhumane conditions, under which they were further denied access to an adversarial system of justice to resolve their plight. For them, captivity was absolute. Camus reasoned that suicide also is a logical reaction to absurdity; and nearly one-third of the Atlanta detainees, in pain, fear, and torment, had tried to kill themselves during the year preceding the riots. For them, life inside the Atlanta Federal Penitentiary was not worth living. Existence had become synonymous with suffering. And no one, from Attorney General Meese's closest advisor down to the cell house guard, ever had raised a voice in formal bureaucratic opposition. This severe breakdown in the institution of law, combined with the deprivation of basic human rights and the absence of fundamental decency in human affairs, had turned Oakdale and Atlanta into living powder kegs waiting to be detonated by an inherently corrupt and stupid foreign policy initiative. It is not surprising, then, that the implementation of this policy also was profoundly stupid.

• • •

At 8:45 A.M. Central Standard Time, November 20, 1987, Oakdale Warden J. R. Johnson received a phone call from the regional director of the Bureau of Prisons informing him that a "repatriation treaty" had been renewed between the U.S. and Cuba. The regional director could not tell Warden Johnson how many of the "Marielitos" in his custody would be deported to the island.[18] Lacking this crucial information, at 12:30 P.M., Johnson and all bilingual staff members circulated to each of the detainee work details and read the following statement:

> The United States and Cuban governments have announced that some Marielitos will be returned to Cuba under a previous agreement. Parole reviews, halfway house and family releases at Oakdale will continue as before [under the terms of "pocket freedom"]. Cubans at Oakdale can help their chances to gain community release through continued positive behavior and respect towards staff and other detainees. We have no details on how many, if any, Cubans at Oakdale will be deported. We will keep you advised as we receive more information [from Washington].[19]

This was followed by a brief period of great confusion among the detainees. Some voiced criticism, many became sullen and quiet, and still others walked off their jobs and gathered in small groups. The next several hours represented an important gestation period for these men who were about to be deported to the alleged "horrors and sadism" of Castro's prison system. Although the depiction of Cuban prisons was inaccurate, it was nevertheless the image that dominated the thinking of the young Oakdale detainees following Warden Johnson's statement, since the vast majority of them had no firsthand experience being locked up in Cuba. Their absorption in the image of Cuban prisons, combined with their own naïveté in the matter, generated extraordinary fear in the minds of the detainees. These powerful emotions were ignited by an intoxicated detainee in the dining room at 6:30, following the NBC "Nightly News."

Had the detainees been given a full explanation of the treaty and an accurate account of what awaited them if they were repatriated, it is quite possible that a riot could have been avoided. The 2,563 Mariels who were affected by the accord had been identified by the INS back in 1984. By November 20, 1987, these 2,563 men were scattered throughout the federal prison system and some were on INS parole to the community. According to INS reports filed after the riots, only ninety-five of the nearly four thousand Cubans of Oakdale and Atlanta (fewer than 5 percent) were actually affected by the repatriation accord.[20]

If the BOP had isolated these ninety-five individuals on November 20, then administrators and staff members could have explained to the remaining majority of detainees that the treaty did not even apply to them, hence, they had nothing to worry about. Had this simple, commonsense management strategy been used, the riots might have been averted altogether. But it was not used because the INS was unable, or unwilling, to share this elementary information with administrative officials of the BOP. This happened despite the facts that (1) the agency had known the names of those Mariels who were on the repatriation list for nearly three years, and (2) it had the computerized management information systems necessary for tracking them. Useem and Kimball argue that small details usually contribute to the onset of prison rioting. At Sante Fe, for example, prison officials had failed to install unbreakable glass around the institution's main control center, and the glass windows surrounding the control center were easily smashed by rioting prisoners with clubs and hammers, allowing them to recapture the area. In the same way, the INS's inability to immediately produce a list of names of those detainees who were "eligible" for repatriation must be considered a major precipitating cause of the Oakdale and Atlanta riots. Whatever their reason for withholding the information, either because of sheer incompetence or because of something more ominous, the INS's decision to do so represents yet another remarkably unintelligent policy choice.

Closer to the Road

Beyond such critical management information problems, a more fundamental set of mistakes contributed to the onset of rebellion. The activities of administrators and staff members at Oakdale and

Atlanta between November 20 and 23 clearly indicate that they did not comprehend the treaty's magnitude in the minds of the detainees. There are at least five examples of this.

First, as the dining room incident was unfolding on the evening of November 20, only five hours after the treaty was announced, most of the Oakdale administrators were either on their way to, or already at, a retirement banquet for two prison employees. Warden Johnson learned of the incident on his car radio en route to the party.[21] Obviously, the Oakdale administrators had failed to recognize any significant sign of unrest or discord among the detainees during the afternoon.

Second, despite the seriousness of the dining room incident, Johnson did not report it to the regional and central offices of the BOP.[22] In other words, the Oakdale administrators dismissed the incident as nothing more than an isolated act of violence committed by a drunken detainee, an incident that they (incredibly) saw as being unrelated to the repatriation accord.

Third, staff members at Oakdale and Atlanta overlooked several obvious signals of the violence to come. And, in so doing, they also contributed to the precipitation of rebellion. On Monday, November 23, guards working in the mail room at Atlanta witnessed an unusually high volume of mail being sent by the detainees. Ordinarily, one bag of mail left the prison each Monday morning, but on this day three bags were being sent from the institution. Most of the mail was packaged and consisted of photographs and other small memorabilia.[23] Given the sentimental value that the detainees placed on these items—and the BOP's history of destroying them in times of conflict—this event should have alarmed the mail room guards enough to report the incident to their superiors. They did not.

Fourth, the fact that detainees at both Oakdale and Atlanta began wearing multiple layers of clothing—and, in Atlanta, tennis shoes—before the riots started, combined with the fact that guards did not return the detainees to their living areas to dress in required prison clothing, is paramount to understanding the precipitating causes of the riots.

Fifth, during the mornings of November 20 (at Oakdale) and November 23 (at Atlanta), BOP officials failed to act on repeated

warnings from inmate informants that a disturbance was immi-
nent. If administrators had taken these warnings seriously, and if
they had understood the full ramifications of the repatriation
treaty, they could have offered the detainees an alternative to their
daily routine. Instead of forcing detainees to brood on the treaty
in isolation—as they stood before their noisy industrial machines
in UNICOR or dug up weeds around the Oakdale perimeter—work
details could have been canceled and replaced with more relaxing
and comforting activities. The detainees might have been allowed,
for example, to return to their cell houses and housing units, or
they could have been allowed to go to the chapel to pray with a
Catholic priest. They might have been allowed to go to the recreation areas to physically work off their stress. They could have
been given access to telephones to call family and friends. Or they
could have been offered the opportunity to simply walk freely
around the prison compound and discuss the treaty with other
inmates and with staff members. At the very least, any of these
activities might have reduced anxieties. At the most, they might
have headed off the coming violence.

After Oakdale and Atlanta had fallen to the Cubans, Director
Quinlan told *Newsweek,* "We instructed the staff to be on the look-
out for signs that there might be problems. They reported none.
. . . We thought we were on top of it."[24] Unfortunately, Meese's
Justice Department was far from being "on top of it." The inability
of the INS to provide timely information on the ill-conceived
treaty and the BOP's insensitivity regarding the implications of
the accord, were the most influential correctional-level precipitating causes of the riots. In a word, the riots can be traced, once
again, to stupidity.

Initiation and Expansion: "Nourishing Greatness"

"The biggest problem facing inmates desiring to start a riot,"
argue Useem and Kimball, "is to get fellow inmates to act in con-
cert."[25] The detainees found two solutions to this problem, and
they came in two distinct phases. Both solutions were derived
from features of the inmate subculture, established before the
riots, that carried over into the initiation and expansion stages.

Phase I: The Euphoria of Revolt

First and foremost, the coordinated effort to seize control of Oakdale and Atlanta was political. The initiators of the riots were motivated by a specific grievance: They were ready to die in U.S. prisons rather than be deported back to Cuba. Thus, the disturbances were rebellions against the breakdown of law and the expected deprivation of human rights that awaited them in Cuba. In the spirit of *el exilio*, the riots were, in fact, a final, desperate attempt to capture the attention of President Ronald Reagan.

But the riots represented an altogether original form of political activism. With the riots came an end to the long, passionate letters to Reagan. Gone, too, were the bitter and painful hunger strikes in his honor. There was no more endless patience waiting for the president to respond to their terrible plight. And, significantly, there were no more suicides. "Revolt," Camus wrote, "proudly rejects suicide and keeps faith with the reality of human senses."[26] Now the Mariels spoke to their beloved president through the language of collective violence.

Through their violence, the detainees experienced the sort of euphoria alluded to time and again with such stunning clarity by Camus. And with the euphoria came the emotional impetus to coordinate and expand the riots. Through revolt, Camus said, "The body, compassion, the created world, action, human nobility will then resume their place in this insane world. . . . Revolt . . . nourish[es] his greatness."[27]

The euphoria of revolt was manifest in the cry of *Somos los Abandanados* as 250 Oakdale detainees stormed the front gate in an attempt to break out and regain their freedom. According to Useem and Kimball, such an event is unprecedented in the American twentieth century. Euphoria also was displayed in the detainees' brave attempts to return the searing tear gas canisters. It showed in the immediate burning of the institution, an act that destroyed more than $6 million worth of federal resources in less than two hours. And it was clear in their excited parading of a guard around the burning compound in a laundry cart, as detainees laughed and banged on the cart with clubs. To understand this euphoria is to understand the essence of *el exilio*.

In Atlanta, the euphoria manifested itself in the fires started in the UNICOR shop, which were meant to burn the huge building to the ground—and they did just that. It also was manifest in the massive show of force that followed, eight hundred Cuban prisoners appeared on the yard armed with everything from machetes to chains and blowtorches. After years of poor food, overcrowding, open toilets, rampant brutality, idleness, and monotony, these men had, for the moment, escaped the absurdity of their lives to reclaim their "human nobility."

Desperate times called for desperate actions. If President Reagan would not pay attention to patience, impassioned letters, hunger strikes, and suicide attempts, then maybe he would notice mass violence. Through his corrupt attorney general, the president would, indeed, soon come to pay very close attention.

Phase II: The Momentum
The second solution to the coordination problem came with the detainees' swift, safe, and successful capture of hostages. According to the BOP, this activity was carried out with "military precision."[28] More accurately, it was carried out with the precision of guerrilla warfare.

At Oakdale, four separate groups of detainees methodically crisscrossed the compound, setting fire to fourteen buildings, arming themselves with tools, makeshift weapons, and gasoline, forcing the SORT squad to exhaust its tear gas supply, and capturing twenty-eight hostages. Oakdale fell to the Cubans in a brief forty-five minutes—and the detainees injured no one in the process. At Atlanta, 1,300 prisoners split into three groups methodically setting fire to the massive UNICOR building, arming themselves with makeshift weapons for the battle to come, and capturing 105 hostages. They gained control of the institution in less than ninety minutes and, again, they injured no one. According to Useem and Kimball, the expansion stage of a riot is marked by prisoners' attempts "to subject as much of what was under the administration's power to their own, as quickly as possible."[29] By this definition, Oakdale and Atlanta were seized with remarkable alacrity and human compassion.

Concomitantly, the detainees also demonstrated a willingness to commit violence that caused the prison security forces of Oakdale and Atlanta to retreat from the central compounds of both institutions. This accomplishment strengthened the internal structure of the initiator culture and provided the momentum necessary to advance to the next stage of rioting.

State Response: The Politics of Restraint

While the breakdown/deprivation theory explains why the detainees initiated and expanded their riots, in the case of Oakdale and Atlanta the theory fails to predict the state's response. That is, there was nothing greedy or stupid about the way prison administrators handled the riots once they had begun. Instead, they exercised great restraint, courage, and compassion for both the detainees and their hostages. Thankfully for the detainees and the hostages, at this point there were no state-organized criminals around to foul things up.

At Atlanta, when prison security forces saw they were outnumbered, they immediately retreated from the compound. At this point, more than a thousand prisoners were loose in the yard, capturing hostages, handcuffing them, and leading them toward the chapel. Amid this pandemonium, tower guards shot and killed one detainee and wounded five others. Then, because of the threat of violence by detainees, the guards stopped firing and no further assaults were made on the initiators. Given what could have happened, the BOP's reaction to the initiation of the Atlanta riot was remarkably restrained. As far as the detainees and their hostages were concerned, the public interest was well served in the ninety minutes it took for the Mariel Cubans to take control of the Atlanta Federal Penitentiary on the morning of November 23.

The same restraint was shown at Oakdale during the initiation and expansion stages and no one was shot, killed, or injured by the state. It was especially obvious in the courageous actions of the yard captain who walked incognito into the midst of the riot to rescue staff members locked in the Food Service Building. And afterward, he handed over a set of keys to a group of initiators so they could save the lives of several fellow detainees trapped in the burning hospital.

Thus, in instructive contrast to the breakdown/deprivation

theory, which explains rioting in terms of administrative greed and stupidity, the state's response to the initiation and expansion of the Oakdale and Atlanta rebellions stands as an example of selfless and intelligent public policy.

State of Siege: "Mr. Reagan, You Will Kill Us"

American prison riots have always occurred far from the scrutiny of the media and the public. It is only after the conflict is over that we begin to learn about the true causes of rebellion. But shortly after the Cuban detainees captured Oakdale, the institution was surrounded by reporters from around the nation. Now, there was a new set of rules to be followed in prisoner protests, and they were established by the men who held control of the Oakdale prison: the detainees themselves.

Enlivened by the euphoria of revolt and the extraordinary momentum it created, the first official act of the detainee "administration" at Oakdale was to clearly express its collective belief in *el exilio*. Early Sunday morning, November 22, three Mariel Cubans climbed to the rooftop of one of the housing units. Armed with wooden clubs, they were dressed like guerrilla fighters, in headbands, baseball caps worn backward, boots, rain jackets, and olive-drab jumpsuits. They positioned themselves before the media's cameras, and one of them yelled, "Here is our statement."

They sat down on the roof and hung their legs over the edge. With the brilliant Louisiana sunrise shining in their faces, they unfurled a white bed sheet with these words printed in bright red:

MR. REAGAN IF <u>YOU</u> DENY OUR FREEDOM YOU KILL US![30]

Notice that the first "you" is emphasized: If *you*, Ronald Reagan yourself, turn your back on us this time, you will kill us! That is the down-to-the-bone expression of *el exilio*. And given Ronald Reagan's ambivalence toward human rabble and his loathing of all things Cuban, the state of mind behind the message was, indeed, phantasmagoric.

· · ·

The sieges at Oakdale and Atlanta lasted for nearly two weeks and were characterized by the same inmate norms and codes of conduct that were established before the riots. Yet, while initiation and expansion sprang from euphoria and momentum, the state of siege was marked by intense psychological blackmail, a complex organization, and a deep mistrust of government.

The detainees employed three interrelated strategies to maintain control over their institutions. The first was elaborate theatrics used to drive home the point that their grievance must be taken seriously. These included the construction of the frightening execution chair, the makeshift acetylene-tank-bomb, and numerous threats to slit the throats of hostages with machetes. The second was the high level of organization that developed among the detainees, including the establishment of their own police force and system of justice. And the third was their spirituality, carried over from their longstanding devotion to the heavenly *orishas*. Together, these strategies led to prevention of defection, humane treatment of hostages, civility in the detainee ranks, orderly provision of food and medicines, playfulness, and continued communication both with each other and with the outside world.

For its part, the state continued its strategy of restraint as the immense federal show of force waited "with endless patience" for the negotiations to work toward a peaceful settlement.

Once again, the breakdown/deprivation theory explains why the detainees were able to maintain a state of siege, but in the case of Oakdale and Atlanta it does not predict the state's response, at least not as far as the BOP was concerned. The problem—the reason the siege continued for so long—relates not to the BOP's performance immediately beyond the walls of the occupied institutions. Instead—and this is highly consistent with the breakdown/deprivation thesis—the problem can be traced to the pre-riot stage: namely, to government policies.

The Politics of Mistrust
It was shortly after 9:30 P.M., Sunday, November 22, that the Oakdale detainees were given their photocopies of Attorney General Meese's letter offering them an "indefinite moratorium" on repatriations and a "full, fair, and equitable review" of each case by the INS, in exchange for their hostages. They would not accept this arrangement until shortly after 2:00 P.M., November 29—

seven days later. The Atlanta detainees received their copy of Meese's letter at approximately 1:00 P.M., Monday, November 23. They would not accept the deal until shortly after midnight, December 4—eleven days later. The terms of the deal did not change during this time. This prolonged state of siege, the longest in the history of American prisons, was the result of the detainees' lack of confidence in the federal government, brought about by years of incredible bungling and outright chicanery on the part of INS and its head, Edwin Meese III.

The detainees had three specific problems with the attorney general and his proposal. First, they did not trust the ability of the INS to be "full, fair, and equitable" about anything. Second, they did not trust Meese's promise to suspend the deportations. And third, Meese repeatedly denied their request to speak with someone they *did* trust.

The Politics of Cruelty

Beginning in 1981, the INS had implemented a number of court-ordered programs to make detainees' sentences commensurate with the seriousness of their parole violations. These reforms were intended to bring logic and structure to the arrest and detention of Mariel Cubans. But for those detainees who occupied the housing units and cell houses of Oakdale and Atlanta during the state of siege, the reforms had amounted to little more than pocket freedom. A major finding by the BOP in its *After-Action Report* on the riots was that the INS's release programs consisted of

> promises about what was necessary to be released, about when they would be released, and about where they would be released. According to [Oakdale and Atlanta] staff, many detainees had attempted to work within the framework of a release program only to see that program end and a new one, with new rules and regulations, initiated.[31]

The detainees made the same point, only more forcefully. The *After-Action Report* goes on to say that

> it was evident that many detainees held deep-seated negative feelings regarding INS. Several [BOP] staff stated that injuries may

have occurred to INS staff if staff had been taken hostage during the riot. Many detainees appeared to believe that they had been unfairly treated, that INS had made them many promises which had not been kept. . . . Detainees repeatedly told hostages that Immigration and Naturalization Services, not the Bureau of Prisons, was the target of their anger and frustration.[32]

When examined in terms of the breakdown/deprivation theory, the detainees' reluctance to accept the moratorium on deportations and the promise of a "full, fair, and equitable review" cannot be blamed on forces within the correctional establishment. Instead, the blame must be laid squarely at the door of the Immigration and Naturalization Service—a door that was owned by business associates of the attorney general.

To argue for such practices is to support a political culture that sends forth professionalized public administrators who have been nourished by institutionalized xenophobia, privilege and perquisite, indoctrination, and specialized training in what Kate Millett so eloquently describes as the "politics of cruelty." According to Millett, state permission is a necessary prerequisite to the practice of cruelty. Without permission, she argues, cruelty

is criminal and to be punished, a merely individual act, without meaning, self-indulgent, aberrant, and forbidden. But with permission it is patriotism, service, laudable activity, salaried, professionalized. Practiced upon "one's own" it would be insanity, treason, inhumanity. Everything depends upon permission. Which is the state.[33]

For the lone Mariel Cuban, already struggling with the formidable problem of assimilating into American society, a politics of cruelty had been incorporated thoroughly into INS policies and procedures. Through special legislation and special state powers, the INS had created a situation in which an innocent act could easily be interpreted as a crime for which the alleged perpetrator had no trial, no legal defender, and no recourse to bail. For him, there was no presumption of innocence. Arrest was tantamount to conviction, sentences were outlandish and absolute, and they had to be served under conditions that might kill him. And in an important way, these conditions resembled the racially tense situation at Attica: In both instances, the great majority of guards were white and the prisoners were black. Not only were the Mariels detained in brutal and inhumane conditions, but their captors knew little of the thought, speech, rituals, and aesthetics of contemporary Cuban culture.

To argue against these policies is to first recognize their inherent racism and utter stupidity. To truly fight them requires organized opposition from within the bureaucracy, or what is commonly referred to as "whistle-blowing." When properly grounded, whistle-blowing in government affairs is a reformist activity consistent with bureaucratic rationality, because organizational oppositions naturally presuppose a normative transformation of the social structure.[34] Someone inside the Justice Department could have blown the whistle on INS policies and practices on the grounds that they were not effective and efficient, or because such policies and practices were immoral and violated fundamental human rights. If they had done so the Oakdale and Atlanta riots might have been avoided. But no one did, despite the fact that the problems associated with indefinite detention were repeatedly raised by congressmen, immigration attorneys, civil rights groups, religious organizations, and journalists. It is little wonder that the Cubans of Oakdale and Atlanta demonstrated "anger and frustration" against the INS because of its legacy of broken promises. It is also little wonder that they refused for nearly two weeks to accept Attorney General Meese's proposal of a "full, fair, and equitable review" of each detainee case regarding their repatriation to Cuba.

Disdain for the Law
Armed with 20/20 hindsight, it is probably safe to conclude that there was no criminal justice administrator in the United States more ill-suited to the task of ending the historic state of siege at Oakdale and Atlanta than Edwin Meese III. From the days of his controversial nomination and confirmation hearings for the post of attorney general, Meese had been routinely disparaged and vilified by many for his misconduct. Starting with the questionable presidential appointments through Wedtech and the bungled

Iraqi pipeline project, Meese had been described as everything from a "pig" and an "ethical pygmy" to "a major infirmity" to good government. The dissection of Meese's character reached its pinnacle on November 17, 1987, with the release of the 690-page Iran-Contra report. This judgment on the infamous arms-for-hostages deal with Iran, widely covered by the media, concluded that Meese had displayed a blatant "disdain for the law" that had become characteristic of the Reagan administration.[35]

Five days later, this same man—one of the most highly-placed individuals of the American 1980s—sent a photocopy of a letter to the Oakdale detainees who were at the time holding machetes to the throats of prison guards and threatening to burn others alive with gasoline. Twelve hours later, he sent a copy of the same letter to the Cubans holding the prison at Atlanta.

It does not take a penologist to understand why the Mariels refused his offer. "We didn't trust Meese," said a leader of the Oakdale riot. "He's a liar." As for the Atlanta detainees, Gary Leshaw remembers that the chief government negotiator was seen as "just incompetent, on the take."[36] "Frankly," said the FBI negotiator Diader Rosario shortly after the siege had ended, "I don't think they [the detainees] were even psychologically or emotionally ready to accept Meese's promised moratorium on deportations."[37] And it doesn't take a sociological theory to explain that the U.S. government's decision to designate this man as its leader in the effort to bring an end to the historic prison riots was extremely stupid.

Third Party Exclusion
This stupidity would eventually be mitigated by the sensibility of a third party: Bishop Agustin Roman. Yet this would not happen until Edwin Meese was gracefully removed from the negotiation process by Michael Quinlan and the Congress. The termination of the state of siege ultimately turned on six crucial events.

First, on November 17, four days before detainees stormed the front gate at Oakdale, Bishop Roman concluded his chairmanship of a Catholic conference in Washington, D.C., on the plight of imprisoned Mariel Cubans. The conference produced a list of more than seven hundred Mariels who had long before completed their sentences for criminal activity but who remained in custody at Oakdale and Atlanta awaiting release to the community, under the terms of the Cuban Review Plan of 1987. The conference delegates appended their list of names to a letter addressed to Attorney General Meese, pleading with him to stop the INS's practice of indefinite detention. Roman's document was delivered by courier and crossed the attorney general's desk at about the same time that Meese received Senator John Tower's Iran-Contra report, which charged the attorney general with "disdain for the law."[38]

Second, on Monday morning, November 23, Oakdale detainees requested a meeting with Bishop Roman to discuss the possibility of laying down their weapons and surrendering their hostages. Sensing a possible breakthrough, Quinlan dispatched a government plane to Miami to fly Roman to Oakdale. Had Bishop Roman made the flight, the Oakdale riot could have ended by noon and perhaps the Atlanta riot could have been avoided altogether. But it is fruitless to second-guess history. As the pilot was preparing for takeoff, he received a last-minute message from Quinlan to cancel the flight, leaving Bishop Roman grounded on a Miami runway.[39] There was only one person who had the authority to override Quinlan's decision to bring Roman into the Oakdale negotiations: the same man whose ethical misconduct had triggered the riots in the first place, Edwin Meese III.

Third, on the morning of November 26, the fifth day of the Oakdale siege and the third day of the siege in Atlanta, Meese invited Bishop Roman to Washington to discuss his possible role in bringing an end to the crisis. In the sanctity of the attorney general's office, Roman expressed again his willingness to help, but Meese refused the bishop's assistance. According to the BOP's *After-Action Report*, Meese was reluctant to allow Bishop Roman to participate in the negotiations because he was "an outspoken critic of INS's policy of indefinite detention."[40]

Fourth, after two more days, when no other resolution to the crisis was forthcoming (or when the attorney general realized that his letters were not having the desired effect), Meese allowed Quinlan to fly Roman to Oakdale. Within an hour of his arrival, the siege was over.

Fifth, several hours later, Roman offered to work the same magic at Atlanta. But the headstrong attorney general directed Quinlan to reject the bishop's offer. As a result, the Atlanta siege continued for another week.

Sixth, and finally, on the morning of December 2, Quinlan (unaccompanied by Meese) was asked to brief a joint committee of Congress on the Atlanta siege. That afternoon, Bishop Roman's audiotape was played on the prison loudspeaker system. The next day, the Atlanta detainees voted to lay down their weapons and surrender.

Had Bishop Roman been allowed immediate access to the detainees, the riots could have ended as quickly as they had begun. To the extent that ending prison riots serves the public good, Roman's involvement must be viewed as an intelligent decision. By the same token, the numerous restrictions actually placed on the bishop's involvement, created solely by the United States attorney general, must be considered nothing less than profoundly counterproductive.

Termination and Aftermath: "Everything Happened, Nothing Happened"

The lessons of history prompted Useem and Kimball to conclude that "the chances for successful resolution [of a prison riot] depend on the skill and organization of the state."[41] The lessons of Oakdale and Atlanta suggest that a third criterion be added to successful resolutions: credibility. The negotiations at Oakdale and Atlanta were not about inmate proposals and administrative counterproposals. Instead, they were about wild greed and deep stupidity. That is, the termination stage of the riots can best be described as an exercise in overcoming the politics of cruelty and mistrust.

If there is an overriding lesson to be learned from the termination of the Oakdale and Atlanta riots, it is that prison officials and guards—those who actually know the prisoners who have captured control from the state—are better prepared to negotiate settlements than bureaucratic officials who are unknown to the prisoners. It is difficult for rioting prisoners, especially those in their twenties, to trust someone they do not know. It is even more difficult to trust someone whose name is routinely associated with scandal and corruption. And it is harder still to trust such a person when he has never himself worked in a maximum-security prison. That is how the detainees of Oakdale and Atlanta perceived Attorney General Meese: as an unreliable outsider who was completely detached from the brutal realities of prison life.

Such a lesson implies that if Meese had turned over the entire negotiation process to director Quinlan and the BOP officials who ran Oakdale and Atlanta, Bishop Roman could have been brought in to negotiate a settlement in a matter of hours. As it turned out, the combined efforts of Bishop Roman (through his peacemaking), the BOP (through its doctrine of restraint and "endless patience"), and the detainees (through their psychological blackmail, sophisticated organization, and spirituality) served to bring about a safe and successful resolution to the ordeal.

In the end, all hostages were released unharmed. The detainees were not repatriated to Cuba. The detainees received their "full, fair, and equitable review"—and eventually the INS streamlined its process of granting community release. In fact, during the seven months following the uprisings, nearly two-thirds of the detainees then in prison were approved for release by the INS.[42] In effect, with their signing of the final agreement ending the state of siege, the detainees were guaranteed more rights in the United States than at any other time since their arrival on the 1980 boatlift. They were relieved of all financial responsibility for damages resulting from the riots and neither the Atlanta Federal Penitentiary nor the Oakdale Detention Center any longer houses Cuban refugees from the port of Mariel. Public awareness of the plight of Mariel Cubans has been raised. And, in a separate move, public opinion eventually drove the unscrupulous attorney general from office. In short, the Oakdale and Atlanta riots could be considered a monumental success.

On the other hand, little has really changed. "For all that has happened," writes Gary Leshaw, "nothing has happened."[43] The policy of indefinite detention still remains. While the INS's processing of Mariel Cubans may have improved, due process has not. Today, some 1,800 Mariels still are being indefinitely detained in

American prisons and jails. As some are released, others take their places. They are confined in such end-of-the-line federal maximum security prisons as Leavenworth, Lompoc, Marion, and Terre Haute, where they are routinely segregated from the general population and are treated with special precautions because they are thought to be extremely dangerous. Confined to their cells for twenty-three hours every day, they are given no access to further education; hence, most of them cannot speak or read English. Without access to vocational education, they have few skills that would help them assimilate into American society.

Institutional abuses also continue. At Leavenworth, detainees recently have been forced to wear signs around their necks reading "Oakdale Leader." Other Mariel prisoners have been fed spoiled and rotted food since the riots. Guards at the Terre Haute Penitentiary recently removed and destroyed hundreds of personal items belonging to Mariels in yet another attempt to break their will. And in March 1992, Cuban detainees waged a two-day riot behind the walls of the Talledega Federal Prison. Once again, it seems, the detainees have begun to contemplate the absurdity of their existence.

Meanwhile, the sociopolitical factors that led to the Freedom Flotilla in the first place have reached another critical point. Compounding these problems, in 1992, former Arkansas Governor Bill Clinton—who had played a major role in the Fort Chaffee incident of 1980—was elected president of the United States on (among others) the promise that "It's time to bring the hammer down on Fidel Castro!"[44]

Conclusions and Recommendations: "Getting Back to Normal"

By adopting a hard line against Castro, President Clinton has violated an essential principle of U.S.–Cuban relations as it was envisioned by his boyhood hero, John F. Kennedy. The historical record reveals that in the fall of 1963, President Kennedy told UN Ambassador William Atwood that he was in favor of "pushing toward an opening toward Cuba. To take Castro out of the Soviet fold and perhaps wiping out the Bay of Pigs and maybe getting back to normal."[45]"Getting back to normal" implies that Kennedy was ready to engage in diplomatic rapprochement with Castro, which meant discontinuing not only the military offensive against Cuba, but also curtailing economic sanctions as well.[46] But with Kennedy's assassination came an abrupt end to the possibility of lifting sanctions; and they remain in place to this day.

Current U.S. policy toward Cuba, then, is frozen in Cold War logic. It features an aggressive economic embargo intended to isolate Cuba, to severely damage that nation's economy, and to make it more difficult for Cuba to support international adventurism on behalf of communism. It also fosters inflammatory rhetoric against the Castro regime, broadcast over the State Department–sponsored television station, Marti (the multimillion dollar successor to Radio Marti), which began operations in 1990. In addition, the Clinton White House has supported even stiffer trade sanctions through the so-called Cuban Democratic Act, which bans trade with Cuba by foreign subsidiaries of U.S. corporations.

Billions of dollars and an extraordinary investment of human capital have been spent to enforce this policy. Yet, by both scholarly and international political consensus, the government's policy not only has failed to accomplish its intended goal, but it is also regarded as extremely inhumane. U.S. policy toward Cuba has been roundly condemned in Latin America and the United Nations for its ruthless oppression of ordinary Cubans.[47] It has also failed to break the back of Castro's government. Far from it. Cuban scholars James Blight, Aaron Belkin, and David Lewis cogently describe this policy failure:

> If the construction of US foreign policy were a science, the Washington hypotheses concerning its Cuba policy would long ago have been refuted. The policy of squeezing Cuba via an economic embargo . . . has failed for almost three decades. Fidel Castro came to power when Dwight Eisenhower was president. Castro is still in power. Politics is not a science, yet it is still difficult to escape the impression that the US government, urged on at every turn by radical elements in the Cuban exile community in the United States, has figuratively been banging its head against a brick wall, getting nowhere, but banging away all the same.[48]

Failed public policies usually lead to human suffering, and the U.S. policy toward Cuba is no exception. Since the collapse of the Soviet Union, Cuba has struggled without its $5 billion annual subsidy—roughly one-fourth of Cuba's GNP.[49] By 1994, Cuba's economy had crumbled and much of the nation's standard of living had reverted to Third World levels. Shortages of food, medicine, and clothing are now a common feature of Cuban life. Dozens of factories have closed because there is no fuel to run machines and no raw materials to process. Sugar and tobacco crops wither and die because there are no fertilizers, no pesticides, and no electricity to pump water for irrigation. There is no fuel to run trucks, so those crops that do survive rot for want of distribution. People travel by bicycle and by horse and buggy. Residents of Havana are forced to live with daily twelve-hour electrical blackouts. There is no soap, no toilet paper, and no paper for writing and drawing.[50] Instead of breaking the back of Castro's Cuba, the effect of U.S. policy has been to make life more wretched for ordinary Cuban men, women, and children—giving them, once again, economic reasons to flee the island.

By the time this book is in print, there very well may have been a replay of the Mariel boatlift. Between January and August 1994, 5,163 Cubans arrived on Florida's coast on boats or rafts—the largest number in a similar period since the Freedom Flotilla of 1980.[51] The U.S. government's initial reaction to this exodus has been to echo the "open arms and open hearts" rhetoric of the Carter years. On August 9, 1994, Pentagon spokesman David Thomas told reporters, "We recognize that people fleeing Castro's tyranny need our help and compassion."[52]

Four days later, thirty-two Cubans drowned in the Atlantic after their dilapidated tugboat was rammed by a Cuban patrol vessel trying to stop their fleeing to Florida. This was followed by the hijacking of three passenger ferries, one from the port of Mariel, by another two hundred Cubans attempting to escape to Florida. At the same time, an unprecedented riot broke out in the streets of Havana, with demonstrators shouting, "Down with Fidel!" Police quelled the uprisings by firing their weapons in the air.[53] Castro has reacted to these developments much the same way he had in 1980. On August 8, 1994, he declared that he would stop putting "obstacles in the way of people who want to leave the country."[54]

Fearing a replay of the Mariel boatlift, both the Clinton administration and the U.S. media have resurrected the language and logic of moral panic. Consider, for example, this recent report filed by the *Los Angeles Times:*

> The Clinton administration is prepared to mount a virtual blockade of the 90-mile-wide strait between Florida and Cuba if Cuban President Fidel Castro launches a repeat of the 1980 Mariel boatlift, *in which he sent thousands of Cuban criminals* to U.S. shores [emphasis added].[55]

Similarly, the editors of the *New York Times* have recently stated that "Mr. Castro encouraged an exodus from Mariel harbor [in 1980] that dumped 125,000 Cuban refugees, including murderers and rapists, on Florida."[56]

The evidence presented in this book portrays a very different picture. Fidel Castro did not send "thousands" of criminals to the United States in 1980; he sent, at most, fewer than four hundred. Those men were not murderers and rapists. They were, rather, a group of ordinary thieves, who happened to be physically fit and profusely illustrated with tattoos. That was the extent of their criminality.

The evidence also shows that the Mariel boatlift created a judicial, administrative, and penological nightmare for thousands of emigrants and their captors, a nightmare that may well have set back by a decade hopes for improved relations between Havana and Washington. Since then, communism has imploded, the Cold War has ended, the former Soviet Union has significantly reduced economic and military assistance to Cuba, and there are no more socialist fronts in Africa or Latin America for Cuba to support. There are no Russian troops in Cuba and there are no Cuban troops in foreign countries. The Cuban armed forces are being reduced in size and they possess no potential for nuclear armament. Fidel Castro is no longer a threat to U.S. security. Is it not time, then, to finally pick up the mantle of John F. Kennedy and normalize official policy on Cuba?

The preponderance of academic literature on the subject shows that the most effective, efficient, and humane way for the United States to avert future Mariel boatlifts would be to change U.S. policy from zero-sum to positive-sum logic—meaning that both countries gain or that there is a recognized interdependence between nations rather than institutionalized strategic defensiveness. Such a U.S. policy would:

(1) Lift economic sanctions against Cuba,
(2) Lift restrictions on American travel to the island,
(3) Permit more Cubans to immigrate legally, and,
(4) Normalize political relations with the Cuban government.

The goal of this policy is simple. It promises to create social conditions inside Cuba that will help Cubans stay at home and avoid a new generation of Abandoned Ones.

Notes

Chapter 1

1. The events described in this chapter and the next are based on the following sources: U.S. Department of Justice, Federal Bureau of Prisons, *A Report to the Attorney General on the Disturbance at the Federal Detention Center, Oakdale, Louisiana and the U.S. Penitentiary, Atlanta, Georgia* (U.S. Department of Justice, BOP, February 1, 1988, hereafter referred to as *After-Action Report*); "A Cuban Explosion," *Newsweek* (December 7, 1987), 38–40; Katie Wood and Brenda L. Mooney, "What Really Happened at the Atlanta Pen," *Fulton County Daily Report* (December 14, 1987), 2–12; various reports from the *Miami Herald*, the *New York Times*, and the *Atlanta Constitution* that appear in *The Commission Pro-Justice Mariel Prisoners: The Mariel Injustice* (Coral Gables, Fla.: The Commission Pro-Justice Mariel Prisoners, 1987); and an interview with Gary Leshaw, attorney for the Cubans, conducted on March 22, 1994. Quotations from prisoners are based on interviews conducted at the U.S. Penitentiary, Terre Haute, in 1988 and 1989.

Chapter 3

1. All quotations from BOP employees are based on interviews conducted at the U.S. Penitentiary at Terre Haute, or at my office in the Criminology Department at Indiana State University.

2. See Mark S. Hamm, "Santeria in Federal Prisons: Understanding a Little Known Religion," *Federal Prisons Journal* 2 (1992), 37–42.

3. Tom Wicker, *A Time to Die* (New York: Quadrangle/New York Times Books, 1975).

4. Sue Mahan, "An 'Orgy of Brutality' at Attica and the 'Killing Ground' at Santa Fe: A Comparison of Prison Riots." In Michael Braswell, Steven Dillingham, and Reid Montgomery, Jr., eds., *Prison Violence in America* (Cincinnati: Anderson, 1985), 73–88.

5. Mark Colvin, *The Penitentiary in Crisis: From Accommodation to Riot in New Mexico* (Albany: State University of New York Press, 1992); Robert Morris, *The Devil's Butcher Shop: The New Mexico Prison Uprising* (New York: Franklin Watts, 1983).

6. Mark S. Hamm, "The Abandoned Ones: A History of the Oakdale/Atlanta Riots." In Gregg Barak, ed., *Crimes by the Capitalist State: An Introduction to State Criminality* (Albany: State University of New York Press, 1991), 145–180.

7. Howard Bidna, "Effects of Increased Security on Prison Violence," *Journal of Criminal Justice* 3 (1975), 33–46; Ralph Conant, "Rioting, Insurrection and Civil Disorderliness," *American Scholar* 37 (1968), 420–433; Ezra Stotland, "Self-Esteem and Violence by Guards and State Troopers at Attica," *Criminal Justice and Behavior* 3 (1976), 85–96; Burt Useem and Peter Kimball, *States of Siege: U.S. Prison Riots, 1971–1986* (New York: Oxford University Press, 1988).

8. Useem and Kimball, *States of Siege*, 34.

9. See Mark S. Hamm, "State Organized Homicide: A Study of Seven CIA Plans to Assassinate Fidel Castro." In William J. Chambliss and Marjorie S. Zatz, eds., *Making Law: The State, the Law, and Structural Contradictions* (Bloomington: Indiana University Press, 1993), 315–346.

10. Useem and Kimball, *States of Siege*, 36.

11. Ibid., 104.

12. Ibid.; Colvin, *The Penitentiary in Crisis;* Morris, *The Devil's Butcher Shop*.

13. Mark S. Hamm, "Ethics, Scholarship and *The Justice Professional:* The Tragic Case of the Mariel Cuban," *The Justice Professional* 6 (1992), 135–154.

14. Useem and Kimball, *States of Siege;* Wicker, *A Time to Die*.

15. Colvin, *The Penitentiary in Crisis;* Useem and Kimball, *States of Siege*.

16. Wicker, *A Time to Die*.

17. Useem and Kimball, *States of Siege*, 55.

18. Ibid., 48.

19. Hamm, "The Abandoned Ones."

20. Colvin, *The Penitentiary in Crisis;* Useem and Kimball, *States of Siege*.

21. Useem and Kimball, *States of Siege*.

22. Morris, *The Devil's Butcher Shop.*

23. Quoted in Useem and Kimball, *States of Siege,* 51.

24. Ibid., 24.

25. Ibid.

26. Mark S. Hamm, "Political Rehabilitation in Cuban Prisons: The Plan Progressivo," *Journal of Correctional Education* 40 (1989), 72–79.

27. Hamm, "The Abandoned Ones."

28. Useem and Kimball, *States of Siege,* 112.

29. Ibid.

30. Ibid., 58.

31. Quoted in Harry E. Allen and Clifford E. Simonsen, *Corrections in America: An Introduction* (New York: Macmillan, 1992), 550; Meese's award is detailed in Mark S. Hamm, "From Wedtech and Iran-Contra to the Riots at Oakdale and Atlanta: On the Ethics and Public Performance of Edwin Meese III," *Journal of Crime & Justice* 14 (1991), 123–148.

32. Hamm, "The Abandoned Ones."

33. Ibid.

34. Quoted in Bernard Gavzer, "Are Human Rights Being Abused in Our Country?" *Parade* (December 12, 1993), 6, 8.

35. Ibid., 6.

36. Quoted in James Miller, *The Passion of Michel Foucault* (New York: Simon & Schuster, 1993), 270.

Chapter 4

1. Claes Brundenius, *Revolutionary Cuba: The Challenge of Economic Growth with Equity* (London: Westview Press, 1984).

2. Ibid.; Barry Sklar, "Cuban Exodus 1980: The Context," in Louis Irving Horowitz, ed., *Cuban Communism* (New Brunswick, N.J.: Transaction Books, 1984), 376–390; Peter Winn, "Is the Cuban Revolution in Trouble?" *Nation* (June 7, 1980), 682–685; John Womack, Jr., "The Revolution Tightens Its Belt," *New Republic* (May 31, 1980), 19–23. With regard to the natural disasters plaguing the Cuban economy during this period, Winn suggests that human hands may have played a role. As he notes, past U.S. Senate investigations have revealed that the last time African swine fever appeared in Cuba, the U.S. Central Intelligence Agency was responsible for its introduction.

3. Sklar, "Cuban Exodus 1980."

4. Ibid., 376.

5. For a discussion of the rationing system, see Ernesto F. Betancourt and Wilson P. Dizard III, "Fidel Castro and the Bankers: The Mortgaging of a Revolution." In Louis Irving Horowitz, ed., *Cuban Communism* (New Brunswick, N.J.: Transaction Books, 1984), 191–209; Carmelo Mesa-Lago, *Cuba in the 1970s: Pragmatism and Institutionalization* (Albuquerque: University of New Mexico Press, 1978); Kenneth Y. Tomlinson, "Freeing Cuba for Freedom," *Reader's Digest* (August 1980), 92–96; and Womack, "The Revolution Tightens Its Belt."

6. Sklar, "Cuban Exodus 1980."

7. Agefi Press Service, *International Bondletter and Eurocurrency Financing Review* 40 (March 27, 1982).

8. Betancourt and Dizard, "Fidel Castro and the Bankers."

9. "Cuba's Tattered Economy—Through Refugee Eyes," *U.S. News & World Report* (May 5, 1980), 21–22; Winn, "Is the Cuban Revolution in Trouble?"; Womack, "The Revolution Tightens Its Belt."

10. Tomlinson, "Fleeing Cuba for Freedom."

11. Womack, "The Revolution Tightens Its Belt."

12. Ibid.

13. Betancourt and Dizard, "Fidel Castro and the Bankers." It is worth noting that Cuba's involvement in Africa was initially endorsed by the United States government. In a television interview on CBS in 1978, Ambassador Andrew Young declared that the Cuban troops "bring a certain stability and order to Angola." Young further stated that "Cuba is in Africa because it really has shared in a sense of colonial oppression and domination." Cited in Clark R. Mollenhoff, *The President Who Failed* (New York: Macmillan Publishing Co., 1980), 224. As events surrounding the Mariel boatlift unfolded, however, it is difficult to believe that the Carter administration approved of this rhetoric by Ambassador Young.

14. Carmelo Mesa-Lago, *The Economy of Socialist Cuba: A Two Decade Appraisal* (Albuquerque: University of New Mexico Press, 1981).

15. Ibid.

16. Ibid.

17. Ibid.

18. Sklar, "Cuban Exodus 1980." 380.

19. Amnesty International, *Political Imprisonment in Cuba* (London: Amnesty International Publications, 1987); Armando Valladares, "The Cuban Gulag." In Irving Louis Horowitz, ed., *Cuban Communism* (New Brunswick, N.J.: Transaction Books, 1984), 790–797.

20. Valladares, "The Cuban Gulag," 791.

21. Ibid. President Castro has often stated that "In a revolution there are no neutrals." Quoted in Lee Lockwood, *Castro's Cuba, Cuba's Fidel* (New York: Vintage Books, 1969), 247. In 1965, Castro indicated that the number of Cubans interned in government jails and prison camps for political crimes or "errors" was listed at twenty thousand and growing. Traditionally, the majority of Cuban political prisoners have not been, as one might assume, individuals of urban backgrounds, but *campesinos*—peasants from the mountains and outlying areas. According to Lockwood's interviews with Castro, the aim of "political rehabilitation" is to "neutralize" prisoners to the point where the government can be reasonably certain that they will not engage in activities against the regime. The main effort, moreover, is to convince prisoners that the Cuban revolution is working to ameliorate social problems for all Cubans, and to show them that in opposing Castro's government, they erred out of ignorance. Once they demonstrate an understanding of this, "they can be restored to society in a frame of mind which will inspire them to work productively" (Lockwood, 250). The tactics used to produce this "frame of mind" have for years been criticized by Amnesty International, the Human Rights Organization of the American States, and scholars throughout the world. Since Fidel Castro came to power in 1959, it has been estimated that 872,000 Cubans have left their homeland primarily to escape this system and to take advantage of political and economic opportunity in the United States. See "Cuban-Haitian Refugees," *U.S. Department of State Bulletin* (August 1980), 79–82.

22. Sklar, "Cuban Exodus 1980." 377.

23. Gary MacEoin, "Playing Politics with 'Refugees,'" *Progressive* (July 1980), 36–37; Womack, "The Revolution Tightens Its Belt."

24. Brundenius, *Revolutionary Cuba;* Mesa-Lago, *The Economy of Socialist Cuba.*

25. Winn, "Is the Cuban Revolution in Trouble?" 682. *Newsweek* reporters spoke with thousands of Mariel refugees during 1980. Said one of the first passengers to arrive in America, "I never knew what blue jeans were until *La Communidad* came home." Quoted in "The Refugee's Lot," *Newsweek* (May 26, 1980), 31.

26. Sklar, "Cuban Exodus 1980"; Womack, "The Revolution Tightens Its Belt."

27. Ibid. The Refugee Act of 1980 was a major foreign policy initiative of the Carter administration. It sought to heal old wounds with several Soviet

bloc nations. See Jerel A. Rosati, *The Carter Administration's Quest for Global Community* (Columbia: University of South Carolina Press, 1987).

28. To the extent that unemployment rates measure the efficacy of this policy, the mass exodus was successful. After the Mariel boatlift of 1980, unemployment decreased in Cuba from 188,000 to 146,000. Female unemployment fell from 12 percent to 7 percent and male unemployment fell to 2½ percent—comparable to the early 1970s, before natural disasters, demographic changes, and military interventions in Africa. See Brundenius, *Revolutionary Cuba;* and Mesa-Lago, *The Economy of Socialist Cuba.* Insofar as political stability measures the success of the massive boatlift, the policy was also successful. Castro had declared in a December 1979 speech that ". . . in a certain way we have been needing an enemy. When we have a clearly defined enemy, engaged in hard-fought combat," he explained, "we are more united, energetic, stimulated." Quoted in Winn, "Is the Cuban Revolution in Trouble?" 684. Thanks to the Freedom Flotilla of 1980, the Cuban government was able to revive its hostility toward the United States, and therefore found an "enemy" once again. Accordingly, Castro seized on the U.S.–Cuban crisis as an opportunity to criticize the political failings of his own leaders and institutions.

29. "Exodus from Cuba," *U.S. Department of State Bulletin* (July 1980), 80–81.

30. Brundenius, *Revolutionary Cuba;* "Cuban Refugees," *U.S. Department of State Bulletin* (August 1980), 68–71.

31. Sklar, "Cuban Exodus 1980." Figures on the actual number of Cuban refugees who came to the U.S. on the Freedom Flotilla vary from the number reported here to 125,262 reported by the INS (see *Time,* October 13, 1980). The figures used by Brundenius and Sklar are derived from Cuban census reports, whereas the figures reported by the INS are based on their own internal documents.

32. "Cuban-Haitian Refugees," *U.S. Department of State Bulletin.* See also Marlys Harris, "A Yanqui Comes Home," *Money* (September 1980) 100–106; Jerry Kishenbaum, "Freedom: Big League Baseball Prospects," *Sports Illustrated* (May 19, 1980); MacEoin, "Playing Politics with 'Refugees' "; Sklar, "Cuban Exodus 1980"; Tomlinson, "Fleeing Cuba for Freedom," and special features on the Freedom Flotilla published by *Newsweek* on May 26 and September 20, 1980.

33. Brundenius, *Revolutionary Cuba.*

34. Sklar, "Cuban Exodus 1980," 380. See also "Cuban Refugees," *U.S. Department of State Bulletin* (July 7, 1980), 70–71.

35. "Cuban Refugees," *U.S. Department of State Bulletin* (July 7, 1980), 71. "We will not," concluded the White House, "permit our country to be used as a dumping ground for criminals who present a danger to society."

36. Sklar, "Cuban Exodus 1980."

37. This pejorative characterization of the Mariel Cuban appears often in press accounts of the Freedom Flotilla. See "Cubans Vote with Their Feet" *Newsweek* (April 21, 1980); "For Cubans: Hospitality and Hostility," *U.S. News & World Report* (May 19, 1980); "For Most Cubans, U.S. a Happy Haven," *U.S. News & World Report* (September 1, 1980); E. Howard Hunt, "Castro's Worms," *National Review* (June 13, 1980), 722–724; John Osborn, "With Open Arms," *New Republic* (June 21, 1980), 6–8; and The Commission Pro-Justice Mariel Prisoners, *Mariel Injustice,* 10–21. For scathing reviews of the United Press International in their treatment of the Mariel Cubans see Milton Mayer, "Massaging the News," *Progressive* (August 1980), 44–45; "A Half-Opened Door," *New Republic* (May 24, 1980); and Winn, "Is the Cuban Revolution in Trouble?"

38. After he left office, President Carter would reflect on the events of May 1980: "Because of problems with Castro's regime, at least 10 percent of the total population of Cuba was trying to escape, and looking for any possible means to come to the United States. Castro began actively encouraging many Cubans to emigrate. Although most of the emigrants were good citizens, we were soon to discover that some were mental patients and criminals." Jimmy Carter, *Keeping the Faith: Memoirs of a President* (New York: Bantam Books, 1982), 533.

39. See *President Carter in 1980.* Congressional Quarterly (1981). As it turned out, President Carter found his handling of the Mariel boatlift "costly in political popularity." Carter, *Keeping the Faith,* 534.

40. "President Says U.S. Offers 'Open Arms' to Cuban Refugees," *The New York Times* (May 6, 1980), A1.

41. Statement of Gary Leshaw, U.S. House Judiciary Committee, Subcommittee on Courts, Civil Liberties, and the Administration of Justice, February 4, 1988, 2.

Chapter 5

1. Carter, *Keeping the Faith;* "Cuban Refugees," *U.S. Department of State Bulletin* (June 1980), 68–71. See also The Minnesota Lawyer's International

Human Rights Committee, *The Freedom Flotilla Six Years Later: From Mariel to Minnesota* (Minneapolis: Minnesota Lawyer's International Human Rights Committee, 1986).

2. "The Cuban Tide Is a Flood," *Newsweek* (May 19, 1980), 28–29; "The Welcome Wears Thin," *Time* (September 1, 1980), 8–10.

3. "Cuban Refugees," *U.S. Department of State Bulletin* (June 1980); "Carter and the Cuban Influx," *Newsweek* (May 26, 1980), 22–28.

4. "Exodus from Cuba," *U.S. Department of State Bulletin* (July 1980), 80–81; "Dispersing Cubans Easier Said Than Done," *U.S. News & World Report* (June 2, 1980); The Minnesota Lawyer's International Human Rights Committee, *The Freedom Flotilla Six Years Later.* Under the terms of the Refugee Act of 1980, an excludable person paroled into the United States differs from a deportable person (a person who has made an entry into the country even if illegally). Excludable persons are considered to have no more rights than someone who is stopped at the border of a country. An excludable person on parole has no rights to a hearing and his parole may be revoked at any time. In contrast, a deportable person is entitled to certain hearing rights under federal law and INS regulations.

5. See ". . . And Trouble with Cuban Refugees Too," *U.S. News & World Report* (August 18, 1980), 9; "Coping with Cuba's Exodus," *Newsweek* (May 12, 1980), 60–63; "Cuba's Boat People—Dilemma for Carter," *U.S. News & World Report* (May 5, 1980), 41–42; "The Cuban Conundrum," *Newsweek* (September 29, 1980).

6. "The Refugees: Rebels with a Cause," *Newsweek* (June 16, 1980), 28–29.

7. Osborne, "With Open Arms"; "The Cuban Tide Is a Flood"; "When Cubans Bolt Refugee Centers," *U.S. News & World Report* (April 21, 1980), 13. The difference between "refugees" and "excludable entrants" is that the law may be interpreted to mean that "refugees" have already been screened and cleared before they reach the U.S. (even if they lack passports or visas).

8. Quoted in "Coping with Cuba's Exodus," 60.

9. "A Half-Opened Door," 5.

10. "When Cubans Bolt Refugee Centers."

11. "Cuban Refugees," *U.S. Department of State Bulletin* (August 1980), 68–71. See also Paul Heath Hoeffel, "Fort Chafee's Unwanted Cubans," *New York Times Magazine* (December 21, 1980), 30–54; "In the Last Days of the Boatlift," *U.S. News & World Report* (June 16, 1980), 29; "The Refugees: Rebels with a Cause."

12. Quoted in Sklar, "Cuban Exodus 1980," 32. See "Cuban Refugees," *U.S. Department of State Bulletin* (August 1980).

13. "Freedom Flotilla: A Brave Skipper, A Grateful Family and Angry Florida Critics," *People* (May 26, 1980), 29.

14. Quoted in "When Cubans Bolt Refugee Centers," 13.

15. Quoted in "The Refugees: Rebels with a Cause," 28.

16. "Freedom Flotilla: A Brave Skipper, A Grateful Family and Angry Florida Critics"; "The Cuban Tide Is a Flood."

17. "In the Last Days of the Boatlift"; "The Refugees: Rebels with a Cause"; "The Welcome Wears Thin."

18. "Camp of Fear in Wisconsin," *Time* (September 8, 1980), 28. These increased security measures had little effect on maintaining order in the relocation camps. On the contrary, violence became a standard feature of the relocation program, producing a series of small riots including an August 6 rebellion at the Fort Indiantown Gap facility that left fifty-eight Mariel Cubans seriously injured. See ". . . And Trouble from Cuban Refugees, Too"; "The Cuban Refugees Move On," *Time* (October 13, 1980), 45.

19. "The Refugees: Rebels with a Cause"; "The Welcome Wears Thin."

20. This conclusion is supported by a *Newsweek* poll conducted in May 1980. Fifty-nine percent of those questioned felt that the influx of Cubans "was bad for the United States," and 40 percent indicated that "the nation should accept no more Cuban Refugees at all." See "Carter and the Cuban Influx," 22.

21. This concern was heightened by the fact that upon release from the relocation camps, sixteen Cubans participated in a spree of airline hijackings during the summer of 1980. In August alone, seven American airliners were hijacked to Havana by members of the Freedom Flotilla. See "Cuban Hijackers—And Those Who Stay," *Newsweek* (September 1, 1980), 26; and "Havana-Bound," *Time* (August 25, 1980), 40.

22. Sklar, "Cuban Exodus 1980"; "The Cuban Refugees Move On."

23. Ibid. See also "For Most Cubans, U.S. a Happy Haven."

24. Kurt Chandler, "Despite INS Parole Plan, Uncertainty Remains for State's Mariel Cubans," *Minneapolis Star and Tribune* (August 23, 1987), 7B; Joe Dolman, "Locking Up Liberty in the Atlanta Pen," *Southern Changes* 8 (December 1986), 1–3; "A Half-Opened Door"; "Refugee Rights," *Time* (January 12, 1981), 52. See also "Cuban Refugees," *U.S. Department of State Bulletin* (August 1980); Scott Shepard, "Cuban Inmate's Rights Violated, Group Says," *Atlanta Constitution* (April 15, 1987), 6B.

25. See generally John Braithwaite, "The Myth of Social Class and Criminality Reconsidered," *American Sociological Review* 46 (1981), 366–376; William J. Chambliss, "A Sociological Analysis of the Laws of Vagrancy," *Social Problems* 12 (1964), 67–77; Richard Quinney, *Class, State and Crime: On the Theory and Practice of Criminal Justice* (New York: David McKay, 1977).

26. Daniel Glaser, "The Counterproductivity of Conservative Thinking about Crime," *Criminology* 16 (1978), 211.

27. U.S. Bureau of Justice Statistics, *Report to the Nation on Crime and Justice* (Washington, D.C.: U.S. Department of Justice, 1988).

28. Carter, *Keeping the Faith,* 533.

29. Statement by Deputy Attorney General Arnold I. Burns, U.S. Department of Justice, December 11, 1987, 1.

30. See Larry M. Eig, *Indefinite Detention of Freedom Flotilla Cubans: A History of the Judicial Response* (Washington, D.C.: Congressional Research Service, Library of Congress, February 25, 1986); Sophie H. Pirie, "The Need for a Codified Definition of 'Persecution' in United States Refugee Law," *Stanford Law Review* 39 (1986), 187–234.

31. Daniel Golden, "U.S. No Haven for These Cuban Refugees," *Boston Globe* (March 29, 1987), A23–26; "Marielitos: The Forgotten Refugees," ABC *Nightline* (broadcast July 3, 1987); "Refugee Rights."

32. Timothy Dwyer, "U.S. Prisons a Limbo for 5,000 Cubans," *Philadelphia Inquirer* (July 13, 1987), 1A–4.

33. Chandler, "Despite INS Parole Plan, Uncertainty Remains for State's Mariel Cubans."

34. John Irwin, *The Jail: Managing the Underclass in American Society* (Berkeley: University of California Press, 1985).

35. U.S. House of Representatives, Subcommittee on Courts, Civil Liberties, and the Administration of Justice, *Atlanta Federal Penitentiary* (Washington, D.C.: U.S. Government Printing Office, 1986) (Hereafter referred to as *The House of Representatives Report*). See also Dolman, "Locking Up Liberty at the Atlanta Pen"; Steven Donzinger, "INS Treatment of Cubans Offends American Sense of Justice," *Atlanta Journal and Constitution* (November 8, 1987), A1; "Fairness of Case Reviews for Cubans Is Challenged," *New York Times* (January 3, 1988).

36. Joan Treadway, " 'The Abandoned' Await Their Chance for a New Life," *New Orleans Times-Picayune* (August 30, 1987), C1–2.

37. Statement by Deputy Attorney General Arnold I. Burns, 1.

38. Quoted in Ann Woolner, "Pat Swindall's Conversion," *Fulton County Daily Report* (February 9, 1988), 8.

Chapter 6

1. Jim Hampton, "Caged Logic on Cuban Prisoners," *Miami Herald* (October 19, 1987), A-12; "Cubans Still Waiting for Fairness," *Atlanta Constitution* (July 9, 1987), 12-A; Cindy McAfee, "Shoob Urges Fairness to Detainees," *Marietta Daily Journal* (February 26, 1986), 1. Since Castro came to power in 1959, no fewer than six policy phases have characterized Cuban emigration to the United States. Each phase has involved the regranting of emigration privileges denied Cubans in the past, or again terminating the regranted privileges. See Thomas D. Boswell and Manuel Rivero, "Cubans in America," *Focus* (April 1985), 2–9.

2. See Henry A. Kissinger, *The Report of the President's National Bipartisan Commission on Central America* (New York: Macmillan, 1984).

3. Kenneth N. Skoug, Jr., "The United States and Cuba." Address before the "Face-to-Face" Program of the Carnegie Endowment for International Peace (December 17, 1984). See also International Security Council, *The Soviet Challenge in Central America and the Caribbean* (New York: CAUSA, 1985); William M. LeoGrande, "Cuba," in Morris J. Blachman et al., eds., *Confronting Revolution: Security Through Diplomacy in Central America* (New York: Pantheon, 1986).

4. "Castro's Challenge to Reagan," *Newsweek* (January 9, 1984), 38–41; Thomas W. Walker, "Nicaraguan–U.S. Friction: The First Four Years, 1979–1983." In Kenneth M. Coleman and George C. Herring, eds., *The Central American Crisis: Sources of Conflict and the Failure of U.S. Policy* (Wilmington, Del.: Scholarly Resources, 1985).

5. Quoted in "Castro's Challenge to Reagan," 38, 39, 41.

6. "U.S., Cuba Resume Normal Migration," *U.S. Department of State Bulletin* (February 4, 1984), 44–46. In addition to these restored migration agreements, on October 17, 1984, the Reagan administration reenacted the 1966 Cuban Refugee Act, which superseded Carter's Refugee Act of 1980. With regard to the Mariel people, Reagan's legislation allowed all those classified as "excludable entrants" (and who were not in prison) to receive permanent U.S. residency status by 1985 (instead of the original 1987 date set forth in the Carter legislation). See Boswell and Rivero, "Cubans in America."

7. Quoted in Skough, "The United States and Cuba," 3. During his administration, Ronald Reagan also would approve a series of measures to

enforce a strict U.S. embargo of Cuba. These measures made it difficult for the Cuban government to obtain U.S. dollars and goods. The objective of the embargo was to deny Castro's government any economic benefit from the U.S. as long as Castro continued to support Marxist-Leninist regimes in Central America. See "Cuba: New Migration and Embargo Measures," *U.S. Department of State Bulletin* (November 1986), 86–87.

8. "Cuba: New Migration and Embargo Measures," *U.S. Department of State Bulletin* (November 1986), 86–87. In response to this policy, and in keeping with his embargo, on August 22, 1986, President Reagan issued a proclamation to prevent the Cuban government from "trafficking in human beings by charging citizens and residents of the United States thousands of dollars to finance the direct travel from Cuba to the U.S." "Cuba: New Migration and Embargo Measures," *U.S. Department of State Bulletin* 86–87.

9. "Seventy-Three of the 201 Cuban Refugees Who Were Deported to Cuba Are Still in Cuban Prisons," *Diario de Las Americas* (June 23, 1986), 1. See also Robert W. Kastenmeier, "Mariel Cubans Deserve Due Process Too," *The Washington Post* (March 24, 1988), 12-A.

10. Eig, *Indefinite Detention of Freedom Flotilla Cubans*; Ann Woolner, "Cuban Detention 'A Disgrace,'" *Fulton County Daily Report* (January 20, 1987), 1–4.

11. Dolman, "Locking Up Liberty in the Atlanta Pen"; Hampton, "Caged Logic on Cuban Prisoners"; "Men Without a Country," *Newsweek* (June 9, 1986), 29; *The House of Representatives Report*.

12. Ibid.

13. Eig, *Indefinite Detention of Freedom Flotilla Cubans*.

14. Ibid.

15. Ibid.

16. *The House of Representatives Report*.

17. Stanley Cohen, *Folk Devils and Moral Panics* (London: Macgibbon and Kee, 1972; see also Jeff Ferrell, *Crimes of Style: Urban Graffiti and the Politics of Criminality* (New York: Garland, 1993).

18. Ralph H. Turner and Samuel J. Surace, "Zoot-Suiters and Mexicans: Symbols in Crowd Behavior," *American Journal of Sociology* 62 (1956), 14.

19. Coramae Richey Mann, *Unequal Justice: A Question of Color* (Bloomington: Indiana University Press, 1993).

20. Herbert Burkholz, "The Latinization of Miami," *New York Times Magazine* (September 21, 1980), 45–47; "The New Wave of Cubans Is Swamping Miami," *Business Weekly* (August 25, 1980), 87–88.

21. Ibid.

22. Ibid.

23. John Lewis, "A Mocking Memory," *Congressional Record* (April 27, 1987).

24. Quoted in National Center on Institutions and Alternatives/Coalition to Support Cuban Detainees, *Project Due Process* (Arlington, Va.: National Center on Institutions and Alternatives, 1987), 15.

25. Burkholz, "The Latinization of Miami."

26. Quoted in "Can Miami Cope with Flood of Refugees?" *U.S. News & World Report* (May 12, 1980), 55.

27. Burkholz, "The Latinization of Miami."

28. Lewis, "A Mocking Memory."

29. James L. Jengeleski, Orlando DeGarcia, and Mellisa A. Sweigert, "Land of Opportunity for Crime: The Cuban Criminal," *The Justice Professional* 1 (1986), 34.

30. Ibid., 39; see also Hamm, "Ethics, Scholarship and *The Justice Professional.*"

31. "Castro's 'Crime Bomb' Inside U.S.," *U.S. News & World Report* (January 16, 1984), 27–30.

32. Ibid., 27.

33. Hamm, "Political Rehabilitation in Cuban Prisons."

34. Castro's 'Crime Bomb' Inside U.S."

35. Ibid.

36. Ibid.

37. Ibid.

38. Ibid.

39. Hamm, "The Abandoned Ones."

40. Quoted in Dwyer, "U.S. Prisons a Limbo for 5,000 Cubans," 4A.

41. Ibid.

42. Quoted in Chandler, "Despite INS Parole Plan, Uncertainty Remains for State's Mariel Cubans," 7B.

43. Ibid.

44. Quoted in "Castro's 'Crime Bomb' Inside U.S.," 30.

45. All yearly figures are taken from the *Budget of the United States Government* (Washington, D.C.: Government Printing Office, 1978–1991).

46. Mark S. Hamm, *American Skinheads* (Westport, Conn.: Praeger, 1993).

47. "The Sleaze Watch," *The New Republic* 198 (May 9, 1988), 8.

48. Hamm, "From Wedtech and Iran-Contra to the Riots at Oakdale and Atlanta."

49. Ibid., 132.

50. Ibid.

51. Ibid.

Chapter 7

1. 1. Eugene Victor Debs, *Wall and Bars* (Chicago: Charles H. Kerr, 1973), 91, 98.

2. James Fuller, *Alcatraz* (San Francisco: Asteron, 1982).

3. Dolman, "Locking Up Liberty at the Atlanta Pen."

4. The following chronology is drawn from *The House of Representatives Report*, Appendices 7 and 8.

5. All conclusions are found in *The House of Representatives Report* and in Gary Leshaw, "Atlanta's Cuban Detainees: A Retrospective," *The Atlanta Lawyer* (Fourth Quarter 1992), 6–28.

6. *The House of Representatives Report*, 7.

7. John P. Conrad, "What Do the Undeserving Deserve?" in Robert Johnson and Hans Toch, eds., *The Pains of Imprisonment* (Prospect Heights, Ill.: Waveland Press, 1988), 315. See also Lee H. Bowker, *Corrections: The Science and the Art* (New York: Macmillan, 1982).

8. Gresham M. Sykes, *The Society of Captives: A Study of a Maximum Security Prison* (Princeton: N.J.: Princeton University Press, 1958), 111.

9. Ibid., 110.

10. See Amnesty International, *Report 1986* (London: Amnesty International Publications, 1986); Gregg Barak, "Crime, Criminology, and Human Rights: Toward an Understanding of State Criminality," in Gregg Barak, ed., *Varieties of Criminology: Readings From a Dynamic Discipline* (Westport, Conn.: Praeger, 1994), 253–268; George F. Cole, Stanislaw J. Frankowski, and Marc G. Gertz, eds., *Major Criminal Justice Systems* (Beverly Hills, Calif.: Sage Publications, 1981); J. W. Cosman, "Declaration of Basic Principles for the Treatment of Prisoners," *Journal of Correctional Education* 40 (1989), 56–61; Mark S. Hamm et al., "The Myth of Humane Imprisonment: A Critical Analysis of Severe Discipline in U.S. Maximum Security Prisons, 1945–1990." In Michael Braswell, Reid Montgomery, Jr., and Lucien X. Lombardo, eds., *Prison Violence in America*, 2d edition (Cincinnati: Anderson Publishing Co., 1994), 163–196; David Kauzlarich, "Prolegomenon to the Criminalization of Nation-States: The International Covenant on Civil and Political Rights." Paper presented at

the annual meeting of the American Society of Criminology (Phoenix, October 1993).

11. Cited in Shela Van Ness, "American Accountability of Human Rights: The Case of Mariel Cuban Detainees." Paper presented at the annual meeting of the American Society of Criminology (Chicago, November 1988).

12. Mann, *Unequal Justice*.

13. The Commission Pro-Justice Mariel Prisoners, *The Mariel Injustice*.

14. Leshaw, "Atlanta's Cuban Detainees," 13.

15. Ibid., 14.

16. Quoted in The Commission Pro-Justice Mariel Prisoners, *The Mariel Injustice*, 59.

17. Quoted in Leshaw, "Atlanta's Cuban Detainees," 15.

18. Sally Sandidge, "On the Road Again," *Atlanta Lawyer* (Fourth Quarter 1992), 9.

19. Quoted in Van Ness, "American Accountability of Human Rights," 28–29.

20. Quoted in The Commission Pro-Justice Mariel Prisoners, *The Mariel Injustice*, 83.

21. Ibid., 86.

22. Ibid.

23. Ibid., 90.

24. Sykes, *The Society of Captives*, 130.

25. U.S. Immigration and Naturalization Service, Cuban Review Plan (unpublished report).

26. Letter from Congressman Pat Swindall to Assistant Attorney General John R. Bolton, December 22, 1987.

27. The preceding chronology was constructed based on information in Tracy Thompson, "Cubans, Guards Trapped in Cycle of Violence in Atlanta Pen," *Atlanta Journal* (April 19, 1987), A1; autopsy reports from the Armed Forces Institute of Pathology, April 21, 1987; the Office of the Medical Examiner, Decatur, Ga., February 20, 1987; the DeKalb County, Ga., Medical Examiner, February 19, 1987; and the Division of Forensic Sciences, Georgia Bureau of Investigation, March 23, 1987; and on an interview with a Cell House E detainee who witnessed the incident.

28. Leshaw, "Atlanta's Cuban Detainees," 28.

29. Quoted in The Commission Pro-Justice Mariel Prisoners, *The Mariel Injustice*, 62.

30. Ibid., 63.

31. Ibid.

32. Ibid.

33. Ibid., 67.

34. Letter from Swindall to Bolton.

35. Statement of Gary Leshaw.

36. Ibid.; see also feature articles in the *New Orleans Times-Picayune* (August 30, 1987). During this period allegations were made by detainees that INS officials were taking bribes in exchange for granting parole to the Cubans. See Leshaw, "Atlanta's Cuban Detainees."

37. Sykes, *The Society of Captives*, 85.

Chapter 8

1. Conrad, "What Do the Undeserving Deserve?" 314.

2. Gresham M. Sykes, *Criminology* (New York: Harcourt Brace Jovanovich, 1978), 500.

3. Ibid.

4. Ibid., 501.

5. Ibid.

6. Ibid., 518.

7. Ibid., 519.

8. The following description is based on William R. Bascom, "The Focus of Cuban Santeria," *Southwestern Journal of Anthropology* 6 (1950), 64–68; Wyatt MacGarrey, *Cuba: Its People, Its Society, Its Culture* (New Haven, Conn.: HRAF Press, 1962); Richard Kennedy, *The International Dictionary of Religion: A Profusely Illustrated Guide to the Beliefs of the World* (New York: Crossroads, 1984); Joseph M. Murphy, "Santeria," in Mircea Eliade, ed., *The Encyclopedia of Religion*, vol. 13 (New York: Macmillan, 1987); Luisah Teish, *Jambalaya* (San Francisco: Harper & Row, 1985); and Claudio Veliz, *Latin America and the Caribbean: A Handbook* (New York: Praeger, 1968).

9. MacGarrey, *Cuba*.

10. Frei Betto, *Fidel and Religion* (New York: Simon & Schuster, 1987).

11. This section draws from Hamm, "Santeria in Federal Prisons."

12. The name Pérez is a pseudonym.

13. Quoted in Gavzer, "Are Human Rights Being Abused in Our Country?" 6.

14. Sykes, *Criminology*, 526.

15. Ibid.

16. Denny McLain, *Strikeout: The Story of Denny McLain* (St. Louis: Sporting News Publishing Co., 1988), 239.

17. Ibid.

18. Howard I. Kushner, *Self-Destruction in the Promised Land: A Psychocultural Biology of American Suicide* (New Brunswick, N.J.: Rutgers University Press, 1989).

19. Quoted in Kushner, *Self-Destruction in the Promised Land,* 108.

20. Ibid.

Chapter 9

1. U.S. Senate, *Nomination of Edwin Meese III* (Washington, D.C.: Government Printing Office, 1984).

2. Ibid., 469.

3. Ibid.

4. Edwin Meese III, *With Reagan: The Inside Story* (Washington, D.C.: Regnery Gateway, 1992), 81.

5. Ibid.

6. U.S. Senate, *Office of the Government Ethics' Review of the Attorney General's Financial Disclosure* (Washington, D.C.: U.S. Government Printing Office, 1987).

7. William Sternberg and Matthew C. Harrison, Jr., *Feeding Frenzy* (New York: Henry Holt, 1989), 30.

8. Ibid., 30–31.

9. Suzanne Garment, *Scandal: The Culture of Mistrust in American Politics* (New York: Doubleday, 1991), 118.

10. Quoted in George Lardner, Jr., and Mary Thorton, "A Wedtech Entanglement: Friendship Drew Meese into Scandal," *Washington Post* (September 3, 1987), A20.

11. Ibid.

12. Sternberg and Harrison, *Feeding Frenzy,* 214.

13. Quoted in Lardner and Thorton, "A Wedtech Entanglement," A20.

14. U.S. Senate, *Office of the Government Ethics' Review of the Attorney General's Financial Disclosure.*

15. Ibid.; Hamm, "From Wedtech and Iran-Contra to the Riots at Oakdale and Atlanta."

16. Lardner and Thorton, "A Wedtech Entanglement."

17. Ibid., A1.

18. Ibid.

19. Sternberg and Harrison, *Feeding Frenzy;* Garment, *Scandal.*

20. Lardner and Thorton, "A Wedtech Entanglement."

21. Quoted in Robert L. Jackson, "Meese Friend Told Wedtech of Influence in Government," *Los Angeles Times* (September 30, 1987), 16.

22. Ibid.

23. Ibid.; Sternberg and Harrison, *Feeding Frenzy.*

24. U.S. Senate, *Nomination of Edwin Meese III;* U.S. Senate, *Confirmation of Edwin Meese III* (Washington, D.C.: Government Printing Office, 1985).

25. Garment, *Scandal.*

26. Meese, *With Reagan,* 323n.

27. Lardner and Thorton, "A Wedtech Entanglement."

28. James B. Stewart, *The Prosecutors: Inside Offices of the Government's Most Powerful Lawyers* (New York: Henry Holt, 1988).

29. U.S. Senate, *Confirmation of Edwin Meese III.*

30. Quoted in Garment, *Scandal,* 88.

31. U.S. Senate, *Confirmation of Edwin Meese III.*

32. Ibid., 153.

33. U.S. Senate, *Filing and Review of Attorney General Edwin Meese's Financial Disclosures* (Washington, D.C.: Government Printing Office, 1987); Ronald J. Ostrow and Robert L. Jackson, "2 Ex-Meese Advisors Indicted over Wedtech," *Los Angeles Times* (December 23, 1987) 1.

34. Ibid. In 1987, the Senate held that the term "limited blind partnership" is a phrase without legal meaning. Because of the way this nonlegal strategy was employed by Chinn, the actual amount of money (if any) invested by Meese in Wedtech is unknown. Likewise, there is no evidence to indicate that Meese actually earned income from Wedtech.

35. Sternberg and Harrison, *Feeding Frenzy.*

36. Ibid., U.S. Senate, *Filing and Review of Attorney General Edwin Meese's Financial Disclosures.*

37. Ostrow and Jackson, "2 Ex-Meese Advisors Indicted over Wedtech."

38. Garment, *Scandal;* Hamm, "From Wedtech and Iran-Contra to the Riots at Oakdale and Atlanta."

39. Ibid.

40. Vernon Walters, United States Mission to the United Nations, Statement by Ambassador Vernon Walters . . . under Item 12, Human Rights in Cuba. Press release, November 26, 1986.

41. Quoted in Steven R. Weisman, "Reagan, in a Radio Speech, Appeals to People of Cuba," *New York Times* (January 6, 1984), A4.

42. Quoted in Tony Platt, "Cuba and the Politics of Human Rights," *Social Justice* 15 (1988), 40.

43. Quoted in U.S. House of Representatives, *Hearings on Human Rights in Cuba* (Washington, D.C.: Government Printing Office, 1984), 1.

44. U.S. Department of State, *Country Reports of Human Rights Practices for 1986* (Washington, D.C.: Government Printing Office, 1986), 459.

45. Quoted in Tony Platt, "The United States, Cuba, and the New Cold War," *Social Justice* 15 (1988), 7.

46. Ibid.

47. Flora Biancalana and Cecilia O'Leary, "Profile of U.S. Press Coverage of Cuba," *Social Justice* 15 (1988), 63–71.

48. Armando Valladares, *Against All Hope: The Prison Memoirs of Armando Valladares,* trans. Andrew Hurley (New York: Knopf, 1986), xv.

49. Quoted in Platt, "The United States, Cuba, and the New Cold War," 8.

50. Hamm, "State-Organized Homicide"; Hamm, "From Wedtech and Iran-Contra to the Riots at Oakdale and Atlanta."

51. Platt, "Cuba and the Politics of Human Rights."

52. Quoted in John Parry, "U.S. Lays out Rights Stance," *Washington Post* (January 20, 1987), A15.

53. John Parry, "Cuba Denounces U.S. Criticisms of Human Rights," *Washington Post* (February 24, 1987), A18.

54. Ibid.

55. Ibid.

56. Ibid.

57. Ibid.

58. Ibid.

59. Platt, "Cuba and the Politics of Human Rights."

60. Joseph B. Treaster, "Cuba and Human Rights," *New York Times* (May 21, 1987), A12.

61. Quoted in Elaine Sciolino, "Reagan's Mighty Effort to Condemn Cuba," *New York Times* (March 24, 1987), A16.

62. Platt, "Cuba and the Politics of Human Rights."

63. Fidel Castro, speech given at the 8th Conference of the American Jurists Association (Havana), September 17, 1987.

64. Sciolino, "Reagan's Mighty Effort to Condemn Cuba."

65. Ibid.

66. Platt, "Cuba and the Politics of Human Rights."

67. Sciolino, "Reagan's Mighty Effort to Condemn Cuba."

68. Ibid.

69. Ibid.

70. Ibid.

71. Ibid.

72. Ibid.

73. Platt, "Cuba and the Politics of Human Rights."

74. Sciolino, "Reagan's Mighty Effort to Condemn Cuba."

75. Quoted in "U.N. Rejects Faulting Cuba," *New York Times* (March 12, 1987), A12.

76. Ibid.

77. Ibid.

78. Quoted in Sciolino, "Reagan's Mighty Effort to Condemn Cuba," A16.

79. Quoted in "U.N. Rejects Faulting Cuba," *New York Times* A12.

80. Castro, speech at the 8th Conference of the American Jurists Association.

81. Ibid.

82. Quoted in Valladares, *Against All Hope,* Epilogue.

83. Institute for Policy Studies, "Cuban Prisons: A Preliminary Report," *Social Justice* 15 (1988), 55–62.

84. Amnesty International, *Political Imprisonment in Cuba* (London: Amnesty International Publications, 1987).

85. Amnesty International, *United States of America: The Death Penalty* (London: Amnesty International Publications, 1987).

86. Tony Platt and Cecilia Platt, "XXXIX International Course in Criminology," *Crime and Social Justice* 30 (1987), 125–127. For further evidence on the humane and constructive aspects of Cuban penology see Hamm, "Political Rehabilitation in Cuban Prisons"; Ervin R. John, "Seeing Oriente in a Jeep: An American in Cuba, Part I," *Nation* 14 (1966), 296–299; Lockwood, *Castro's Cuba, Cuba's Fidel*; and The Human Rights Project, *Report on Boniato Penitentiary Santiago Cuba (October 9)* (Washington, D.C.: The Human Rights Project, 1987).

87. Institute for Policy Studies, "Cuban Prisons," 59.

88. Amnesty International, *Political Imprisonment in Cuba.*

89. Ibid.; Institute for Policy Studies, "Cuban Prisons."

90. Quoted in Hamm, "Political Rehabilitation in Cuban Prisons," 78.

91. John P. Wallach, "Fidel Castro and the United States Press." In Wil-

liam E. Ratliff, ed., *The Selling of Fidel Castro* (New Brunswick, N.J.: Transaction Books, 1987), 144.

92. Cited in Lardner and Thorton, "A Wedtech Entanglement."

93. Ibid.

94. See Andy Pasztor, "Memo to Meese in 1985 Described Plan to Make Pipeline Payments to Israel," *Wall Street Journal* (February 24, 1988), 18E.

95. Garment, *Scandal;* Sternberg and Harrison, *Feeding Frenzy.*

96. Ibid.

97. U.S. Senate, *Office of Government Ethics' Review of the Attorney General's Financial Disclosure.*

98. Ibid., 2–4.

99. Garment, *Scandal.*

100. Ibid.

101. Cited in Dan Morain, "Wallach Seen as a Successful Attorney," *Los Angeles Times* (December 28, 1987), 4.

102. Quoted in Lardner and Thorton, "A Wedtech Entanglement," A20.

103. Quoted in Morain, "Wallach Seen as a Successful Attorney," 4.

104. Ibid.

105. Quoted in Ostrow and Jackson, "2 Ex-Meese Advisors Indicted over Wedtech," 1.

106. Garment, *Scandal.*

107. Quoted in Ostrow and Jackson, "2 Ex-Meese Advisors Indicted over Wedtech," 17.

108. Ibid.; Garment, *Scandal;* Sternberg and Harrison, *Feeding Frenzy.*

109. Hamm, "From Wedtech and Iran-Contra to the Riots at Oakdale and Atlanta"; Platt, "Cuba and the Politics of Human Rights."

110. Ibid.

111. Meese, *With Reagan,* 285.

112. Ibid.

113. Stewart, *The Prosecutors.*

114. Platt, "Cuba and the Politics of Human Rights."

115. U.S. State Department, "U.S., Cuba Resume Normal Migration."

116. Ibid.

Chapter 10

1. Useem and Kimball, *States of Siege,* 5–6.

2. Ibid.

3. Ibid., 235.

4. Ibid., 5.

5. Ibid.

6. Ibid.

7. Ibid.

8. Ibid., 235.

9. Vincent Ostrom, *The Intellectual Crisis in Public Administration* (University: University of Alabama Press, 1974).

10. Quoted in Dwight Waldo, *The Enterprise of Public Administration: A Summary View* (Novato, Calif.: Chandler & Sharp, 1980), 99.

11. Kenneth J. Meier, *Politics and The Bureaucracy: Policymaking in the Fourth Branch of Government* (North Scituate, Mass.: Duxbury Press, 1979), 164.

12. Quoted in Douglas W. Kmiec, *The Attorney General's Lawyer: Inside the Meese Justice Department* (New York: Praeger, 1992), 193.

13. Edwin Meese III, Foreword to Kmiec, *The Attorney General's Lawyer*, xi.

14. Hamm, "From Wedtech and Iran-Contra to the Riots at Oakdale and Atlanta."

15. See Garment, *Scandal;* Sternberg and Harrison, *Feeding Frenzy.*

16. Kmiec, *The Attorney General's Lawyer*, 194.

17. Ibid., 194–195.

18. *After-Action Report.*

19. Ibid., Oakdale-13.

20. Ibid.

21. Ibid.

22. Ibid.

23. Ibid.

24. "A Cuban Explosion," 40.

25. Useem and Kimball, *States of Siege*, 210.

26. Quoted in John Cruickshank, *Albert Camus and the Literature of Revolt* (New York: Oxford University Press, 1969), 62.

27. Albert Camus, *Le Mythe de Sisyphe* (Paris: Gallimard, 1942), 75.

28. *After-Action Report.*

29. Useem and Kimball, *States of Siege*, 211.

30. "A Cuban Explosion," 38.

31. *After-Action Report*, Oakdale-10.

32. Ibid., Oakdale-9, Atlanta-66.

33. Kate Millett, *The Politics of Cruelty: An Essay on the Literature of Political Imprisonment* (New York: Norton, 1994), 36.

34. Mark S. Hamm, "Whistleblowing in Corrections," *Sociological Viewpoints* 5 (1989), 35–45.

35. U.S. President's Review Board. *Review of the President's Special Review Board* (Washington, D.C.: U.S. President's Review Board, 1987). Also known as the "Tower Commission Report."

36. Interview with Leshaw, March 1994.

37. Quoted in Wood and Mooney, "What Really Happened at the Atlanta Pen," 3.

38. The Commission Pro-Justice Mariel Prisoners, *The Mariel Injustice*.

39. Ibid.; *After-Action Report*.

40. Ibid.

41. Useem and Kimball, *States of Siege*, 216.

42. Leshaw, "Atlanta's Cuban Detainees."

43. Ibid., 15.

44. Speech delivered at a Miami fundraiser for the Cuban-American Foundation, September 15, 1992. See Pamela S. Falk, "Exiles Set Policy Agenda on Cuba for Next Administration," *Wall Street Journal* (October 16, 1992), A15; Pat M. Holt, "Put Policy Toward Cuba on a More Rational Basis," *Christian Science Monitor* (February 4, 1993), 18; Jorge Dominguez, "Cuba's Helper," *Washington Post* (March 7, 1994), A19.

45. Quoted in Hamm, "State-Organized Homicide," 326. This was the John F. Kennedy of the post-MONGOOSE era, when his administration made several attempts to assassinate the Cuban leader.

46. History shows that Castro was just as receptive to such an initiative in 1963 (see Hamm, "State-Organized Homicide"), as he is today. On May 1, 1993, Castro directly appealed to President Clinton to lift U.S. economic sanctions against Cuba. See "Castro Seeks End of Embargo," *New York Times* (May 2, 1993), A18.

47. See Eugene A. Carroll, Jr., "Lift the Embargo While Castro is Still Boss," *Los Angeles Times* (October 25, 1993), B7.

48. James G. Blight, Aaron Belkin, and David Lewis, "Havana Ground Rules: The Missile Crisis, Then and Now." In Wayne S. Smith, ed., *The Russians Aren't Coming: New Soviet Policy in Latin America* (Boulder, Colo.: Lynne Rienner Publishers, 1992), 171–172.

49. "Clinton's Fidel Problem," *Wall Street Journal* (December 31, 1992), A6.

50. Johanna McGeary and Cathy Booth, "Cuba Alone," *Time* (December 6, 1993), 43–54.

51. "27 Cubans Picked up at Sea in a Boat Reported Hijacked," *New York Times* (August 10, 1994), A12.

52. Quoted in "Cubans Hijack Ship, Set Sail for U.S.," *Bloomington Herald-Times* (August 10, 1994), A5.

53. "Cubans, and Cuba Policy, Lost at Sea," *New York Times* (August 11, 1994), A14.

54. Quoted in Steven Greenhouse, "Cubans Who Seize Boat Win Asylum," *New York Times* (August 11, 1994), A8.

55. "U.S. Prepared to Stop Boatlift with Blockade," *Bloomington Herald-Times* (August 11, 1994), A4.

56. Cubans, and Cuba Policy, Lost at Sea," A14.

References

". . . And Trouble With Cuban Refugees Too." 1980. *U.S. News & World Report,* August 18, 9.

Allen, Harry E., and Clifford E. Simonsen. 1992. *Corrections in America.* New York: Macmillan.

Amnesty International. 1987. *Political Imprisonment in Cuba.* London: Amnesty International Publications.

———. 1987. *United States of America: The Death Penalty.* London: Amnesty International Publications.

———. 1986. *Report 1986.* London: Amnesty International Publications.

Barak, Gregg. 1994. "Crime, Criminology, and Human Rights: Toward an Understanding of State Criminality." In *Varieties of Criminology: Readings From A Dynamic Discipline,* edited by Gregg Barak. Westport, Conn.: Praeger.

Bascom, William R. 1950. "The Focus of Cuban Santeria." *Southwestern Journal of Anthropology* 6:64–68.

Bentancourt, Ernesto F., and Wilson P. Dizard III. 1984. "Fidel Castro and the Bankers: The Mortgaging of a Revolution." In *Cuban Communism,* edited by Louis Irving Horowitz. New Brunswick, N.J.: Transaction Books.

Betto, Frei. 1987. *Fidel and Religion.* New York: Simon and Schuster.

Biancalana, Flora, and Cecilia O'Leary. 1988. "Profile of U.S. Press Coverage of Cuba." *Social Justice* 15:63–71.

Bidna, Howard. 1975. "Effects of Increased Security on Prison Violence." *Journal of Criminal Justice* 3:33–46.

Blight, James G., Aaron Belkin, and David Lewis. 1992. "Havana Ground

Rules: The Missile Crisis, Then and Now." In *The Russians Aren't Coming: New Soviet Policy in Latin America*, edited by Wayne S. Smith. Boulder, Colo.: Lynne Rienner Publishers.

Boswell, Thomas D., and Manuel Rivero. 1985. "Cubans in America." *Focus*, April, 2–9.

Bowker, Lee H. 1982. *Corrections: The Science and the Art*. New York: Macmillan.

Braithwaite, John. 1981. "The Myth of Social Class and Criminality Reconsidered." *American Sociological Review* 46:366–76.

Brundenius, Claes. 1984. *Revolutionary Cuba: The Challenge of Economic Growth with Equity*. London: Westview Press.

Budget of the United States Government. 1978–1991. Washington, D.C.: Government Printing Office.

Burkholz, Herbert. 1980. "The Latinization of Miami." *New York Times Magazine*, September 21, 45–47.

Burns, Arnold I. 1987. Statement by Deputy Attorney General Arnold I. Burns, December 11. Washington, D.C.: U.S. Department of Justice.

"Camp of Fear in Wisconsin." 1980. *Time*, September 8, 28.

Camus, Albert. 1942. *Le Mythe de Sisyphe*. Paris: Gallimard.

"Can Miami Cope with Flood of Refugees?" 1980. *U.S. News & World Report*, May 12, 55.

Carroll, Eugene J. 1993. "Lift the Embargo While Castro Is Still Boss." *Los Angeles Times*, October 25, B7.

Carter, Jimmy. 1982. *Keeping the Faith: Memoirs of a President*. New York: Bantam Books.

"Carter and the Cuban Influx." 1980. *Newsweek*, May 26, 22–28.

Castro, Fidel. 1987. Speech presented at the 8th Conference of the American Jurists Association, Havana, Cuba, September 17.

"Castro Seeks End of Embargo." 1993. *New York Times*, May 2, A18.

"Castro's Challenge to Reagan." 1984. *Newsweek*, January 9, 38–41.

"Castro's 'Crime Bomb' Inside U.S." 1984. *U.S. News & World Report*, January 16, 27–30.

Chambliss, William J. 1964. "A Sociological Analysis of the Laws of Vagrancy." *Social Problems* 12:67–77.

Chandler, Kurt. 1987. "Despite INS Parole Plan, Uncertainty Remains for State's Mariel Cubans." *Minneapolis Star and Tribune*, August 23, 7B.

"Clinton's Fidel Problem." 1992. *Wall Street Journal*, December 31, A6.

Cohen, Stanley. 1972. *Folk Devils and Moral Panics*. London: Macgibbon and Kee.

Cole, George F., Stanislaw J. Frankowski, and Marc G. Gertz, eds. 1981. *Major Criminal Justice Systems*. Beverly Hills, Calif.: Sage Publications.

Colvin, Mark. 1992. *The Penitentiary in Crisis: From Accommodation to Riot in New Mexico*. Albany: State University of New York Press.

Commission Pro-Justice Mariel Prisoners. 1987. *The Mariel Injustice*. Coral Gables, Fla.: Commission Pro-Justice Mariel Prisoners.

Conant, Ralph. 1968. "Rioting, Insurrection and Civil Disorderliness." *American Scholar* 37:420–433.

Conrad, John P. 1988. "What Do the Undeserving Deserve?" In *The Pains of Imprisonment*, edited by Robert Johnson and Hans Toch. Prospect Heights, Ill.: Waveland Press.

"Coping with Cuba's Exodus." 1980. *Newsweek*, May 12, 60–63.

Cosman, J. W. 1989. "Declaration of Basic Principles for the Treatment of Prisoners." *Journal of Correctional Education* 40:56–61.

Cruickshank, John. 1969. *Albert Camus and the Literature of Revolt*. New York: Oxford University Press.

"Cuba's Boat People—Dilemma for Carter." 1980. *U.S. News & World Report*, May 5, 41–42.

"Cuba's Tattered Economy—Through Refugee Eyes." 1980. *U.S. News & World Report*, May 5, 21–23.

"The Cuban Conundrum." 1980. *Newsweek*, September 29, 24–27.

"A Cuban Explosion." 1987. *Newsweek*, December 7, 38–40.

"Cuban Hijackers—And Those Who Stay." 1980. *Newsweek*, September 1, 26.

"The Cuban Refugees Move On." 1980. *Time*, October 13, 45.

"The Cuban Tide Is a Flood." 1980. *Newsweek*, May 19, 28–29.

"Cubans, and Cuba Policy, Lost at Sea." 1994. *New York Times*, August 11, A14.

"Cubans Hijack Ship, Set Sail for U.S." 1994. *Bloomington Herald-Times*, August 10, A4.

"Cubans Still Waiting for Fairness." 1987. *Atlanta Constitution*, July 9, 12A.

"Cubans Vote with Their Feet." 1980. *Newsweek*, April 21, 17–18.

Debs, Eugene V. 1973. *Walls and Bars*. Chicago: Charles H. Kerr.

"Dispersing Cubans Easier Said Than Done." 1980. *U.S. News & World Report*, June 2, 3–5.

Dolman, Joe. 1986. "Locking Up Liberty in the Atlanta Pen." *Southern Changes*, December, 1–3.

Dominguez, Jorge. 1994. "Cuba's Helper." *Washington Post*, March 7, A19.

Donzinger, Steven. 1987. "INS Treatment of Cubans Offends American Sense of Justice." *Atlanta Journal and Constitution,* November 8, A1.

Dwyer, Timothy. 1987. "U.S. Prisons a Limbo for 5,000 Cubans." *Philadelphia Inquirer,* July 13, 1A-4.

Eig, Larry M. 1986. *Indefinite Detention of Freedom Flotilla Cubans: A History of the Judicial Response.* Washington, D.C.: Library of Congress, Congressional Research Service.

"Fairness of Case Reviews for Cubans Is Challenged." 1988. *New York Times,* January 3, A1.

Falk, Pamela S. 1992. "Exiles Set Policy Agenda on Cuba for Next Administration." *Wall Street Journal,* October 16, A15.

Ferrell, Jeff. 1993. *Crimes of Style: Urban Graffiti and the Politics of Criminality.* New York: Garland.

"For Cubans: Hospitality and Hostility." 1980. *U.S. News & World Report,* May 19, 6–8.

"For Most Cubans, U.S. a Happy Haven." 1980. *U.S. News & World Report,* September 1, 4–5.

"Freedom Flotilla: A Brave Skipper, a Grateful Family and Angry Florida Citizens." 1980. *People,* May 26, 29.

Fuller, James. 1982. *Alcatraz.* San Francisco: Asteron.

Garment, Suzanne. 1991. *Scandal: The Culture of Mistrust in American Politics.* New York: Doubleday.

Gavzer, Bernard. 1993. "Are Human Rights Being Abused in Our Country?" *Parade,* December 12, 4–6.

Glaser, Daniel. 1978. "The Counterproductivity of Conservative Thinking about Crime." *Criminology* 16:210–220.

Golden, Daniel. 1987. "U.S. No Haven for These Cuban Refugees." *Boston Globe,* March 29, A23–26.

Greenhouse, Steven. 1994. "Cubans Who Seized Boat Win Asylum." *New York Times,* August 11, A8.

"A Half-Opened Door." 1980. *New Republic,* May 24, 4.

Hamm, Mark S. 1993. *American Skinheads: The Criminology and Control of Hate Crime.* Westport, Conn.: Praeger.

———. 1993. "State Organized Homicide: A Study of Seven CIA Plans to Assassinate Fidel Castro." In *Making Law: The State, The Law, and Structural Contradictions,* edited by William J. Chambliss and Marjorie S. Zatz. Bloomington: Indiana University Press.

————. 1992. "Ethics, Scholarship and *The Justice Professional:* The Tragic Case of the Mariel Cuban." *The Justice Professional* 6:135–154.

————. 1992. "Santeria in Federal Prisons: Understanding a Little Known Religion." *Federal Prisons Journal* 2:37–42.

————. 1991. "The Abandoned Ones: A History of the Oakdale/Atlanta Riots." In *Crimes by the Capitalist State: An Introduction to State Criminality,* edited by Gregg Barak. Albany: State University of New York Press.

————. 1991. "From Wedtech and Iran-Contra to the Riots at Oakdale and Atlanta: On the Ethics and Public Performance of Edwin Meese III." *Journal of Crime & Justice* 14:123–148.

————. 1989. "Political Rehabilitation in Cuban Prisons: The Plan Progressivo." *Journal of Correctional Education* 40:72–79.

————. 1989. "Whistleblowing in Corrections." *Sociological Viewpoints* 5:35–45.

Hamm, Mark S., Terese Coupez, Frances E. Hoze, and Corey Weinstein. 1994. "The Myth of Humane Imprisonment: A Critical Analysis of Severe Discipline in U.S. Maximum Security Prisons, 1945–1990." In *Prison Violence in America,* edited by Michael Braswell, Reid Montgomery, Jr., and Lucien X. Lobardo. 2d ed. Cincinnati: Anderson.

Hampton, Jim. 1987. "Caged Logic on Cuban Prisoners." *Miami Herald,* October 19, A12.

Harris, Marlys. 1980. "A Yanqui Comes Home." *Money,* September, 100–106.

"Havana-Bound." 1980. *Time,* August 25, 40.

Hoeffel, Paul Heath. 1980. "Fort Chafee's Unwanted Cubans." *New York Times Magazine,* December 21, 30–54.

Holt, Pat M. 1993. "Put Policy Toward Cuba on a More Rational Basis." *Christian Science Monitor,* February 4, 18.

Human Rights Project. 1987. *Report on Boniato Penitentiary Santiago Cuba (October 9).* Washington, D.C.: Human Rights Project.

Hunt, E. Howard. 1980. "Castro's Worms." *National Review,* June 13, 722–724.

"In the Last Days of the Boatlift." 1980. *U.S. News & World Report,* June 16, 29.

Institute for Policy Studies. 1988. "Cuban Prisons: A Preliminary Report." *Social Justice* 15:55–62.

International Bondletter and Eurocurrency Financing Review. March 27, 1982.

International Security Council. 1985. *The Soviet Challenge in Central America and the Caribbean.* New York: CAUSA.

Irwin, John. 1985. *The Jail: Managing the Underclass in American Society*. Berkeley: University of California Press.

Jackson, Robert L. 1987. "Meese Friend Told Wedtech of Influence in Government." *Los Angeles Times*, September 20, 16.

Jengeleski, James L., Orlando DeGarcia, and Mellisa A. Sweigert. 1986. "Land of Opportunity for Crime: The Cuban Criminal." *Justice Professional* 1:33–44.

John, Ervin R. 1966. "Seeing Oriente in a Jeep: An American in Cuba, Part I." *Nation*, 14, 296–299.

Kastenmeier, Robert W. 1988. "Mariel Cubans Deserve Due Process Too." *Washington Post*, March 24, 12A.

Kauzlarich, David. 1993. "Prolegomenon to the Criminalization of Nation-States: The International Covenant on Civil and Political Rights." Paper presented at the annual meeting of the American Society of Criminology, Phoenix.

Kennedy, Richard. 1984. *The International Dictionary of Religion*. New York: Crossroads.

Kishenbaum, Jerry. 1980. "Freedom: Big League Baseball Prospects." *Sports Illustrated*, May 19, 6–8.

Kissinger, Henry A. 1984. *The Report of the President's National Bipartisan Commission on Central America*. New York: Macmillan.

Kmiec, Douglas W. 1992. *The Attorney General's Lawyer: Inside the Meese Justice Department*. New York: Praeger.

Kushner, Howard I. 1989. *Self-Destruction in the Promised Land: A Psychocultural Biology of American Suicide*. New Brunswick, N.J.: Rutgers University Press.

Lardner, George, Jr., and Mary Thorton. 1987. "A Wedtech Entanglement: Friendship Drew Meese into Scandal." *Washington Post*, September 3, A1–A20.

LeoGrande, William M. 1986. "Cuba." In *Confronting Revolution: Security Through Diplomacy in Central America*, edited by Morris J. Blackman et al. New York: Pantheon Books.

Leshaw, Gary. 1992. "Atlanta's Cuban Detainees: A Retrospective." *Atlanta Lawyer*, Fourth Quarter, 6–28.

———. 1988. Statement before U.S. House Judiciary Committee, Subcommittee on Courts, Civil Liberties, and the Administration of Justice, February 4.

Lewis, John. 1987. "A Mocking Memory." *Congressional Record*, April 27.

Lockwood, Lee. 1969. *Castro's Cuba, Cuba's Fidel*. New York: Vintage Books.

MacEoin, Gary. 1980. "Playing Politics with 'Refugees.'" *Progressive*, July, 36–37.

MacGarrey, Wyatt. 1962. *Cuba: Its People, Its Society, Its Culture*. New Haven, Conn.: HRAF Press.

Mahan, Sue. 1985. "An 'Orgy of Brutality' at Attica and the 'Killing Ground' at Sante Fe: A Comparison of Prison Riots." In *Prison Violence in America*, edited by Michael Braswell, Steven Dillingham, and Reid Montgomery, Jr. Cincinnati: Anderson.

Mann, Coramae Richey. 1993. *Unequal Justice: A Question of Color*. Bloomington: Indiana University Press.

"Marielitos: The Forgotten Refugees." 1987. Nightline (ABC), July 3.

Mayer, Milton. 1980. "Massaging the News." *Progressive*, August, 44–45.

McAfee, Cindy. 1986. "Shoob Urges Fairness to Detainees." *Marietta Daily Journal*, February 26, 1.

McGeary, Johanna, and Cathy Booth. 1993. "Cuba Alone." *Time*, December 6, 43–54.

McLain, Denny. 1988. *Strikeout: The Story of Denny McLain*. St. Louis: Sporting News Publishing Co.

Meese, Edwin, III. 1992. Foreword to *The Attorney General's Lawyer: Inside the Meese Justice Department*, by Douglas W. Kmiec. New York: Praeger.

———. 1992. *With Reagan: The Inside Story*. Washington, D.C.: Regnery Gateway.

Meier, Kenneth J. 1979. *Politics and the Bureaucracy: Policymaking in the Fourth Branch of Government*. North Scituate, Mass.: Duxbury Press.

"Men without a Country." 1986. *Newsweek*, June 9, 29.

Mesa-Lago, Carmelo. 1981. *The Economy of Socialist Cuba: A Two Decade Appraisal*. Albuquerque: University of New Mexico Press.

———. 1978. *Cuba in the 1970's: Pragmatism and Institutionalization*. Albuquerque: University of New Mexico Press.

Miller, James. 1993. *The Passion of Michel Foucault*. New York: Simon and Schuster.

Millett, Kate. 1994. *The Politics of Cruelty: An Essay on the Literature of Political Imprisonment*. New York: Norton.

Minnesota Lawyer's International Human Rights Committee. 1986. *The Freedom Flotilla Six Years Later: From Mariel to Minnesota*. Minneapolis: Minnesota Lawyer's International Human Rights Committee.

Mollenhoff, Clark R. 1980. *The President Who Failed*. New York: Macmillan.

214 • • • References

Morain, Dan. 1987. "Wallach Seen as a Successful Attorney." *Los Angeles Times*, December 28, 4.

Morris, Robert. 1983. *The Devil's Butcher Shop: The New Mexico Prison Uprisings*. New York: Franklin Watts.

Murphy, Joseph M. 1987. "Santeria." In *The Encyclopedia of Religion*, edited by Mircea Eliade. Vol. 13. New York: Macmillan.

National Center on Institutions and Alternatives/Coalition to Support Cuban Detainees. 1987. *Project Due Process*. Arlington, Va.: National Center on Institutions and Alternatives.

"The New Wave of Cubans Is Swamping Miami." 1980. *Business Weekly*, August 25, 87–88.

Osborn, John 1980. "With Open Arms." *New Republic*, June 21, 6–8.

Ostrom, Vincent. 1972. *The Intellectual Crisis in Public Administration*. University: University of Alabama Press.

Ostrow, Ronald J., and Robert L. Jackson. 1987. "2 Ex-Meese Advisors Indicted over Wedtech." *Los Angeles Times*, December 23, 1.

Parry, John. 1987. "U.S. Lays Out Rights Stance." *Washington Post*, January 20, A15.

———. 1987. "Cuba Denounces U.S. Criticisms of Human Rights." *Washington Post*, February 24, A18.

Pasztor, Andy. 1988. "Memo to Meese in 1985 Described Plan to Make Pipeline Payments to Israel." *Wall Street Journal*, February 23, 18E.

Pirie, Sophie H. 1986. "The Need for a Codified Definition of 'Persecution' in United States Refugee Law." *Stanford Law Review* 39:187–234.

Platt, Tony. 1988. "Cuba and the Politics of Human Rights." *Social Justice* 15:38–54.

———. 1988. "The United States, Cuba, and the New Cold War." *Social Justice* 15:4–21.

Platt, Tony, and Cecilia Platt. 1987. "XXXIX International Course in Criminology." *Crime and Social Justice* 30:125–127.

"President Carter in 1980." 1981. Washington, D.C.: Congressional Quarterly.

"President Says U.S. Offers 'Open Arms' to Cuban Refugees." 1980. *New York Times*, May 6, A1.

Quinney, Richard. 1977. *Class, State and Crime: On the Theory and Practice of Criminal Justice*. New York: David McKay.

"Refugee Rights." 1981. *Time*, January 12, 52.

"The Refugee's Lot." 1980. *Newsweek*, May 26, 31.

"The Refugees: Rebels with a Cause." 1980. *Newsweek*, June 16, 28–29.

Rosati, Jerel A. 1987. *The Carter Administration's Quest for Global Community.* Columbia: University of South Carolina Press.

Sandidge, Sally. 1992. "On the Road Again." *Atlanta Lawyer,* Fourth Quarter, 8–9.

Sciolino, Elaine. 1987. "Reagan's Mighty Effort to Condemn Cuba." *New York Times,* March 24, A16.

"Seventy-Three of the 201 Cuban Refugees Who Were Deported to Cuba Are Still in Cuban Prisons." 1986. *Diario de Las Americas,* June 23, 1.

Shepard, Scott. 1987. "Cuban Inmate's Rights Violated, Group Says." *Atlanta Constitution,* April 15, 6B.

Sklar, Barry. 1984. "Cuban Exodus: The Context." In *Cuban Communism,* edited by Louis Irving Horowitz. New Brunswick, N.J.: Transaction Books.

Skoug, Kenneth N., Jr. 1984. "The United States and Cuba." Address presented to "Face-to-Face" Program, Carnegie Endowment for International Peace, December 17.

"The Sleaze Watch." 1988. *New Republic,* May 9, 8.

Sternberg, William, and Matthew C. Harrison, Jr. 1989. *Feeding Frenzy.* New York: Henry Holt.

Stewart, James B. 1988. *The Prosecutors: Inside Offices of the Government's Most Powerful Lawyers.* New York: Henry Holt.

Strotland, Ezra. 1976. "Self-Esteem and Violence by Guards and State Troopers at Attica." *Criminal Justice and Behavior* 3:85–96.

Swindall, Pat. 1987. Letter to Assistant Attorney General John R. Bolton, December 22.

Sykes, Gresham M. 1978. *Criminology.* New York: Harcourt Brace Jovanovich.

———. 1958. *The Society of Captives: A Study of a Maximum Security Prison.* Princeton, N.J.: Princeton University Press.

Teish, Luisah. 1985. *Jambalaya.* San Francisco: Harper and Row.

Thompson, Tracy. 1987. "Cubans, Guards Trapped in Cycle of Violence in Atlanta Pen." *Atlanta Journal,* April 19, A1.

———. 1987. "Prison Officials Get 2nd Autopsy on Cuban Inmate." *Atlanta Constitution* April 19, 1A.

Tomlinson, Kenneth Y. 1980. "Fleeing Cuba for Freedom." *Reader's Digest,* August, 92–96.

Treadway, Joan. 1987. " 'The Abandoned' Await Their Chance for a New Life." *New Orleans Times-Picayune,* August 30, C1–C2.

Treaster, Joseph B. 1987. "Cuba and Human Rights." *New York Times,* May 21, A12.

Turner, Ralph H., and Samuel J. Surace. 1956. "Zoot-Suiters and Mexicans: Symbols in Crowd Behavior." *American Journal of Sociology* 62:14–20.

"27 Cubans Picked Up at Sea in a Boat Reported Hijacked." 1994. *New York Times,* August 10, A12.

"U.N. Rejects Faulting Cuba." 1987. *New York Times,* March 12, A12.

U.S. Bureau of Justice Statistics. 1988. *Report to the Nation on Crime and Justice.* Washington, D.C.: U.S. Department of Justice.

U.S. Department of Justice. Federal Bureau of Prisons. 1988. *A Report on the Disturbance at the Federal Detention Center, Oakdale, Louisiana and the U.S. Penitentiary, Atlanta, Georgia.* U.S. Department of Justice, Federal Bureau of Prisons.

U.S. Department of State. 1986. *Country Reports of Human Rights Practices for 1986.* Washington, D.C.: Government Printing Office.

———. 1986. "Cuba: New Migration and Embargo Measures." November, 86–87. Washington, D.C.: Government Printing Office.

———. 1984. "U.S., Cuba Resume Normal Migration." February 4, 44–46. Washington, D.C.: Government Printing Office.

———. 1980. "Cuban-Haitian Refugees." August, 79–82. Washington, D.C.: Government Printing Office.

———. 1980. "Cuban Refugees." June, 68–71. Washington, D.C.: Government Printing Office.

———. 1980. "Cuban Refugees." July, 70–71. Washington, D.C.: Government Printing Office.

———. 1980. "Exodus from Cuba." July, 80–81. Washington, D.C.: Government Printing Office.

———. 1980. "Cuban Refugees." August, 68–71. Washington, D.C.: Government Printing Office.

U.S. House of Representatives. 1984. *Hearings on Human Rights in Cuba.* Washington, D.C.: Government Printing Office.

U.S. House of Representatives. Judiciary Committee. Subcommittee on Courts, Civil Liberties, and the Administration of Justice. 1986. *Atlanta Federal Penitentiary.* Washington, D.C.: Government Printing Office.

"U.S. Prepared to Stop Boatlift with Blockade." 1994. *Bloomington Herald-Times,* August 11, A4.

U.S. President's Review Board. 1987. *Review of the President's Special Review Board.* Washington, D.C.: U.S. President's Review Board.

U.S. Senate. 1987. *Filing and Review of Attorney General Edwin Meese's Financial Disclosures.* Washington, D.C.: Government Printing Office.

———. 1987. *Office of the Government Ethics' Review of the Attorney General's Financial Disclosure.* Washington, D.C.: Government Printing Office.

———. 1985. *Confirmation of Edwin Meese III.* Washington, D.C.: Government Printing Office.

———. 1984. *Nomination of Edwin Meese III.* Washington, D.C.: Government Printing Office.

Useem, Burt, and Peter Kimball. 1988. *States of Siege: U.S. Prison Riots, 1971–1986.* New York: Oxford University Press.

Valladares, Armando. 1986. *Against All Hope: The Prison Memoirs of Armando Valladares.* Translated by Andrew Hurley. New York: Knopf.

———. 1984. "The Cuban Gulag." In *Cuban Communism,* edited by Irving Louis Horowitz. New Brunswick, N.J.: Transaction Books.

Van Ness, Shela. 1988. "American Accountability of Human Rights: The Case of Mariel Cuban Detainees." Paper presented at the annual meeting of the American Society of Criminology, Chicago.

Veliz, Claudio. 1968. *Latin America and the Caribbean: A Handbook.* New York: Praeger.

Waldo, Dwight. 1980. *The Enterprise of Public Administration: A Summary View.* Novato, Calif.: Chandler and Sharp.

Walker, Thomas W. 1985. "Nicaraguan–U.S. Friction: The First Four Years, 1979–1983." In *The Central American Crisis: Sources of Conflict and the Failure of U.S. Policy,* edited by Kenneth M. Coleman and George C. Herring. Wilmington, Del.: Scholarly Resources.

Wallach, John P. 1987. "Fidel Castro and the United States Press." In *The Selling of Fidel Castro,* edited by William E. Ratliff. New Brunswick, N.J.: Transaction Books.

Walters, Vernon. 1986. United States Mission to the United Nations, Statement by Ambassador Vernon Walters . . . under Item 12, Human Rights in Cuba. Press release, November 26.

Weisman, Steven R. 1984. "Reagan, in a Radio Speech, Appeals to People of Cuba." *New York Times,* January 6, A4.

"The Welcome Wears Thin." 1980. *Time,* September 1, 8–10.

"When Cubans Bolt Refugee Centers." 1980. *U.S. News & World Report,* April 21, 13.

Wicker, Tom. 1975. *A Time to Die.* New York: Quadrangle/New York Times Books.

Winn, Peter. 1980. "Is the Cuban Revolution in Trouble?" *Nation,* June 7, 682–685.

Wood, Katie, and Brenda L. Mooney. 1987. "What Really Happened at the Atlanta Pen." *Fulton County Daily Report,* December 14, 2–12.

Woolner, Ann. 1988. "Pat Swindall's Conversion." *Fulton County Daily Report,* February 9, 5.

———. 1987. "Cuban Detention 'A Disgrace.'" *Fulton County Daily Report,* January 20, 1–4.

Womack, John. 1980. "The Revolution Tightens Its Belt." *New Republic,* May 31, 19–23.

Chronology
of Events

1975–1979	The Cuban government wages a military offensive in Ethiopia and Angola.
January–March 1979	More than 115,000 Cuban-Americans are allowed to visit family members on the island of Cuba, leading to increased consumerism, feelings of loss for loved ones, and a general demoralization among many Cubans who are struggling to earn a living under Castro's regime.
July 1, 1979	The Cuban government implements a series of economic reforms that include the establishment of worker-relocation camps in rural areas, where theft and worker absenteeism become commonplace.
December 21, 1979	President Castro tells the Cuban people that economic hardship will prevail in their country for years to come.
December 1979	Anti-Castro posters and leaflets begin to appear on the streets of Havana, signaling a growing dissatisfaction with economic and social conditions in Cuba. Meanwhile, a Cuban prisoner named Armando Valladares begins to publish books in foreign markets that testify to a regular

pattern of torture and extralegal execution in the Cuban prison systems.

April 20, 1980   The Cuban government announces that evacuation of those who want to leave Cuba will be permitted via the port of Mariel. More than 120,000 join the "Freedom Flotilla" bound for the United States.

May 1, 1980   U.S. Immigration and Naturalization officials in Key West begin to notice Cuban men who are "more hardened and rougher in appearance" than those who had come on earlier vessels from Mariel.

May 5, 1980   President Carter welcomes the Freedom Flotilla with "an open heart and open arms."

May 14, 1980   The Carter administration accuses Fidel Castro of "taking hardened criminals out of prison and mental patients out of hospitals and forcing boat captains to take them to the United States."

May 19, 1980   President Castro responds to Carter's accusation by calling the refugees from Mariel not criminals but, rather, "anti-social" and "anti-government reactionaries." He further claims that all mental patients passing through the port of Mariel have been requested by family members in the United States.

June 1, 1980   More than seventy thousand Mariels are backed up in U.S. relocation camps waiting to settle in America.

June 6, 1980   Mariel Cubans go on a rampage at Fort Chafee, Arkansas, leaving one dead and fifty-five seriously injured.

June 7, 1980   The Carter administration explains that the Fort Chafee incident was caused by "some hardened criminals exported to the United States by Fidel Castro."

June 8, 1980   President Carter orders expulsion proceedings against the Fort Chafee rioters and sends 3,700 Air Force personnel to stand guard over the relocation camps.

August 6, 1980   Mariel Cubans riot at Fort Indiantown Gap, Pennsylvania, leaving fifty-eight seriously injured.

August 15–17, 1980   Miami, which eventually becomes home for about 35 percent of the entire Freedom Flotilla, experiences four days of rioting, which results in hate and distrust of Mariels within the Cuban-American community.

August 17–30, 1980   Seven American airliners are hijacked to Havana by members of the Freedom Flotilla.

October 30, 1980   A total of 120,737 Mariel refugees have been processed into the United States. Fewer than one-half of 1 percent of them are found to have serious criminal backgrounds. Meanwhile, the Carter administration and the U.S. media continue to foster the belief that many refugees are, in the words of the press, "murderers, vagrants, homosexuals, and scum."

January 1981   Federal Bureau of Prisons officials decide against tearing down the outdated penitentiary at Atlanta because bed space is suddenly needed for a large number of Mariel Cubans who have failed to meet the conditions of their "parole" in America.

March 1981   Attorneys for the Cubans in Atlanta begin winning due-process rights for their clients in federal district court.

February 1982   Edwin Meese, general counsel to President Reagan, directs a plan that leads to a $32 million contract for a tool and die company called Wedtech Corporation.

July 28, 1983   President Castro tells French and American journalists that there are no human rights violations in Cuba.

October 22, 1983	The United States launches a military invasion of Grenada that leaves nineteen U.S. Marines and more than two hundred Cubans dead, and 784 Cuban soldiers and civilians taken captive. President Castro calls this a "cowardly and ridiculous act" and suspends all diplomatic relations with the United States.
January 2, 1984	The Reagan administration launches an aggressive political attack against human rights violations in Cuba.
July 1984	Atlanta attorney Gary Leshaw files a suit in U.S. District Court arguing that Mariels in Atlanta are being inhumanely treated by the federal government.
October 16– November 1, 1984	Cuban detainees start several small fires in their cellblocks at the Atlanta prison. In response, the prison administration removes and destroys every item of personal property belonging to Cuban detainees. The prisoners are then teargassed and beaten with batons.
December 14, 1984	Limited diplomatic relations suddenly are restored between the U.S. and Cuba. A treaty is signed that allows the United States to receive more than twenty thousand Cubans, including three thousand "political prisoners." In return, the U.S. agrees to deport 2,746 "excludable entrants," beginning with 1,500 Cubans who are incarcerated in the Atlanta Penitentiary.
January–April 1985	A total of 201 Mariel prisoners from Atlanta are deported to Cuba, where seventy-three of them are immediately reimprisoned.
January–May 1985	The U.S. District Court in Atlanta is "outraged" at the Reagan administration's "unseemly haste" in trying to deport Cubans before they have received fair trials.
February 5, 1985	Edwin Meese is confirmed as attorney general of the United States.

May 10, 1985   President Castro is angered by antagonistic messages delivered over the CIA-operated "Voice of America" program on Radio Marti. In response, Castro suspends the 1984 U.S.–Cuban emigration accord.

October 1985   The U.S. Supreme Court denies the right of due process to imprisoned Mariel Cubans.

December 30, 1985   The federal penitentiary at Atlanta is filled far beyond capacity with nearly two thousand Cubans in custody.

January 1986   Two Mariel detainees are brought to trial for their part in the 1984 Atlanta riot. Both are acquitted. According to jurors, "the living situation of the detainees was shameful."

January–June 1986   A number of Mariel prisoners write letters to President Reagan and engage in hunger strikes to get his attention concerning human rights abuses in both Cuba and the United States.

February 3, 1986   Congressman Robert W. Kastenmeier conducts an oversight investigation of the Atlanta Penitentiary and concludes that none of the detainees are serving criminal sentences—yet "current living conditions for Cubans . . . [are] intolerable considering even the most minimal correctional standards."

March 1986   The Bureau of Prisons begins to accept Cuban inmates at the medium-security Oakdale Detention Center in order to accommodate the overflow of nonviolent Cuban offenders from the Atlanta Penitentiary.

May 1986   Alfred A. Knopf publishes *Against All Hope: The Prison Memoirs of Armando Valladares*.

December 11, 1986   President Reagan hosts "Human Rights Day" at the White House and is joined in his vilification of Cuba by Armando Valladares and the U.S. press.

December 1986   Ambassador Vernon Walters testifies before the United Nations General Assembly that Cuba "operates a vast network of prisons . . . and firing squads to keep itself in power." Walters later withdraws his condemnation of Cuba for lack of support within the UN.

February 8, 1987   Detainee Santiago Peralta-Ocana is murdered by prison guards at the Atlanta Penitentiary.

February–March 1987   The Reagan administration withdraws its chief counsel at the U.S. Interests Section in Cuba and the State Department releases a special report on "widespread violations of human rights" in Cuba, including torture and state-authorized murder.

February–March 1987   The UN Human Rights Commission convenes in Geneva. The UN offensive against human rights violations under communism is led by U.S. delegate E. Robert Wallach. Wallach's allegation of human rights abuses in Cuba also fails to gain UN backing.

February–July 1987   Fidel Castro wages a diplomatic offensive against the U.S. by inviting a number of international delegations to tour the Cuban prison system. None of the delegations can corroborate claims of torture or random executions in Cuba. On balance, the Cuban prisons are found to be more humane than the Atlanta Penitentiary at that time.

April 4, 1987   A guard is stabbed in the back by a Mariel Cuban in the Atlanta Penitentiary.

April 4–19, 1987   Atlanta guards shake down all detainee cells and find a number of machetes, ropes, clubs, and saw-blades.

June–November 1987   Attorney General Meese appears five times before a congressional panel investigating the Wedtech scandal.

June 22, 1987   The Cuban Review Plan is implemented at the Atlanta

Penitentiary. Between July and November, only eighty Cuban detainees are released under this plan; another eight hundred receive "pocket freedom."

July 3, 1987   The INS reports that "some 2,700 Marielitos [in Oakdale and Atlanta] have been guilty of serious crime."

July 13, 1987   The INS reports that "Marielitos are hard-core deviates that do strange things." Further, the INS proposes "keeping all these people in jail for the rest of their lives."

July 17, 1987   E. Robert Wallach is forced to resign his position as U.S. representative to the UN Human Rights Commission because of his involvement in the Wedtech scandal.

August 23, 1987   The INS describes the imprisoned Mariels as "the most dangerous group the Federal Bureau of Prisons has ever had."

November 16–19, 1987   State Department officials meet with representatives of the Cuban government in Mexico City to reactivate emigration accords established in 1984.

November 17, 1987   Bishop Agustin Roman and the Catholic conference draft a letter to Attorney General Meese pleading with him to stop the indefinite detention of Mariel Cubans in American prisons.

November 17, 1987   The Iran-Contra Report is released, accusing Attorney General Meese of "disdain for the law" in the United States.

November 20, 1987   News of the reactivated emigration accord is received by the Department of Justice, the INS, and the BOP; representatives of the media are alerted. The detainees learn about the new accord first from Warden Johnson at Oakdale, and later from Tom Brokaw on the NBC "Nightly News." Within minutes of Brokaw's announcement, an intoxicated detainee at Oakdale starts a small riot in the prison cafeteria. This incident is ignored by BOP officials at Oakdale because it is seen as simply the activity of a lone, drunken prisoner.

November 21, 1987

Cuban detainees riot and gain control of the Oakdale Detention Center, taking twenty-eight hostages and burning more than half the forty-seven-acre complex.

November 22, 1987

The BOP is contacted by Bishop Roman, who offers his help in seeking a resolution to the Oakdale crisis. Federal officials reject Roman's assistance and Attorney General Meese sends a copy of a letter to Oakdale detainees offering "an indefinite moratorium on deportations to Cuba" in exchange for hostages. The detainees, however, reject Meese's offer and continue to hold the hostages.

November 23, 1987

Cuban detainees riot and gain control of the Atlanta Penitentiary, taking more than a hundred hostages and burning three buildings. One detainee is killed, several others are injured, and eight Bureau of Prisons staff are injured. In exchange for hostages, the detainees are also offered, but do not accept, a moratorium on deportations to Cuba by Attorney General Meese.

November 23, 1987

Detainees at Oakdale ask to speak with Bishop Roman. Bureau of Prisons Director Michael Quinlan dispatches a plane to Miami to fly Roman to the Oakdale crisis, yet the travel arrangements are suddenly cancelled by the attorney general, leaving the bishop stranded on an airport runway in Miami.

November 24, 1987

Detainees holding control of the Oakdale compound threaten to burn a hostage to death in full view of all hostages, detainees, and government officials. Meanwhile, six hostages suffering from medical complications are released by detainees in Atlanta.

November 25,   Another hostage in Atlanta is released because of health
1987   problems.

November 26,   Attorney General Meese meets with Bishop Roman at the
1987   Department of Justice in Washington.

November 27,   Live television coverage of the Oakdale siege begins.
1987

November 29,   Bishop Roman is allowed to visit and speak with rioting
1987   Cubans at Oakdale. Within an hour, he convinces them to
                 lay down their weapons and surrender all hostages.

November 29,   Director Quinlan denies Bishop Roman access to the Ma-
1987   riel Cubans who have control of the Atlanta Penitentiary.

December 1,   One Atlanta hostage is released as a birthday present to
1987   Carla Dudeck, founder of the Coalition to Support Cuban
                 Detainees.

December 2,   Director Quinlan briefs members of the congress on the
1987   Cuban riots. Within hours of Quinlan's presentation,
                 Bishop Roman is allowed to deliver a three-minute audio
                 tape to the Atlanta detainees.

December 3,   Atlanta detainees vote to end the ten-day siege.
1987

December 4,   Bishop Roman is allowed to speak with Atlanta detainees
1987   and is able to facilitate the signing of an agreement to end
                 the crisis.

December 11,   Assistant Attorney General Arnold I. Burns tells reporters
1987   in Washington that "while most Mariel Cubans have been
                 law-abiding productive citizens, some 7,600 have ended up
                 in federal or state correctional institutions."

Index

Abrams, Elliott, 131, 137, 148
Afghanistan, 124, 149
Africa, 47, 48, 104, 106, 180, 186n, 188n
American Bar Association, 39
American Civil Liberties Union, 39, 94
American Correctional Association, 38, 88
Amnesty International, 38, 141, 142, 187n
Angola, 48, 149, 186n
Argentina, 50, 138
Arma, Alberto, 100
Atlanta Federal Penitentiary, 9, 60, 68, 81, 84; conditions of confinement, 32, 37, 62–63, 64, 88–89, 91–96, 97, 110, 113, 115–16, 118, 119, 160, 166, 171–72; detainee adaptations, 102–3, 113, 119; detainee code of conduct, 104, 110, 113, 117–18; detainees of, xii, 9, 24, 27, 37, 41, 45, 59, 62–63, 65–69, 71–73, 85–87, 88–89, 91–101, 112, 118, 130, 131, 143, 146, 149, 156, 160, 162, 173–74, 176, 197n; human rights violations at, 91–92, 94, 103, 108, 113, 115, 119, 138, 143, 155, 160,
172; paroles from, 80, 100–101; renovations of, 93, 97; riot of 1984, 85–87, 89; staff of, 63, 80, 83, 85–87, 89, 93, 94, 95, 97–100, 104, 108–9, 115–16, 162–63, 166–67, 175–76; suicides and suicide attempts at, 63, 64, 65, 88, 92, 97, 100, 114–19, 160
Atlanta riot, xi, 45, 62, 63, 66, 67, 79, 87, 94, 102, 108, 112, 115, 153; compared to Attica and Sante Fe, 30, 33–40, 172; and detainee organization, 15, 18–23, 27, 32–34, 67–68, 118, 169, 176; and hostages, 10–13, 15–19, 20, 22–23, 28, 33–34, 93, 166, 169, 176; initiation and expansion stages, 10–11, 164–68, 172, 174; media coverage of, 13, 19, 20–23; negotiations, 11–13, 14, 22–24, 25–29, 33, 36, 169–75; spirituality of, 15, 23, 27, 32–34, 169, 176; state of siege, 15–29, 35, 168–75, 176; success of, 40, 176; termination stage, 175–76; theatrical events, 15, 17, 18, 28–29, 40, 169; triggering event, 120, 133, 139, 148–49, 155–56, 158, 162, 174
Attica riot, xiv, 30, 31, 33, 34, 35, 36–37, 38, 114, 172

Atwood, William, 177

Baker, James A., III, 122
Ball, Peter, 140
Barrack, Thomas J., Jr., 126
Batista, Fulgencio, 132
Baum, David, 143
Belkin, Aaron, 178
Bender, Howard, 82
Bermudez, Oscar, 100
Biancalana, Flora, 131
Blight, James, 178
Brokaw, Tom, 3, 149
Bumpers, Dale, 56
Bureau of Prisons (BOP), 38, 69, 77,
    80, 83, 84; and Atlanta riot, 10,
    17, 21, 25, 30, 166, 167, 169, 176;
    and detainees, xii, 3, 99, 100,
    116; employees of, 58, 183n; half-
    way houses of, 67, 96, 101; and
    implementation of repatriation
    treaty, 161–64; and Edwin Meese,
    82, 95, 159; and Oakdale riot, 5,
    8, 9, 20, 30, 166, 167, 169, 176;
    procedures of, 18, 86, 98; reports
    of, 88, 96, 170, 174
Burns, Arnold, 65, 69
Bush, George, 55, 81, 95, 131

Camus, Albert, 155, 160, 165
Capone, Al, 84
Carter, Jimmy, xv, 39, 49, 113; and
    Edwin Meese, 127, 144; reaction
    to Freedom Flotilla, 52, 53, 56,
    57, 59–60, 189n; and Ronald
    Reagan, 52, 71, 122
Carter administration, 51–52, 179,
    186n, 187n–88n; and resettlement
    of Mariel Cubans, 54–55, 75
Castro, Fidel, 37, 46, 75, 78, 148;
    anti-Reagan speeches by, 71, 139;
    assassination attempts against, 68,
    134, 135, 205n; and Cuban politi-
    cal prisoners, 142, 187n; and
    Freedom Flotilla, 50–52, 59,
    179–80; and human rights, 140;
    and religion, 107–8; and U.S. re-

lations, 49, 56, 70–71, 72, 78,
    130–31, 148–49, 158, 177–80,
    188n, 193n, 205n
Central America, 70, 71
Chicago, 58, 84
Chinn, W. Franklyn, 129–30, 145,
    200n
Clinton, Bill, 56, 177, 205n
Clinton administration, 178–79, 180
CNN, 12, 21, 22
Coalition to Support Cuban Detain-
    ees, xi, xv, 21
Cohen, Stanley, 74
Combinado del Este Prison, 48, 61
Communidad, 49, 187n
Conner, Roger, 80
Conrad, John, 90, 102
Conyers, John, 94
Cortazar, Julio, 43
Cruz, Rafael, 117
Cuba: economic problems of, 45–48,
    59, 65, 71, 155, 178–79, 185n,
    188n, 205n; Escambray Moun-
    tains of, 98, 111; history of,
    104–5; military of, 47–48, 70, 180,
    188n, 194n; political prisoners
    (plantados) in, 23, 48, 50, 71, 131–
    32, 134, 136–37, 138, 141–42,
    149, 155–56, 187n; rationing sys-
    tem in, 46, 60, 186n; religion in,
    104–5, 107–8; rural relocation
    camps in, 47, 48, 112; support of
    communism by, 47–48, 70, 178,
    180, 186n; and U.S. relations, 78,
    180–81, 194n. See also Castro,
    Fidel, and U.S. relations
Cuban Democratic Act, 178
Cuban prisons, 144, 148, 161, 202n;
    executions in, 48, 130, 132–33,
    134, 137, 139, 140, 142, 148, 155;
    inmates of, 51, 60, 61, 72, 77, 98,
    112; political rehabilitation in, 49,
    187n; torture in, 48–49, 131–33,
    134, 136, 137, 139, 140, 142–43,
    148, 155; and U.S. media, 131–33;
    violence in, 60, 98, 141
Cuban Refugee Act, 193n

Cuban Review Plan of 1987, 96–97, 100–101, 156, 174

Deaver, Michael K., 122
Debs, Eugene V., 84
Dellums, Ronald, 94
Diouf, Abdou, 137
Dobbin Air Force Base, 22
Dudeck, Carla, xv, 21, 22
Dunn, Marvin, 75

El exilio, 43, 119, 133, 165, 168
Elgin Air Force Base, 54, 56
Espy, Mike, 94
Ethics in Government Act of 1978, 127, 145, 157
Eve, Arthur, 34

Fahy, Reverend Joseph A., 100
FBI, 54, 146; at Atlanta, 11, 12, 13, 17, 25, 28, 100; at Oakdale, 7, 8, 16
Ferre, Maurice, 76
Ferrer, Rafael, 66
Fort Chaffee, 54, 55–56, 177
Fort Indiantown Gap, 54, 56–57, 191n
Fort McCoy, 54, 56
Fort Walton Beach, 54, 55, 56, 62
Foucault, Michel, 40–41
Fox, Vernon, 154
Frank, Barney, 94
"Free Speech Movement," 121
Freedom Flotilla (Mariel boatlift), 81, 179, 180, 186n, 188n; economic causes of, 45–48, 59; political causes of, 50–51, 59, 177; refugees of, 39, 45, 50–51, 53–55, 56, 59–67, 74–76, 91, 98, 112, 187n, 188n, 189n, 191n; social causes of, 48–50, 59, 177; U.S. reaction to, 51–52, 53, 55, 189n

Garment, Suzanne, 123
Giuliani, Rudolph W., 145, 146
Glaser, Daniel, 58–59
Gonzalez, Guzman, 67

Great American Bank of California, 126–27
Grenada, 70–71, 130, 139
Guerilla warfare, 33, 37, 40, 67, 166, 168

Hamilton, Alexander, 156–57
Hanberry, Jack, 87, 88, 89
Harding, Warren G., 84
Harrison, Matthew, 122, 124
Havana, 48, 60, 61, 134, 179, 180, 191n
Hendin, Herbert, 118
Hernandez, José, 86
Herrera, Alberto, 60–65, 98, 110, 112, 133
Hiatt, Howard, 140
Holtzman, Elizabeth, 55, 56
Human Rights Organization of the American States, 187n

Indefinite detention, 98, 133, 148; detainee adaptations to, 58, 63, 93, 113, 114–19; legal basis for, 66–67, 68, 72–73, 91–92, 160, 176–77; protests against, 38–39, 85, 93, 94–95, 138, 172, 174
Indiana State University, xi, 183n
Inman, Mike, 1, 79
Institute for Policy Studies, 140–41, 142
International Course in Criminology, 39th, 141–42
Iran-Contra Committee Report, 83, 173, 174; and scandal, 122, 146, 147
Irwin, John, 72

Jackson, George, 97
Jefferson, Thomas, 156–57
Johnson, J. R., 161, 163
Johnson White House, 121

Kastenmeier, Robert W., 87–89, 93, 95, 114
Kennedy, Edward, 54–55
Kennedy, John F., 177–78, 180, 205n

Key West, Florida, 51, 52, 53, 62
Kimball, Peter, 32–33, 34, 35, 36–37, 38; and riot stages, 154–55, 162, 164, 165, 166, 175; and theories of rioting, 153–54, 155
Kmiec, Douglas, 159
Koppel, Ted, 1
Ku Klux Klan, 56

La Cabaña Prison, 61
Las Vegas, 68, 74, 77, 78
Leavenworth Federal Prison, 177
Leshaw, Gary, xv, 12, 19, 24, 92–93, 173, 183n; as attorney for detainees, 87, 99, 176; as negotiator, 13, 22, 23, 28, 29
Lewis, David, 178
Lewis, John, 94
Lompoc Federal Prison, 68, 177
Los Angeles, 58, 74, 77, 78

Maby, Reverend Russ, 93
McCune, Gary, 29
McKay, James C., 145, 146
McLain, Denny, 114–15
Madison, James, 156–57
Mariel, Cuba, 45, 50, 59, 84, 160, 176, 179; and Cuban criminals, 50, 61, 81; and Fidel Castro, 51
Mariel Cubans, 45, 62, 63, 130, 133, 138; deportations of, 70, 92, 162, 164, 171; government descriptions, of 51–52, 55, 56, 60, 74; media descriptions of, 59, 60, 180, 187n, 189n; parole violations of, 54, 58, 66; resettlement of, 53–58, 65, 74–76, 191n, 193n. See also Freedom Flotilla, refugees
"Marielitos," 45, 74, 76, 78, 87, 160, 161
Marion Federal Prison, 68, 177
Mas, Jorge, 23
Meese, Edwin, III: as attorney general, 27, 38, 114, 118, 129–30, 147–48, 159, 174, 185n; and attorney general hearings, 125–29, 159, 172; background of, 120–22;

ethics of, 82–83, 92, 120, 127–28, 143–44, 145, 147–48, 157–59, 170, 173, 174; finances of, 126–27, 128–29, 130, 144–45, 171, 200n; as general counsel to the president, 122–25; and Iran-Contra scandal, 147, 173, 174; media coverage of, 128; as negotiator at Oakdale and Atlanta, 7, 9, 11–13, 15, 23–26, 28–29, 35–36, 41, 169–75, 176; and Wedtech scandal, 82, 83, 122–25, 129–30, 144–46, 147, 159, 172
Meese, Ursula, 82, 126, 127, 129
Metzenbaum, Howard, 39
Mexico, 47, 138
Mexico City, 3, 149
Mfume, Kweisi, 94
Miami, 8, 29, 53, 58, 67, 74, 93, 174; Cuban-Americans of, 23, 24, 49, 131, 178; cultural conflict in, 75–76
Miami Police Department, 76, 77, 78
Millett, Kate, xv, 151, 171
Milosz, Czeslaw, 43
Mitterand, François, 137
Mondale, Walter, 71, 77
Moye, Charles A., 72

National Guard, 56; at Atlanta riot, 12, 17, 26, 28, 29; at Oakdale riot, 16, 20, 24
Neier, Aryeh, 140
Nelson, Alan, 94, 95
New York City, 118, 140, 144, 149, 153, 158; Howard Beach incident, 134; Mariel Cubans of, 58, 68, 74; South Bronx, 122, 125, 126
New York City Police Department, 77, 78
North, Oliver, 156

Oakdale Alien Detention Center, 3, 60, 81; conditions of confinement at, 32, 110; construction of, 68, 69, 77, 81, 96; detainee adaptations, 102, 113; detainee code of conduct, 104, 110, 113, 118; detainees of, xii, 9, 13, 37, 39, 41, 45, 59, 65–66, 68, 130, 131, 143, 146, 148, 149, 156, 160, 162, 173–74, 176, 177, 183n; human rights violations at, 138, 143, 155, 160, 172; paroles from, 80; staff of, 31, 80, 83, 104, 108–9, 161, 162–63, 165, 166–67, 173, 175–76. See also Indefinite detention

Oakdale riot, xi, 43, 79, 80, 83, 102, 153; compared to Attica and Sante Fe, 30, 32–40, 162; detainee organization, 15, 18, 20, 33, 68, 118, 169, 176; hostages, 5, 6, 8, 14, 18, 19, 20, 22, 23, 24, 25, 166, 169, 176; initiation and expansion stages, 4–9, 164–68, 172; media coverage of, 9–10, 13, 19, 20, 22, 24, 168; negotiations, 7–9, 14, 23, 24, 36, 169–75; spirituality of, 15, 23, 33–34, 108, 169, 176; state of siege, 8, 15–25, 35, 69, 168–74, 176; success of, 40, 176; termination stage, 175–76; theatrical events, 15–17, 18, 40, 169; triggering event, 120, 133, 139, 148–49, 155–56, 158, 162, 174

Office of Government Ethics, 82, 145

O'Leary, Cecilia, 131

Oswald, Russell, 34, 35, 36

Peña, José, 10–11, 13

Pentagon, 26, 54, 56, 179

Peralta, Santiago, 97–100, 111, 197n

Perez, Ernesto, 22

Perez, Robert Martin, 23

Petrovsky, Joseph F., 99, 100

Pi, Antonio, 115–17

Pickard, Marc, 12, 13, 21, 22, 23, 28, 29

Pocket freedom, 27, 37, 96, 101, 161, 170

Powell, Jody, 55, 56

Prior, Pedro, 66

Quinlan, Michael, as manager of riots, 11, 17, 22, 23, 24, 25, 26, 27–28, 35–36, 164, 173–75; as negotiator at Atlanta, 12–13, 15, 23, 25, 26, 27–28; as negotiator at Oakdale, 7, 8, 9, 15

Radio Marti, 72, 178

Raynsford, Craig, 80

Reagan administration, 69, 74; background of, 120, 122, 123; criminal justice policies of, 76, 77, 83; Cuban policies of, 3, 70–71, 193n, 194n; and human rights offensive against Cuba, 130–31, 133–39, 142–43, 147, 148–49, 156, 158; and Iran-Contra scandal, 147, 173; and Edwin Meese, 122, 127, 129, 147, 157; prison reforms of, 95, 96, 100–101; Small Business Administration of, 125, 126, 130, 144; and E. Robert Wallach, 130, 156

Reagan, Ronald: anti-Castro speeches of, 1, 43, 72, 130–31, 133, 148–49; and detainees of Oakdale and Atlanta, 37, 81, 165, 166, 168; and Grenada, 70–71; and human rights offensive against Cuba, 130, 137, 141, 142, 147, 149; and Edwin Meese, 120–22, 123, 125, 166; political campaigns of, 52, 55, 71, 77; suicide and suicide attempts in his honor, 63, 116–19, 133, 165; and Wedtech, 126

Reno, Janet, 39

Richard, Louis, 79, 80

Roa, Raul, 135–36, 138, 148

Rochester, New York, 58, 66

Rockefeller, Nelson, 35, 36

Rodriguez, Felix, 34–35

Roman, Bishop Agustin: background of, 8–9, 173; detainee reliance on, 9, 33, 41, 174; as negotiator at Atlanta, 25, 26, 27–29, 35, 87, 175, 176; as negotiator at Oakdale, 9, 24–25, 35, 174, 175, 176

Roosevelt, Franklin D., 157, 159

Rosario, Diader, 12, 13, 17, 21, 23, 25, 28, 29, 173

San Francisco, 84, 122, 123, 145–46
Sandidge, Sally, xv, 94
Santeria: background of, 104–8; and body tattoos, 61, 64, 110; case study of, 111–12; charms of, 107, 108; and detainees of Oakdale-Atlanta, 31, 107–8, 119; and *orisha* spirits, 105–7, 108, 110, 111–12, 119, 169; rituals of, 106–7, 108; and "Stones of the Saints," 106, 111
Sante Fe riot (New Mexico State Prison), xiv, 30, 31, 33, 34–35, 36, 38, 162
Schiltgen, Thomas, 80
Schwartz, Herman, 34, 140
Seal, Bobby, 34
Shoob, Marvin, 72–73, 93
Sikorski, Gerry, 82, 145
Silversteen, Thomas, 19–20
Sklar, Barry, 49, 188n
Smith, William French, 125
Soviet Union, 70, 71, 155, 179, 180
Spain, 50, 104
Sputnik Satellite System, 70–71
Stein, Jacob A., 127, 128
Sternberg, William, 122, 124
Suarez, Xavier L., 95
Swindall, Pat, 69, 197n
Sykes, Gresham, 90, 96, 101; theory of prison riots, 90–91, 92, 102–3, 113, 114, 115–16, 120, 154

Thomas, David, 179
Thomas, Edwin W., 127
Thornburgh, Richard, 55
Tweed, "Boss", 158

United Nations, 91, 94, 124, 130, 137, 149, 178
United Nations Commission on Human Rights, 23, 38, 130, 142, 147; Geneva Convention of, 134–39, 140, 142, 143, 148, 149, 158

U.S. Air Force, 26, 58
U.S. Army, 26, 58, 124
U.S. Central Intelligence Agency (CIA), 54, 56, 72, 134, 185n
U.S. Congress, 147, 157; and Atlanta riot, 27, 173, 175; and detainees, 81, 87, 94–95, 97; and indefinite detention, 38, 94–95
U.S. Defense Department, 124, 143
U.S. House of Representatives, xiii, 55, 68, 69, 121, 131; report on the Atlanta Federal Penitentiary (*House of Representatives Report*), 77, 87–89, 96
U.S. Immigration and Naturalization Service (INS), 26, 82, 92; budgets of, 81–82; and deportations of Mariel Cubans, 72, 92, 162, 164, 171; moral panic against Mariel Cubans, 51, 56, 62, 67, 74, 76, 78–83, 92, 94–95, 101, 103, 115, 118, 160; processing of Mariel Cubans, 53–69, 73, 176, 190n; relocation figures of, 58, 59, 60, 65, 77–78, 188n; review panels/policies of, xi, xiii, 64–65, 92, 94, 95–97, 99, 100–101, 116, 159, 170, 171–72, 174, 176, 198n; role in U.S.–Cuban migration policy, 71, 149
U.S. Justice Department, 110, 156; and INS, 79, 81, 82; and Edwin Meese, 26–27, 82–83, 114, 124, 147–48, 159, 160, 164, 172; reports of, xiii, 114; staff of, 22, 117–18
U.S. Penitentiary at Talladega, xiv, 58, 62, 98, 112, 177
U.S. Penitentiary at Terre Haute, xi, xv, 109–113, 177, 183n
U.S. Refugee Act of 1980, 50, 53–55, 57–58, 69, 187n–88n, 190n
U.S. Senate, xiii, 54, 55, 82, 122, 147, 185n; and Edwin Meese, 125–29
U.S. State Department, xiii, 22, 53, 71; and Cuba, 131, 137, 148, 178

U.S. Supreme Court, 73–74, 110
U.S.–Cuban migration policy, 70, 78, 133, 181, 193n. *See also* U.S.–Cuban Treaty of 1987; U.S. Refugee Act of 1980
U.S.–Cuban Treaty of 1987, 3, 24, 37, 38, 40, 69, 148–49; implementation of, 155, 158, 159–60, 162–63, 171; reaction at Atlanta, 10, 11, 13, 23, 26–27, 37, 164, 165, 172; reaction at Oakdale, 4, 7, 9, 23, 37, 163–64, 165, 172
Universal Declaration of Human Rights, 91
University of California at Berkeley, 120–21
University of Wisconsin at Whitewater, 57
Useem, Bert, 32–33, 34, 35, 36–37, 38; and riot stages, 154–55, 162, 164, 165, 166, 175; and theories of rioting, 153–54, 155

Valladares, Armando: as Cuban political prisoner, 48–49, 131–33, 136; as U.S. human rights ambassador, 23, 24, 147, 148
Vance, Cyrus, 53
Vance, Robert, 73
Vietnam, 121, 130

Wallach, E. Robert: as attorney for Edwin Meese, 125–30, 144–46, 158, 159; background of, 122–23; criminality of, 139, 143–44, 145–46, 148; as human rights ambassador, 124, 130, 133–140, 142, 143, 145, 146, 148, 149, 158; memos of, 124, 125–26; as Wedtech lobbyist/board member, 122, 126, 129–30, 139, 144–46
Wallach, John, 142
Walters, Vernon E., 130, 134, 135, 139
Washington, D.C.: and Cuba, 137, 140, 180; and detainees, 134, 173; and Edwin Meese, 126, 127, 129, 143, 144, 174; and Reagan era, 123, 129; and Wedtech, 124, 144
Washington, George, 157, 159
Watergate, 122, 157
Wedtech Corporation (Welbilt), 82, 122–26, 129–30, 144, 158; and Edwin Meese, 129, 200n
Wicker, Tom, 34
Winn, Peter, 49, 185n
Woodstock, 121

Yoruba slaves, 104–5, 108, 113
Young, Andrew, 186n

Zoot-suiters, 74